Innovation and Competition in Zimbabwean Pentecostalism

Bloomsbury Studies in Black Religion and Cultures

Series Editors: Anthony B. Pinn and Monica R. Miller

Bloomsbury Studies in Black Religion and Cultures advances innovative scholarship that reimagines and animates the global study of black religions, culture, and identity across space and time. The series publishes scholarship that addresses the mutually constitutive nature of race and religion and the social, cultural, intellectual, and material effects of religio-racial formations and identities. The series welcomes projects that address and foreground the intersectional and constitutive nature of black religions and cultures and privileges work that is inter/transdisciplinary and methodologically intersectional in nature.

Black Transhuman Liberation Theology, Philip Butler

Forthcoming books in this series:

Black Gospel Music in Britain,
Dulcie A. Dixon McKenzie

Decolonizing Contemporary Gospel Music,
Robert Beckford

New Black Godz,
Monica Miller

Innovation and Competition in Zimbabwean Pentecostalism

Megachurches and the Marketization of Religion

Edited by Ezra Chitando

BLOOMSBURY ACADEMIC
LONDON • NEW YORK • OXFORD • NEW DELHI • SYDNEY

BLOOMSBURY ACADEMIC
Bloomsbury Publishing Plc
50 Bedford Square, London, WC1B 3DP, UK
1385 Broadway, New York, NY 10018, USA
29 Earlsfort Terrace, Dublin 2, Ireland

BLOOMSBURY, BLOOMSBURY ACADEMIC and the Diana logo are trademarks of Bloomsbury Publishing Plc

First published in Great Britain 2021
Paperback edition published 2022

Copyright © Ezra Chitando and contributors, 2021

Ezra Chitando and contributors have asserted their right under the Copyright, Designs and Patents Act, 1988, to be identified as Authors of this work.

For legal purposes the Acknowledgements on p. x constitute an extension of this copyright page.

Series design by Maria Rajka
Cover design: Ben Anslow
Cover images: Golden texture background © Katsumi Murouchi, Closeup of dark black grunge textured background © R.Tsubin (Getty Images), *Dove on the Sun* © DeAgostini/Getty Images

All rights reserved. No part of this publication may be reproduced or transmitted in any form or by any means, electronic or mechanical, including photocopying, recording, or any information storage or retrieval system, without prior permission in writing from the publishers.

Bloomsbury Publishing Plc does not have any control over, or responsibility for, any third-party websites referred to or in this book. All internet addresses given in this book were correct at the time of going to press. The author and publisher regret any inconvenience caused if addresses have changed or sites have ceased to exist, but can accept no responsibility for any such changes.

A catalogue record for this book is available from the British Library.

Library of Congress Control Number: 2020949131

ISBN:	HB:	978-1-3501-7601-0
	PB:	978-1-3502-1327-2
	ePDF:	978-1-3501-7604-1
	eBook:	978-1-3501-7603-4

Series: Bloomsbury Studies in Black Religion and Cultures

Typeset by Integra Software Services Pvt. Ltd.

To find out more about our authors and books visit www.bloomsbury.com and sign up for our newsletters

Contents

List of contributors   vii
Acknowledgements   x

Introduction: Innovation and competition in Zimbabwean Pentecostalism
Ezra Chitando   1

1. Pentecostalism in Zimbabwe and the revitalization of African traditional religions: A comparative analysis of the newer religious movements
   Kudzai Biri   21

2. Miracles, *muti* and magic: An inquiry into the analogous nature of Pentecostal miracles and African traditional beliefs
   Obert Bernard Mlambo and Clive Tendai Zimunya   33

3. 'The devil is on fire': Analysing Pentecostalism as a place of refuge amidst economic and political turmoil in Zimbabwe
   Lovemore Ndlovu   45

4. Pentecostal Prophets Emmanuel Makandiwa and Walter Magaya: Masculinity, competition and the postcolonial state in Zimbabwe
   Ezra Chitando   61

5. Religion in a new era: Pentecostalism and innovation in the Prophetic Healing and Deliverance Ministries in Zimbabwe
   Tabona Shoko   75

6. Rebranding Pentecostalism: An analysis of the United Family International Church and Prophetic Healing Deliverance Ministries
   Molly Manyonganise   89

7. Survival of the fittest: A comparative analysis of United Family International Church and Prophetic and Healing Deliverance Ministries
   Fungai Chirongoma   103

8. Old wine in new wine skins: Continuities and discontinuities of African traditional anthropological beliefs in the DiVineyard Church of His Presence
   Fortune Sibanda   117

9	Competition and complementarity in newer Zimbabwean Pentecostal ministries	
	Tenson Muyambo	135
10	The quest for a unique identity: The case of Prophetic Healing and Deliverance Ministries in Zimbabwe	
	Martin Mujinga	149
11	'Serve God full time and overtime': Pentecostalism in Zimbabwe and the reconfiguration of the gospel of prosperity	
	Kudzai Biri	163
12	Older and newer Zimbabwean Pentecostal churches' focus on the prosperity gospel: A comparative analysis	
	Phillip Musoni	175
13	At the mercy of 'the Man of God'? Sexual and gender-based violence in Zimbabwean Pentecostalism	
	Tapiwa Praise Mapuranga	191
14	Lampooning prophetic Pentecostal Christianity in Zimbabwe: The case of Bustop TV	
	Ezra Chitando and Kelvin Chikonzo	203
Notes		216
References		218
Index		238

Contributors

Kudzai Biri is an associate professor at the University of Zimbabwe, Department of Religious Studies, Classics and Philosophy. She has held the Alexander von Humboldt Fellowship at the University of Bamberg, Germany. Her research interests are in religion and gender, and religion and politics.

Kelvin Chikonzo is a senior lecturer in the Department of Theatre Arts at the University of Zimbabwe. His research and publication interests cover identity, resistance studies, performance history, subaltern studies, democracy and cultural studies within theoretical frameworks of post-linearity (postcolonialism), post-feminism, post-nationalism, postmodernism, post-dramatic semiotics, psychoanalysis, narratology, Marxism, Gaze and Afrocentricity.

Fungai Chirongoma is a PhD student at the University of Cape Town, South Africa. Her research interests are in religion, gender and development. Fungai's PhD focus is on the interventions of faith-based organization in addressing violence against women. She is a tutor of the Religion, Sexuality and Gender course in the Department of Religious Studies at the University of Cape Town.

Ezra Chitando is a professor of history and phenomenology of religion at the University of Zimbabwe and World Council of Churches Ecumenical HIV and AIDS Initiatives and Advocacy Theology Consultant for Southern Africa. He publishes on HIV, Pentecostalism, gender, security, climate change, sexuality and development.

Molly Manyonganise holds a PhD in biblical and religious studies from the University of Pretoria. She is a senior lecturer in the Department of Religious Studies and Philosophy at the Zimbabwe Open University. Her research interests cover religion and politics, gender and religion, as well as African Christianity.

Tapiwa Praise Mapuranga is an associate professor at the University of Zimbabwe, Department of Religious Studies, Classics and Philosophy. Her research and publication interests include religion and gender, politics, method and theory in the study of religion and women in new religious movements.

Obert Bernard Mlambo is a member of the Department of Religious Studies, Classics and Philosophy at the University of Zimbabwe. He is currently an awardee of the Humboldt Return Fellowship and a visiting scholar at the Global South Studies Centre in the University of Cologne, Germany. His research interests include Roman history, veterans and post-war conflicts, and comparative studies of classical and contemporary African societies. He is a recipient of the Fondation Hardt's Young Researchers Fellowship (Geneva, Switzerland) and the Nordic Africa Institute's Guest Scholar Fellowship (Uppsala, Sweden).

Martin Mujinga is the academic dean of the United Theological College in Harare, Zimbabwe. He is a research fellow of the Research Institute for Theology and Religion, University of South Africa. His research interests include Methodist history and theology, African spirituality, the role of religion in transforming societies, theologies of migration, human trafficking, chaplaincy ministry, as well as African liberation, political theologies and ecotheology.

Phillip Musoni is the holder of a Doctor of Philosophy degree from the College of Human Sciences at the University of South Africa in Pretoria, South Africa. He is a post-doctoral research fellow in the Department of Christian Spirituality, Church History and Missiology, University of South Africa. His research and publication interests include African indigenous churches (AICs) and African spiritualities, AICs and politics, AICs and gender, AICs and sexuality, and AICs and the prosperity gospel.

Tenson Muyambo is a PhD holder in gender and religion from the University of KwaZulu Natal. He is currently a lecturer at Great Zimbabwe University, Department of Teacher Development. His research interests are in gender and religion, indigenous knowledge systems, African Pentecostalism and African indigenous religion.

Lovemore Ndlovu is an independent researcher in the study of religion. His research interests lie in the interconnectedness of religion and other institutions such as religion and education, religion and gender, religion and politics, etc. He has studied Pentecostal churches in Zimbabwe and published on the impact of religion on public life, gender and sexualities.

Tabona Shoko is a professor of African traditional religion in the Department of Religious Studies, Classics and Philosophy in Harare, Zimbabwe. His research and publication interests include African Pentecostalism, religion and human rights, and religion and environment.

Fortune Sibanda is an associate professor in the Department of Philosophy and Religious Studies, Great Zimbabwe University, Masvingo, Zimbabwe. Professor Sibanda received his DPhil in Arts (Religious Studies) from the University of Zimbabwe in 2015. Sibanda has published widely in Refereed journals and book chapters. His research interests include new religious movements, African Pentecostalism, human rights issues, religion and the environment, law and religion. Sibanda is a member of a number of academic associations including the American Academy of Religion (AAR), African Consortium for Law and Religion Studies (ACLARS), International Consortium for Law and Religion Studies (ICLARS), African Theological Institutions in Southern and Central Africa (ATISCA), Association for the Study of Religion in Southern Africa (ASRSA) and African Association for the Study of Religion (AASR).

Clive Tendai Zimunya is a philosophy lecturer at the National University of Lesotho in the Department of Philosophy. He holds a PhD in philosophy from the University of KwaZulu-Natal, South Africa. Research interests include African philosophy, logic, epistemology, philosophy of religion and ethics.

Acknowledgements

This volume emerges from two research projects, namely 'Innovation and Competition: Changing Religiosity from African Traditional Religious Beliefs to Pentecostalism in Harare, Zimbabwe', which was led by Tapiwa Praise Mapuranga, and 'Propelled by the Spirit: Pentecostalism, Innovation and Competition in Kenya, South Africa and Zimbabwe', which had Ezra Chitando, Damaris Parsitau, Henrietta Nyamnjoh and the editor as the lead researchers. Both projects were supported by the Nagel Institute for the Study of World Christianity at Calvin College. The chapters in this volume, however, emerge from the Zimbabwean section of the later project. The editor and the researchers/contributors are most grateful for the support.

Prof Joel Carpenter and Nellie Kooistra provided motivation and guidance that facilitated the completion of the two research projects. Prof Afe Adogame, Dr Abel Ugba, Dr Parsitau, Prof Francis Nyamnjoh and Dr Henrietta Nyamnjoh all proffered valuable insights into innovation and competition in African Pentecostalism.

Any shortcomings of this publication, however, must not be attributed to any of the individuals named above.

Introduction: Innovation and competition in Zimbabwean Pentecostalism

Ezra Chitando

Background and context

Zimbabwean Pentecostalism, being firmly located within the larger African Pentecostalism, has been receiving attention from academics who approach the phenomenon from different disciplines and angles. Thus, scholars such as Maxwell (2006), Chitando et al. (2013c), Shoko (2015), Machingura et al. (2018), Togarasei (2018) and Mapuranga (2018) have explored different aspects of Zimbabwean Pentecostalism. These dimensions include history, interface with politics, gender, economic impact and others. Beyond Zimbabwe, some scholars such as Adogame (2013), Kaunda (2018), Asamoah-Gyadu (2015), Kroesbergen (2017, 2019), Afolayan et al. (2018) and others have reflected on the dynamic character of African Pentecostalism. On his part, Ukah (2015) interrogated the policing of miracles in the media by entrepreneurial Nigerian Pentecostal miracles. Ukwuegbu et al. (2014) critique the focus on prosperity in Nigerian Pentecostalism. The rise of mega churches (Hunt 2020) has taken place within the Pentecostal strand of Christianity, necessitating the type of closer analysis undertaken within this volume.

African Pentecostalism has emerged as a highly proliferated phenomenon, taking the sub-Saharan African region by storm within the last two decades. Although a separate narrative is required in order to do justice to its key tenets, for the purposes of this introduction I shall draw attention to the emergence or recasting of the figure of the 'Man of God' or prophet. A comparative analysis across different countries and contexts shows the prophet as mostly a young, charismatic and sophisticated man. He is often associated with miracles, particularly healing, and preaches prosperity and upward social mobility, and provides motivation for his followers. In a highly competitive environment, mega prophets have emerged in some of the hotbeds of African Pentecostalism. These include Nigeria, Ghana, Kenya, Uganda, Zambia and South Africa. Seeking to address socio-economic, political, spiritual and other challenges, the prophets have been something of a spectacle, bringing colour and glamour to the religious scene.

As noted above, Zimbabwe has not been left out of the latest wave of African Pentecostalism. It has become clear that Pentecostalism is now a very strategic player on the Zimbabwean and African religious market. I use the term 'market' deliberately, as it echoes the major thrust of this volume. In economics, the market is an arena where those who are selling different products bring them out for diverse consumers to make a choice. The concept of the religious market has been used in the economics of religion where the assumption has been that religion will be more vibrant in those contexts where it is less regulated (Chaves and Cann 1992; Iannaccone 1998).

Religion is regarded as a phenomenon that is affected by factors such as brands, consumers and markets (Gauthier and Martikainen 2013). The volume edited by Jelen (2002) brings together some of the key themes on the economics of religion. On their part, Nyamnjoh and Carpenter (2018) have explored how shifting attention to the religious market enables scholars to appreciate the innovation and competition that characterize much of contemporary Africa. Crucially, innovation has been undertaken in different facets of African life. Thus, there has been innovation in both the material and immaterial forms in Africa (Gewald et al. 2012: 6). This volume focuses on immaterial innovation within Pentecostalism in Zimbabwe and how it has coloured forms of religious expression in the country.

It is vital to acknowledge that the competition and innovation that characterize Zimbabwean Pentecostalism are being experienced in other African (and global) settings. Within the specific context of Africa, Pentecostalism is characterized by intense competition and innovation in countries such as Nigeria, Ghana, Uganda, Zambia and South Africa (among others). As this volume highlights, such competition and innovation have generated considerable controversy, with some critics wondering whether freedom of religion must be acknowledged as absolute or whether the state must regulate religious practice. Furthermore, competition has necessitated specialization and branding within the Pentecostal movement. Writing from within Kenya, Damaris Parsitau, who herself has invested heavily in understanding newer Pentecostal churches, draws attention to the internal competition when she says:

> Deliverance ministries are always in competition to attract followers to their healing services, hence creating stiff competition between various churches. This competition has necessitated the creation of niche ministries where a particular pastor or pastoress will emphasise certain special powers to woo members. So, some will teach deliverance, others will teach money and prosperity, while others focus on sexual purity and end-time theologies.
>
> (Parsitau 2019)

Parsitau succeeds in underscoring the ultra-competitive nature of African Pentecostalism. However, there are some movements that have sought to combine all the dimensions that she has itemized in the foregoing citation. They have sought to provide a 'supermarket' where clients with specific needs can access their goods of choice, all under one roof. Thus, as this volume illustrates, such movements teach deliverance, money and prosperity, while emphasizing purity and end-time theologies. Admittedly, they place more emphasis on some dimensions, such as deliverance and prosperity. However, they seek to retain and increase their membership in an environment characterized by intense competition.

As Pentecostalism attracts more adherents and clients in Zimbabwe (and in other parts of the world), competition among its propagators has intensified. As different ministries multiply and announce their presence on the market, they are challenged either to attract new adherents and clients or to retain them. Competition generates innovation, as the different Pentecostal prophets seek to demonstrate why they are 'the only game in town'. In Zimbabwe and South Africa, for example, this competition has sometimes generated problematic practices. For example, in order to demonstrate their grip/hold or power over their members, some prophets have led to challenging claims such as resurrecting a member from the dead, having the ability to 'dial God's very own number', having the capacity to levitate, possessing 'spiritual spectacles', selling/distributing anointed pens and condoms (Kaunda 2016), and other claims of the capacity to achieve stupendous feats. All these have been undertaken in the context of the emerging ministries wanting to increase their market share. Central to these processes is aggressive and sophisticated marketing. The following has been noted in relation to the religious market in the United States of America and it is applicable to Zimbabwe. Thus:

> The growth of the megachurch can be attributed to many factors, not the least of which is the sophisticated marketing that these churches have embraced. Marketing research, segmentation, positioning, branding, product development,

integrated marketing communications and distribution strategy are clearly understood and utilized in the marketing strategies of successful megachurches.
(Kuzma et al. 2009: 2)

Studying innovation and competition in Zimbabwean Pentecostalism contributes towards clarifying the phenomenon in the country, within Southern Africa and beyond. This is due to the fact that there is a lot of movement of personalities and ideas within Pentecostalism. For example, two of the leading personalities in Zimbabwean Pentecostalism (whose movements are the main focus of this volume), namely Emmanuel Makandiwa of the United Family International (UFI) Church and Walter Magaya of the Prophetic Healing and Deliverance (PHD) Ministries, are well known in the Southern African region. They are popular for their religious, economic and social programmes. In 2017, the University of South Africa (UNISA) awarded Magaya an honorary doctorate in theology, while in 2019 Magaya was the guest speaker at a UNISA graduation ceremony. It is clear that Makandiwa and Magaya represent a new wave of prophetic Pentecostalism in Africa. Therefore, it is strategic to pay attention to their creativity and innovation as this provides insights into this rapidly expanding phenomenon.

To a very large extent, this volume focuses on 'inter-divine industry and inter-religious competition' in Zimbabwe. Thus, most of the essays concentrate on the intense competition between two of the 'megachurches' in Zimbabwe, namely the United Family International Church (UFIC) of Emmanuel Makandiwa and the Prophetic Healing and Deliverance (PHD) Ministries of Walter Magaya. These were the two largest Pentecostal churches at the time the essays were finalized. They serviced hundreds of thousands of congregants and clients and were two of the most significant players from within the Pentecostal fold. However, there was intense competition between them, although a separate narrative could focus on the collaboration between them (Chitando and Biri 2016). In this regard, the reference to 'healthy competition' by Yidana and Issahaku (2014: 5) can, therefore, be justified.

There appears to be a tacit realization that an attack on one of the prophets/ministries is, by extension, an attack on the other. In other words, their adherents and defenders are painfully aware of the fact that if one prophet is brought down (e.g. by being accused of making false prophecies), the entire prophetic movement faces the risk of being brought into disrepute. However, this does not remove the dimension of fierce internal competition between the prophets. There is both subtle and open competition between these two prophets, as well as others who are jostling for a share of the market. Consequently, in order to retain their share of the market, or to grow it, the prophets must be innovating continually.

Since each chapter that focuses on Makandiwa and Magaya provides at least some background information on these personalities, providing a detailed discussion of these two major personalities here would result in further duplication. However, I shall draw attention to some of the key dimensions that have made these two the leading exemplars of prophetic Pentecostalism in Zimbabwe. Indeed, the close similarities between these two have necessitated branding in an endeavour for each one to stand out on his own. Nonetheless, from a comparative perspective, it is possible to identify some major common features. These are elaborated on in the different chapters in this volume.

These two have emerged as mega-prophets due to their extensive appropriation of the media and aggressive marketing. They have private television stations and are also widely covered by both the private and public media. It is clear that they are newsmakers and their opinion on various aspects of life, including politics, is widely sought. They have been able to capture a large share of the spiritual market, with many members of mainline churches taking time to listen to or view their performances of miracles or motivational talks. To this end, therefore, Makandiwa and Magaya are public spectacles, beyond the religious field in which they are significant players. It is for this reason that most of the chapters in this volume are on these two key religious actors or performers.

Outlining the definitional predicament: Characterizing Zimbabwean Pentecostalism

The academic study of religion has been characterized by a stubborn and persistent admission, namely that most of the leading concepts in the discipline remain open to debate and ongoing clarification. The critical terms for the study of religion (Taylor 1998) have not generated any consensus regarding their meaning and application within the field. The debate over terminology continues to rage, particularly in relation to African/Zimbabwean Pentecostalism. Perhaps one of the biggest challenges has been due to the attempt by scholars to provide an exhaustive and universal definition of Pentecostalism. Such an effort is ultimately futile, as one will not be able to say what Pentecostalism has been in the past, is currently and shall be in the future, for all adherents of Pentecostalism in Zimbabwe and elsewhere (cf Platvoet 1999 on defining religion). Definitions that seek to be comprehensive and binding run the risk of being too wide and prescriptive.

This volume operates with an open or working definition of Zimbabwean Pentecostalism (cf Comstock 1984 on open definitions of religion). Such a definition does not claim any finality but is employed to facilitate discussion. Contributors to this volume focused more specifically on the 'third wave' of Zimbabwean Pentecostalism, namely those ministries that emerged after 2008. Justifying his choice of concentrating on these newer/younger Pentecostal churches, which he dubs 'neo-Pentecostal', Fenga (2018) makes the following assertion:

> There is a wave of Christianity in Zimbabwe which is current, which the research will refer to as the 'Third Wave' of Pentecostalism to distinguish from traditional Pentecostal Christianity in Zimbabwe. These churches are 'neo' because they were founded five years ago, and most of them came from the traditional Pentecostal churches.
>
> (Fenga 2018: 32)

Some very helpful historical perspectives on the growth of Pentecostalism in Zimbabwe from the early 1900s, across the 1960s and the 1980s, as well as new developments in the 2000s, have been provided by Maxwell (2006) and Togarasei (2018) and will not be repeated here. What needs to be underscored is the point that Zimbabwean Pentecostalism is a combination of external influences (particularly from the United States of America via South Africa) and indigenous factors (as illustrated by the opening chapters in this volume).

Some of the key characteristics of Zimbabwean Pentecostalism, particularly what I have termed 'prophetic Pentecostalism' in Chapter 4 in this volume, include the following: emphasis on the Holy Spirit as the enabler of prosperity, healing and deliverance, the power and authority of the prophet as a unique 'Man of God' and the extensive use of media technologies to publicize specific movements. I briefly outline these characteristics below, since they are also elaborated on in many of the chapters in this volume.

First, the emphasis on the Holy Spirit has been central to Pentecostalism across the different historical periods. Indeed, the entire Pentecostal movement might be seen as 'Spirit-driven'. Histories of African Pentecostalism (see e.g. Kalu 2008) or global Pentecostalism (see e.g. Anderson 2013) have rightly drawn attention to the primacy of the Holy Spirit to Pentecostalism. The Holy Spirit, the third person of the trinity, is at the centre of Pentecostalism. The Holy Spirit is regarded as transforming the individual in the experience of conversion and as inspiring a deep sense of mission/spreading the gospel. Thus:

> The key theological contribution of the modern Pentecostal movement is, without doubt, in pneumatology. As Pentecostalism has challenged theologically the widespread notion that the gifts of the Spirit have ceased, its most significant contribution is the reviving of the dynamic work of the Holy Spirit in Christian life and practice. As a result the Pentecostal contribution of pneumatological missiology has changed the global Christian landscape in the last century.
> (Ma 2017: 227)

Second, the theme of prosperity, healing and deliverance features prominently in Zimbabwean Pentecostalism. Whereas the early missionaries had taught a gospel that placed emphasis on salvation as a future event, contemporary Pentecostalism is predominantly 'this-worldly'. In keeping with the African approach to salvation (Maimela 1985), contemporary Zimbabwean Pentecostalism regards prosperity as a mark of divine favour. Thus, converts and clients are encouraged to attain material prosperity this side of the grave. Through investing financially in the ministry, fasting and prayer, confronting and resisting evil spirits, utilizing protective objects from the prophet and other strategies, they are believed to be strategically placed to achieve and retain prosperity. Although this dimension of Pentecostalism has attracted criticism, some scholars such as Togarasei (2011) contend that the idea of prosperity does have its positive side. He maintains that, like Weber's views on the Protestant ethic and how it inspired capitalism, the message on prosperity can galvanize Africans to tackle poverty.

Third, healing and deliverance is another major feature of the latest wave of Zimbabwean Pentecostalism. Commenting on the situation in Nigeria, Diara and Onah (2014: 399) argue that although there are a number of factors responsible for Pentecostal church growth, healing miracles played the most prominent role, especially in Nigeria. This is also true of the Zimbabwean situation. The expulsion of demonic forces that frustrate the elect of God is quite pronounced. 'Principalities and powers' are believed to suffuse the created order. Their major focus is to stop converts and clients from enjoying life in abundance, as promised by the gospel. These negative forces include ancestral/generational curses, misfortunes generated by wicked people such as witches and other malevolent spiritual powers. African Pentecostalism has capitalized on the pre-existing indigenous beliefs in these spiritual powers to promote healing and deliverance. Writing from the context of Ghana, but applying the idea to Africa in general, Baffour makes the following submission:

> In Africa (Ghana inclusive), both good health and sickness can be likened to two sides of the same coin. Good health is considered the wellbeing of the mind, body and spirit, living in harmony with one's neighbour, the environment and oneself, and in all levels of reality – physical, social, spiritual, natural and supernatural. In other words healing and deliverance aim at restoring disturbed persons to proper functioning order, and it is symptomatic of correct relationship with one's environment.
>
> (Baffour 2018: 269)

Fourth, and intricately related to the foregoing, is the emphasis on the power and authority of the 'Man of God' in Zimbabwean Pentecostalism. Indeed, the label 'prophetic Pentecostalism' (adopted by Chitando in Chapter 4) emerges from this feature. The prominent ministries are inseparable from their charismatic prophetic founders. It is these prophets who drive their movements and ensure that converts and clients derive divine blessings. What Klaits (2017: 242–3) observes of African American pastors is applicable to the prophets in Zimbabwean Pentecostalism: they regard themselves as vessels used by God to deliver relevant and life-transforming messages to God's people. Writing from the context of Zambia, but applying the idea to Southern Africa in general, Kroesbergen makes the following submission:

> Nowadays, the focus is not on the equal access of every congregant to God but on the person of the pastor – often referred to as 'man of God' or 'woman of God'. This is the one who is linked to God, this is the one who prays to God, and this is the one who delivers God's good gifts to the ordinary congregants.
>
> (Kroesbergen 2019: 238)

Although every phenomenon is best understood within its own context, from the foregoing, it is possible to locate Zimbabwean prophetic Pentecostalism within the larger setting of African prophetic Pentecostalism. By outlining the key characteristics of Zimbabwean prophetic Pentecostalism and showing how these are consistent with features of African prophetic Pentecostalism, I have illustrated patterns of continuity between the two. Of course, as the chapters in this volume amplify, it remains necessary to cull the peculiar historical, socio-economic, religio-cultural and political factors that have given rise to Zimbabwean prophetic Pentecostalism.

Innovation and competition in Zimbabwean Pentecostalism

The Zimbabwean religious market is characterized by radical pluralism. Alongside African indigenous religions, major missionary religions such as Christianity and Islam have established a significant market share. Furthermore, the Baha'i Faith, Hinduism, Buddhism, Rastafari and other religions are also present on the same market. Consequently, 'Pentecostalism has had to negotiate with the beliefs and practices of its competitors on the religious market' (Chitando 2018: 16). This means that Pentecostalism does not have free rein on the religious market: its entry and expansion are contested and resisted. Furthermore, the competition is not only with external players; it is also very much within Pentecostalism itself. In a helpful analysis on the religious market in Ghana (which they call the divine industry), Yidana and Issahaku (2014) draw attention to the different categories of competition. They write:

> Religious competition amongst the various actors in the divine industry, as the case may be, are categorised into three: inter-divine industry, intra-divine industry and inter-religious competition. To put it another way, competition is faced from within Pentecostal divine industries in particular and orthodox divine industries as a whole and competition from outside where they compete with other religious bodies such as the traditional African and Islamic religions.
>
> (Yidana and Issahaku 2014: 5)

Alongside internal competition, Pentecostal churches must contend with the resilience of African indigenous religions. As recent studies have indicated (Orobator 2018; Grillo et al. 2019), African indigenous religions have remained highly active and continue to be a force to reckon with. It is the 'African map of the universe' that continues to influence African converts to Pentecostalism, as the doyen of African Pentecostalism, Kalu (2008) observed. In competing with African indigenous religions, particularly with its world view and sacred practitioners, Pentecostal prophets have had to demonstrate a lot of creativity. This has involved adaptation, reformulation and outright rejection of certain aspects of African indigenous religions. What is clear, however, is that African Pentecostalism (and any other religion in Africa) must always be prepared to engage with African indigenous religions.

Although this particular volume does not engage with the extent to which innovation and competition in Pentecostalism have had a bearing on the historical mainline churches (Protestant and Catholic) in Zimbabwe, it is clear that the Pentecostal movement has left an indelible mark on the mainline churches. For example, there has been a clear influence by way of the tension over speaking in tongues and the adoption of mass prayer (especially the Lord's Prayer) by the mainline churches. Furthermore, the gospel of prosperity has spilled over from Pentecostal churches to mainline churches, particularly as younger pastors from the latter seek to establish themselves on the religious market. In addition, members of Pentecostal churches put bumper stickers declaring that they are 'Proudly [Methodist/Catholic/Anglican/Reformed, etc.]' in response. Thus, members of mainline churches have been forced to be on the defensive by their counterparts from the Pentecostal churches. Writing about the phenomenon of the megachurch in the United States of America, Kuzma et al. make the following submission:

> The growth of the megachurch can be attributed to many factors, not the least of which is the sophisticated marketing that these churches have embraced. Marketing research, segmentation, positioning, branding, product development, integrated marketing communications and distribution strategy are clearly understood and utilized in the marketing strategies of successful megachurches. In fact, some critics have dismissed the so-called slick marketing of megachurches as evidence of how such churches are somehow not religious enough.
>
> (Kuzma et al. 2009: 2)

The socio-economic and political context: An overview

Innovation and competition do not take place in a socio-economic and political vacuum. In the specific case of Zimbabwe, there were major socio-economic and political developments that are relevant for one to gain an appreciation of the upsurge in Pentecostalism. First, there was serious economic turbulence in the country. From the early 2000s, Zimbabwe had experienced economic challenges that were compounded by the fast-track land reform programme (FTLRP), isolation from the international community through sanctions and record-breaking hyperinflation. There was, indeed, a real plunge (Bond and Manyanya 2002) and unemployment ballooned. With former President Robert Mugabe (he was removed from office in November 2017, and died on 06 September 2019) adopting populist policies and engaging in dangerous rhetoric, Zimbabwe's economy was in free fall.

On the political front, bickering and contestation continued unabated. Mugabe's long tenure as the sole leader of the country since independence in 1980 generated a lot of antipathy. Externally, younger opponents were challenging his grip on power through different platforms. These included formal opposition political parties, trade unions, loose coalitions of youth activists, as well as independent/radical religious leaders (Tarusarira 2016). Internally, his long-serving assistants were becoming impatient with him. However, his praise singers insisted that not even the grave would stop him from presiding over Zimbabwe. This generated factionalism in his party (Nyambi 2016). In turn, this affected the delivery of government programmes.

As citizens struggled to cope, Pentecostalism reasserted its presence on the market through the emergence of vibrant prophetic ministries, such as UFIC and PHD Ministries. Older Pentecostal churches such as the Apostolic Faith Mission (AFM) and the Zimbabwe Assemblies of God Africa (ZAOGA) had offered spiritual guidance and shared economic principles across the years. However, the arrival of young, dynamic and forceful prophets such as Makandiwa and Magaya changed the character of Pentecostalism in Zimbabwe in a decisive way. It was in this context that was characterized by angst and loss of hope that the young prophets arrived to proclaim hope and deliverance. They galvanized their followers and clients to anticipate prosperity. This prosperity would be for both individuals and the country. This was reinforced by some Pentecostal gospel musicians who were 'singing positivity' (Gukurume 2017) in very challenging contexts.

Youthful Pentecostal prophets announced their presence on the Zimbabwean religious market by promising to tackle the most pressing socio-economic challenges in a depressing political environment. Where pessimists were writing off Zimbabwe due to rampant corruption, unemployment and political wrangles, they prophesied hope and dynamic.

They charged that, like the proverbial bones in Ezekiel, Zimbabwe would rise yet again. Individual problems relating to health, unemployment, struggles in relationships, childlessness and others would be overcome, they proclaimed. This phenomenon has been observed in other African contexts. For example, Afe Adogame (2012) has analysed how one particular Pentecostal church in Nigeria emphasizes deliverance in its rhetoric. Similarly, Magaya's PHD Ministries, for example, made deliverance a central feature of its practice.

While trying to heal individuals, families, communities and the nation on the social front, on the economic front the Pentecostal prophets sought to equip individuals with ideas for empowerment. They also proffered models for national prosperity (Wariboko 2012). Pentecostal prophets encouraged individuals to defy the oppressive economic context and to come up with innovative projects. As the volume by Mapuranga (2018) demonstrates, Pentecostal churches sought to equip women in particular with knowledge and skills to run their own businesses. Overall, therefore, an appreciation of the prevailing socio-economic and political context facilitates an understanding of the innovation and competition that characterized Pentecostal interventions.

The interface between the young male Pentecostal prophets and politics is more complicated than the straightforward narrative of complicity with the ruling elite that some critics insist on. In this scheme, the prophets are at the service of the politicians and are holding back their members from engaging in positive social change. They preach about self-control and are trying to achieve personal transformation without changing the political structures of the day, critics charge. Thus:

> Firstly, the prophets spiritualise the material; they reverse the normal perception of things. Instead of confronting the physical hegemony, they focus on the spiritual realm, thus, instead of taking action against the real oppressor, people pray, fast and wait for gods to do the rest. In Zimbabwe, the church for the past 10 years must be given credit for pacifying people from being politically active. Instead of demonstrating and sloganeering against Mugabe, the church encouraged people to fast and to pray. In many of their assemblies, the prophets and preachers redefine power dynamics; power is not a physical confrontation against Mugabe, but in prayer.
>
> (Dube 2015: 3)

In practice, however, the prophets have sought to equip their members with the right mindset to survive in turbulent political contexts. In particular, they call upon Pentecostals to be vigilant citizens who shun corruption and uphold high ethical values. Pentecostal prophets have sought to engineer profound social transformation. While I acknowledge that they have not always been successful, I am impressed by their commitment to creating a new social order.

Writing in the context of Zambia, Kaunda (2018) has highlighted the extent to which Pentecostalism seeks to develop a new political culture. Granted that such projects are always fraught with internal contradictions (often seen in different interpretations of political power), the effort must be acknowledged.

A note on the gender dimension

Like most societies in the world, Zimbabwean society is predominantly patriarchal. Men tend to dominate public space, particularly in politics, business and religion. It is, therefore, not surprising that the prophetic leaders who emerged were mostly men. Although there are some women who are heading Pentecostal ministries in Zimbabwe (Mapuranga 2013a), the field is dominated by young men. To a large extent, although women feature prominently within the Pentecostal movement in Zimbabwe (and in Africa), they mainly do so as clients seeking the services of the 'mighty Men of God'.

The dominant gender ideology facilitates the dominance of young male prophets in Zimbabwean Pentecostalism. The social construction of men as leaders enables young male prophets to find a niche on the religious market. At the same time, equally gifted young women struggle to get a share of the market due to the same gender ideology. However, it is important to acknowledge that there has been debate over the extent to which Pentecostalism has challenged the dominant gender ideology (see e.g. Soothill 2007; Gabaitse 2015).

The young male Pentecostal prophets have, to their credit, been willing to critique toxic expressions of masculinity in Zimbabwe. In particular, they have challenged the tendency to normalize men's extramarital relationships. They have also challenged men to adopt 'Transformative Masculinities', namely those ways of being men that promote the health and well-being of women and children. For example, while the dominant position in Zimbabwean Christianity has always been that 'God hates divorce' (Malachi 2: 16), Makandiwa has said the extreme levels of violence that some men have shown call for a new approach to divorce. On his part, Magaya has called for men to reform and accept women as partners. This rethinking of Pentecostal masculinity confirms an emerging trend that has been observed in other parts of Africa, including, for example, in Zambia (Van Klinken 2016) and Kenya (Chitando and Kilonzo 2018).

The male identity of the prophets grants them a certain level of authority that derives from the patriarchal dividend. This is the privilege that boys and men enjoy by virtue of being male (Connell 1995, 2005). As men, they already have the advantage of being identified with leadership, power and authority. All these dimensions are greatly magnified when the religious dimension is added. The prophets are 'representatives of God' and this elevates their standing in society. Furthermore, it grants them a measure of security in innovation, as they are (to some extent) sheltered from scepticism by virtue of being male.

However, as I shall highlight below, their youthful outlook has rendered them vulnerable. Some critics are quick to draw attention to their age in debates over their authenticity.

Key dimensions of innovation and competition

A longer narrative is required in order to do justice to the dimensions of innovation and competition that characterize the religious market in contemporary Zimbabwe. Chapters in this book go a long way in highlighting some of the key features of innovation and competition in the religious sector in the country. First, there has been a notable growth in Pentecostal megachurches. As has been alluded to already, the UFIC and PHD Ministries constitute two of the largest and most consistent younger Pentecostal churches in Zimbabwe. With headquarters in Harare, but expanding throughout the country, into the Southern African region (particularly in South Africa, Botswana, Namibia and beyond), these churches are attracting tens of thousands of worshippers to their services.

Second, there has been fierce competition for adherents and clients between these two (and other emerging) Pentecostal churches. Indeed, the fierce competition has generated innovation as the churches seek to increase their respective market shares. This has led to branding in order to ensure that each particular prophet (and his distinctive church/products) can stand alone and be identified as autonomous. Such branding has been by way of holding services at distinctive centres (City Sports for UFIC) and Zindoga Business Centre in Waterfalls (PHD Ministries). Also, the branding has led to separate television stations (Christ TV for UFIC and Yadah TV for PHD Ministries). This dimension is particularly important, as scholars of global and African Pentecostalism have highlighted the centrality of the media to the operations of Pentecostal churches (Ukah 2003b; Kay 2009; Obayi and Odogor 2016).

Third, there is innovation on the delivery of the message of prosperity, healing and deliverance within younger Pentecostal churches. Whereas older Pentecostal churches such as the Apostolic Faith Mission (AFM) and the Zimbabwe Assemblies of God Africa (ZAOGA) had been preaching the prosperity gospel for many years, the younger prophets have been more aggressive in communicating the message of prosperity (see the chapter by Musoni in this volume).

Fourth, some emerging Pentecostal prophets (beyond Makandiwa and Magaya who feature prominently in this volume) have been creative around the theology of retribution. This is the theology of 'back to sender' where the evil that would have been designed against one returns to the schemer. Kangwa (2016) has examined this phenomenon in Zambia. It is informed by the indigenous world view where the traditional healer can cause those who intend to harm others to endure the pain they intended to cause to others.

Fifth, the rise of Pentecostal prophets such as Makandiwa and Magaya has instigated the rise of notable traditional healers such as Sekuru (honorific title, 'Grandfather') 'Dr' Kamwelo Banda. Banda, a practising Muslim, is anchored in traditional healing. Like other traditional healers, he has claimed that some of the popular Pentecostal prophets utilize his services by the dark of night. Thus, prophetic Pentecostalism has not enjoyed a smooth ride in its rise to ascendancy on the Zimbabwean spiritual market. Sacred practitioners from African traditional religions (ATRs) and African Initiated Churches have emerged to compete against the 'mega prophets'.

Sixth, there is innovation in some of the products offered by the Pentecostal prophets. For example, Magaya's Aguma product, released amidst serious controversy in 2018, sought to combine the three therapeutic systems found in Zimbabwe into one. Thus, it sought to harmonize Western medicine, spiritual healing and traditional healing into a single product. Magaya claimed that Aguma could heal HIV, cancer and other diseases. He claimed that it had been tested (and confirmed) in scientific laboratories. He (the prophet) had been led to the tree (traditional) in a dream. Thus, Magaya sought to harmonize Western medicine, spiritual healing and traditional medicine through his Aguma product. Although the Ministry of Health challenged him and forced him to apologize, it is clear that he hoped to develop a more integrated product.

Finally, innovation and competition within prophetic Pentecostal Christianity in Zimbabwe have generated considerable controversy. Indeed, a separate study is necessary to do justice to the contentions. These range from the claim that African Pentecostal prophets in general are simply after making money. Thus, they are accused of 'Pentecostapreneurship'. In contexts such as Nigeria, Ghana, Kenya, Zambia, Zimbabwe and others, there have been accusations that many individuals are using the gospel as a resource for self-enrichment. Thus:

> In Pentecostal conceptualization, every born again Christian is empowered for Christian witnessing. For this reason, pentecostapreneurship has two levels of expression. The first level of expression drives some presumed born again Christians (Pentecostals) into active pastoral ministry as ministers with the assumption that the Holy empowers and calls them into such ministries. Such drive encourages the development of *pastorpreneuship* and *evangeconomics*. Pastorpreneurship is the business of using the word of God or God's name to make money, earn a living and/or extort money/other material goods from unsuspecting admirers and adherents. Evangeconomics is business in religion and business through religion and this operates like a franchise.
> (Iheanacho and Ughaerumba 2016: 289–90. Italics original)

Alongside the critique that there is a focus on money, others have raised the charge of false miracles, the abuse of women, uncritical approach to political power, faulty interpretation of scripture and, concomitantly, the preaching of poor theology and others. Among others, for example, Masvotore (2016) has alleged that the newer Pentecostal churches preach a gospel that enslaves rather than saves. Although more space is required to both outline and debate these allegations, it is clear that innovation and competition within the prophetic Pentecostal movement in Zimbabwe (and in Africa) have generated their fair share of controversy.

A Zimbabwean gospel musician from the African indigenous churches, Mambo Dhuterere (real name Darlington Mutseta), gained popularity in 2019 for releasing music which charged that the young Pentecostal prophets were 'selling the gospel for profits'. His music called upon Christians to read the Bible for themselves and to turn away from the Pentecostal prophets. Dhuterere charged that these prophets were claiming to be selling the blood of Christ to their followers, yet salvation was the free gift of God to humanity. Dhuterere's scathing criticism of prophetic Pentecostalism in Zimbabwe must be understood within the context of the competition within the religious sector in Zimbabwe, as he represents African indigenous churches. However, some scholars also find prophetic Pentecostalism problematic. Critiquing the excesses of the movement in South Africa and Zimbabwe, Dube writes as follows:

> Stories of 'Prophets' spraying 'Doom' insecticide on their followers in church services – asking congregants to eat rats, grass, drink petrol – touching female congregants inappropriately in deliverance sessions – abusing and raping congregants – profiteering, among others, abound. These have become commonplace.
>
> (Dube 2019: 29)

However, from a phenomenological perspective, where our focus is on the religious experience of the adherent, we can only concede that the initiatives of the young Pentecostal prophets have generated a wave of excitement and renewed hope for their adherents and clients. They have succeeded in reinvigorating the religious market in Zimbabwe and have demonstrated remarkable creativity and resilience in creating a niche for themselves in a market that had been dominated by the missionary churches, as well as the older indigenous and Pentecostal churches.

Chapters in this volume

The chapters in this volume have been organized thematically. The chapters in the earlier part of the volume focus on the persistence of African traditional religions in the face of competition with prophetic Pentecostalism. These are followed by the chapters in the larger segment that concentrate on understanding innovation and competition within and between the two dominant faces of the movement, namely the UFIC and PHD Ministries. In order to broaden the understanding of Zimbabwean prophetic Pentecostalism beyond these two, a few other churches are also discussed. While there is some overlap among chapters examining UFIC and PHD Ministries, each of the chapters has a specific thrust and concentrates on definitive dimensions of these churches. The last part of the volume comprises chapters that reflect on criticisms that have been levelled against prophetic Pentecostalism in Zimbabwe.

In Chapter 1, Kudzai Biri explores the persistence of African traditional religions within the newer Pentecostal churches in Zimbabwe. She traces the emergence of two of the most prominent Pentecostal churches and highlights the survival of aspects of African traditional religions. For Biri, innovation in these two churches can be seen in how they have successfully repackaged indigenous beliefs and practices and presented them in new forms. Whereas at the theological level the prophets maintain that ATRs must be of no consequence to their adherents, in practice they have been creative and innovative in responding to the demands of ATRs, Biri argues.

This theme is picked up by Obert Bernard Mlambo and Clive Tendai Zimunya in Chapter 2. They reflect on the interpretation of miracles that is common to both African traditional religions and the newer prophetic Pentecostal churches. Mlambo and Zimunya place emphasis on how competition between the specialists of African traditional religions and those of Pentecostalism has led to innovation. They argue that the trying economic situation has motivated religious actors to rebrand themselves in order to remain relevant and appealing. This chapter highlights the impact of the fierce competition between sacred specialists of ATR and those of Pentecostalism that has led to reconfiguring of different offices in these religious traditions.

In Chapter 3, Lovemore Ndlovu seeks to understand the popularity of Pentecostalism in Zimbabwe by using sociological theory. He contends that the socio-economic crisis of the decade 2000–2010 instigated the robust expansion of Pentecostalism. Ndlovu reflects on the close interplay between the crisis and the turn to Pentecostalism. As citizens struggled to make sense of life in a depressing environment, Pentecostal pastors seemed to provide sustainable solutions.

Ezra Chitando follows a similar line of argument in Chapter 4 where he uses the concept of masculinity and the struggles of the state to explain the emergence of Pentecostal prophets in Zimbabwe. He argues that whereas former president Robert Mugabe had been identified as the 'Father of the Nation' in the first two decades of independence, a deepening economic and political crisis led to a re-evaluation of this standing. Subsequently, younger male Pentecostal prophets emerged as better placed to provide healing and hope for many of the citizens. Chitando maintains that the younger male prophets must be located within the patriarchal postcolonial state where the father figure remains dominant.

In Chapter 5, Tabona Shoko analyses innovation within PHD Ministries. Shoko is convinced that this Pentecostal movement, like many others, sources from the indigenous world view. He outlines the main phenomena that are derived from African traditional religions that are found within PHD Ministries. However, Shoko is keen to highlight dimensions of innovation within the movement. In Chapter 6, Molly Manyonganise undertakes an analysis of competition between UFIC and PHD Ministries. She contends that these two movements have rebranded Pentecostalism in Zimbabwe. According to her, the personalities of the founders and artefacts have been used in the battle for superiority in the two churches. Fungai Chirongoma pursues the comparative dimension further in Chapter 7. She argues that, like commercial businesses, these churches compete for consumers. Due to the stiff competition on religious market, they promote their brands at their highest selling points in a bid to get customers (believers). In Chapter 8, Fortune Sibanda shifts attention to continuities and discontinuities of African Traditional anthropological beliefs in a different Pentecostal movement, namely DiVineyard Church of His Presence. Sibanda highlights the tenacity of indigenous anthropological beliefs within the newer Pentecostal theological outlook. This chapter serves to highlight the similarities and differences within the newer prophetic Pentecostal churches in Zimbabwe. Competition has meant that each emerging Pentecostal church seeks to highlight its specific area of (spiritual) competence.

In Chapter 9, Tenson Muyambo compares the UFIC and PHD Ministries in terms of their prophetic, healing and deliverance characteristics. While retaining the dominant motif of competition, Muyambo also contends that it is possible to regard the two movements as complementary. Chapter 10, by Martin Mujinga, interprets the popularity of PHD Ministries in the context of the quest for identity. He maintains that PHD Ministries entered a religious market that was already dominated by earlier players. Consequently, it has sought to project a distinct identity in order to attract and retain its members and clients. Chapter 11 by Biri contends that the newer Pentecostal churches are reconfiguring the gospel of prosperity. Biri challenges the dominant critique of the Pentecostal gospel of prosperity in Zimbabwe. She argues that critics have not done justice to this theme and seeks to highlight the positive dimensions of this gospel.

The last three chapters focus on some of the major critiques of prophetic Pentecostalism in Zimbabwe. In Chapter 12, Phillip Musoni compares the approaches to prosperity between older Pentecostal churches and the newer Pentecostal churches. He maintains that the older Pentecostal churches (such as the ZAOGA) tended to promote more effective approaches to prosperity than the newer Pentecostal churches. Musoni charges that the newer Pentecostal churches appear to promote the empowerment of the prophet ahead of the empowerment of the ordinary members. In Chapter 13, Tapiwa Praise Mapuranga discusses the issue of the abuse of women in Zimbabwean Pentecostalism in general. She highlights the extent to which some Pentecostal prophets have been accused of abusing women. In Chapter 14, Ezra Chitando and Kelvin Chikonzo reflect on the caricature of prophetic Pentecostalism in selected comic strips. They maintain that these critiques of prophets in Zimbabwean Pentecostalism suggest that their dominance has not been without contest.

While there are some unavoidable overlaps between and across some chapters (given that the focus was principally on the two dominant movements), each chapter retains adequate details on the relevant background factors to enable it to stand on its own. Furthermore, each chapter has been written from each author's point of view and has been guided by the author's own interests. This enables each chapter to have its own freshness and novelty, even as it discusses a theme that is covered by other chapters. Thus, each chapter has its own insights and unique perspective on the newer Pentecostal churches. At any rate, Shona (one of the indigenous languages of Zimbabwe) offers some epistemological insights into repetition when proclaiming that '*dzokororo ine simba*' (there is power in repetition!).

Overall, this volume provides a detailed and in-depth review of contemporary Zimbabwean prophetic Pentecostalism in general and two of its dominant forms of expression (at the time of writing), namely UFIC and PHD Ministries, in particular. It is envisaged that the insights gained herein can contribute towards clarifying the larger phenomena of African and global Pentecostalism, as well as the role of innovation and competition in religion.

1

Pentecostalism in Zimbabwe and the revitalization of African traditional religions: A comparative analysis of the newer religious movements

Kudzai Biri

Introduction

Studies of Pentecostalism in Zimbabwe abound. Several scholars have focused on different areas, ranging from politics (Chitando et al. 2013b), prophecy (Manyonganise 2016a), religious geography and technology (Biri 2013a) and gender (Mapuranga 2018), among others. The vibrancy and creativity of Pentecostalism have also been noted. Of significance is the contribution by Biri (2012) on the resilience of traditional beliefs and practices among the Shona people that have found avenues of expression among the Pentecostals. Biri carried out a comparative analysis of this resilience of African traditional religions (ATRs) in the Zimbabwe Assemblies of God Africa (ZAOGA) of Ezekiel and Eunor Guti, one of the oldest Pentecostal churches in the country, and the United Family International Church (UFIC) of Emmanuel and Ruth Makandiwa, one of the newer Pentecostal churches. Building on insights from this earlier study, this chapter focuses on examining persistence of ATRs in the UFIC and Walter Magaya's Prophetic Healing and Deliverance (PHD) Ministries.

I argue that these two newer Pentecostal churches have refused to write off traditional beliefs and practices. Shona traditional religious beliefs and practices are examined within the broader context of ATRs because of their commonalities and persistence in the newer Pentecostal churches. Magaya has insisted that his PHD Ministries is not a church, as assumed by many people. He maintains that it is simply a ministry addressing the three key areas of prophecy, healing and deliverance, as expressed by the name. Such a designation enables him to be innovative, as he is not limited by the traditional definition of a church as an institution with a fixed structure and unchanging beliefs and practices. This chapter makes use of the teachings, sermons and analysis of beliefs and practices sourced from members of the UFIC and PHD in Harare, the headquarters of the two major Pentecostal groups in Zimbabwe.

The major question is: How do these churches interact with the traditional beliefs and practices? Through interpretive phenomenological analysis, the chapter enables a critical analysis of the innovation of UFIC and PHD that has attracted converts to these movements. I need to point out that this chapter is not exhaustive of all beliefs and practices in the UFIC and PHD, but the chapter has selected some in order to establish the revitalization of indigenous beliefs and practices. The vibrancy of the newer Pentecostal movements warrants constant revisits and analysis of new developments in relation to this interaction between ATR and Pentecostalism. This chapter pays attention to specifically the naming system and the use of religious artefacts within the locus of personal and social rebirth as purveyed in the prophetic, healing and deliverance ministries of the two churches.

The backgrounds of the United Family International Church and the Prophetic Healing and Deliverance Ministries

This chapter does not provide a detailed analysis of the emergence of these two newer churches and the rise of the founders, as this is beyond its scope. Also, Biri (2012) and Chitando et al. (2013c) have provided detailed descriptions of these aspects. The focus of this chapter is to point to how the backgrounds of the two leaders inform the beliefs and practices in the two churches. The founders of UFIC are Emmanuel and Ruth Makandiwa. They founded their church in May 2010 after breaking away from the Apostolic Faith Mission in Zimbabwe. Emmanuel Makandiwa grew up in Muzarabani, one of Zimbabwe's rural areas that is associated with the tenacity of indigenous religious beliefs and practices. On the other hand, Walter Magaya was born and grew up in rural Mhondoro. It suffices to say that rural areas are places where the belief in witchcraft activities is very strong. This study affirms observations by Gifford (2004) that are significant in studies on relation between Christianity and African traditional religions. He points out that any analysis that neglects the village life is not complete.

This is very important in examining aspects of the traditional religion in Zimbabwe. People continue to hold on to African traditional beliefs and practices, particularly the witchcraft beliefs and anything that affects the health and well-being of the individual. The belief continues to be strong such that even the urban culture has not managed to write off the traditional world view. It is this persistence of traditional beliefs that seems to inform the UFIC and PHD Ministries on prophecy, healing and deliverance. Although Pentecostalism has become a global phenomenon, African expressions of Pentecostal spirituality have distinctive features that are particularly manifest in prophecy, healing and deliverance. This is important because it discredits the Americanization thesis whereby African Pentecostal leaders are accused of regurgitating Western theologies. Also, comparatively, the use of traditional symbols and artefacts that are absent in North American Pentecostalism is a mark of innovation in African Pentecostalism. This points to how they have negotiated the indigenous spirituality while appropriating Pentecostal spirituality. Furthermore, this demonstrates the extent to which African Pentecostals continue to operate within the locus of the traditional world view regardless of the modernized Pentecostal movements. This negotiation is handled in ways that are sometimes similar and other times different and highlights the complexity with which UFIC and PHD negotiate indigenous spirituality.

The naming system and its significance

The names of the two churches deserve attention. UFIC is a significant name when using traditional worldview. According to Pongweni (1983), names are not given randomly but convey meaning among the Shona (and most other communities throughout the world). The quest for identification as a family is very crucial in the UFIC. Makandiwa is referred to as *Papa* (father). Thus, in him members of the church see a father figure. The status of Makandiwa as father is important because he becomes the rallying point and unifying symbol of all his 'children' (see the chapter by Chitando in this volume). The name UFIC is also very important. Pentecostals have been accused of destroying the traditional family (Van Dijk 2001) and creating a family of the born again, a place of new beginnings and belonging. Thus, in this way some have managed to break away from their traditional extended families, traditional obligations, and assume a new identity in UFIC.

Although the chapter affirms these observations, Makandiwa's naming of his church and the activities of the church mirror the traditional set-up of a family. His followers are identified as a family, calling him *papa*. The members see themselves as brothers and sisters under the leader of their *papa*. These people are not from the same blood (lineage), which is important in identifying the roots and belonging. However, UFIC members become a family through their belief in Jesus. But more important is not belief in Jesus (because that could translate to being a family with all the other Christians), but the figure of Makandiwa is important for this new identity. Makandiwa creates a family where his figure/persona is the unifying symbol. The notion of extended family is important in the traditional family, but external forces of modernity have destroyed and continue to destroy the traditional fabric which rests on communalism. Makandiwa thus reinvents and revitalizes the concept of both family and extended family in his church, manifest in the naming of the church. This quest for a family finds affirmation as people in the UFIC are tied together through their *papa*.

Regalia make them identify each other easily and the church acts as a job breaker for members. This is crucial because the breakdown of the traditional family structure mostly cherished by many people means they easily get attracted to the new family where they can belong. Most people continue to cherish the beauty of the traditional communal life against the background of external forces that have destroyed the traditional socio-economic structures. This is made worse by severe challenges that are faced by many people in sub-Saharan Africa, which in turn have given birth to individualism. At the same time, the Pentecostals want to cope with forces of modernity through what Van Dijk (2001) describes as 'technologies of the self'. In such contexts of suffering and the breakdown of family structures that support the individual, the need for supporting structures for individuals ceases to be an option. Thus, the traditional communal life becomes the most cherished dimension and a source of inspiration to many people, since it offers a haven of belonging and comfort in a terrifying world that is characterized by many vicissitudes of life. The UFIC fulfils that quest for belonging and identity for many Pentecostal believers.

Prophecy, healing and deliverance

Several scholars have drawn attention to the centrality of healing, prophecy and deliverance in African traditional religion. The name PHD attracts a lot of people because the three words constitute areas that are at the heart of the African salvific agenda. The traditional healer (*n'anga*) is central in dealing with all the pressing challenges of life. It is in this context there comes the role of Makandiwa and Magaya as self-enthroned *n'angas* in their respective churches. The section below unravels the status and role of a *n'anga* in the traditional religion in order to shed light on how it has a bearing on Makandiwa and Magaya.

The traditional healer: Status, role and significance

There is a lot of misconception about traditional healers among the Shona. The confusion and misconceptions are caused by Western missionaries and other agents from the West who were pioneers in giving reports and writing about African traditional religions and cultures. These confusion and misconceptions are manifest in the naming of the traditional healer by the missionaries. Chavunduka (1978) points out that many missionaries saw the *n'anga* as the greatest threat to salvation. This is because they were very central to the lives of the Africans. Consequently, the practice of divining and healing was frowned upon as demonic by some of the missionaries. Some of these misleading terms include 'herbalist', 'medicine man' and 'diviner', among others.

Yet other *n'anga*s (plural) had a multiplicity of roles; for example, some did not use herbs and did not even divine. Thus, the terms are either limiting or misleading. It is beyond the scope of this chapter to analyse the types of *n'anga*. What is important is to highlight that they were diverse; some used herbs and others were divining specialists. Some *n'anga* could embody all the roles above, making them very popular. It is the contention of this chapter that when Magaya names his ministry 'PHD', he knows what is central among the Shona people and the prevailing concerns that are caused by external forces of modernity, globalization and urbanization, among others.

Yet these two prophets are not preoccupied with the challenges, but to find explanation of modern challenges with traditional goggles of spiritualizing all negative challenges. Zimbabweans are generally attracted to prophecy, healing and deliverance from causes of misfortunes. In naming his ministry, Magaya taps into the traditional world view and reflects an awareness of what the people cherish most. Shoko (2007) validly points out that the quest for health and well-being is at the heart of African cosmology, and the *n'anga* as the sacred practitioner is central in mediating this health and well-being. This has had the effect of attracting many people from outside the two churches who are searching for prophecy, healing and deliverance. It is no doubt that Magaya is seen as a *n'anga* and often visited by people who want to ascertain their future. This parallels the Shona practice of visiting the *n'anga* for divining purposes. However, Magaya claims that he discovered that he has the gift of prophecy in 2013 (*Daily News* 6 November 2015). Thus, the Pentecostals discredit and demonize *n'angas*, but the founders of Pentecostal ministries enthrone themselves as the new sacred practitioners that can mediate the health and well-being of their members. These developments are a mark of the creativity within African Pentecostalism and this discredits the popular Americanization thesis that is often advanced by some Western scholars.

Designation: The significance of titles

Magaya and Makandiwa are referred to as 'Prophets' by their followers. Awarding such a title means believers have sacralized the lives of Magaya and Makandiwa. The relation of the two prophets to Kusi Victor Boateng from Ghana and Temitope Bolugun Joshua from Nigeria, popularly known as TB Joshua, as mentors and spiritual fathers has a lot of significance. The two mentors are controversial figures who have been accused of using occultism in their ministries in West Africa. The title itself is a source of attraction to many Zimbabweans whose traditional backgrounds are accustomed to visiting a diviner who can foretell. Makandiwa has set aside Wednesdays as days of prophesying to the people, just as a *n'anga* (who has divining expertise) can set aside days for different services, such as healing and divining.

Distributing/selling anointed oil

Both Makandiwa and Magaya pray and distribute holy oil for their members. In 2014, eleven people died at Magaya's gathering when people scrambled for the holy oil in Kwekwe. Most members of these two churches have faith in the oil, and interviews carried out by the researcher show that members believe the oil offers protection from evil forces and opens doors for their prosperity. The pressure for holy oil for protection is testimony of a strong awareness of spiritual forces that can negate progress in life. The use of the anointed oil supplements prayers offered and is very popular because it resonates with protective mechanisms or charms in the traditional religion and culture.

Anointed artefacts

As pointed out by Kalu (2008) and applicable to Pentecostals in Zimbabwe, the Pentecostals demonize African Independent Churches (AICs) as *amademoni* (demonic churches). Not only do they demonize AICs, which are the earliest expression of Pentecostalism in Africa, but they also attack Shona traditional religion (Biri 2013a). In the traditional religion, artefacts in the wrists, neck, waistline and those kept in the homes are basically for protection and they have spiritual significance. They link the living with the timeless living (Bakare 2007) or the living dead (Mbiti 1969). Pentecostalism denounces the use of these artefacts both in the traditional religions and AICs. The use of artefacts such as traditional clay pots (*hari/mbiya*) is associated with worshipping 'false spirits' or ancestral spirits. UFIC and PHD are well known for putting on wristbands that have inscriptions that prop up these particular Pentecostal groups. For example, in UFIC, it is common to see inscriptions such as '*Ndiri mwana wemuporofita*' (I am a child of a prophet) and the portraits of Makandiwa and his wife. Interestingly, this seems to have been adapted from the political circles, particularly in the ruling party where there are portraits of former president, Robert G. Mugabe (up to November 2017), and from then on, those of the new president, Emmerson D. Mnangagwa.

In PHD, regalia have the name of the church and the portrait of Walter Magaya, as his wife Tendai does not feature prominently in the public space. There are also wristbands and other forms of inscription that are a mark of identity, a new identity that they have acquired by denouncing the past. Therefore, the two churches reinvent the traditional symbols and give them new meaning within the Christian set-up in order to attract clientele. This is a mark of genius by the two young leaders because most believers are familiar with the artefacts that they get from the traditional sacred practitioners, particularly the *n'anga*. UFIC and PHD give new meanings to their artefacts, but the appropriation of these traditional symbols defies the myth of making a 'complete break from the past', as the Pentecostal ideology seeks to maintain. Hence, this is the revitalization of the indigenous beliefs and practices within the Pentecostal matrix.

Anointed cloths and regalia

In the UFIC, members bought cloths that Makandiwa prayed for and they give testimonies of miracles that were enabled by such cloths. Biri (2012) documents testimonies from UFIC members that claimed miracles that include the reworking of cooking stoves. It is important to point out that Apostles in the New Testament used handkerchiefs to heal. However, the ways of the modern-day prophets show that the believers tap more into traditional view of artefacts than the biblical concept. This is because the handkerchiefs were not given to believers to stay with them. Staying with the cloth is a mark of belief in traditional religion where there is the practice of keeping artefacts for protection, success and healing. However, these artefacts are sold and mostly are not given for free. Also, T-shirts with portraits of the two leaders and sometimes their wives are common in both the churches. Putting on regalia with the portrait of 'the Man of God' is a way of marketing the founders and their movements, apart from the belief that one is blessed to be with the regalia that feature 'the Man/Woman of God'.

The artefacts described above complement deliverance prayers. Days are set aside for deliverance sessions. While there is controversy surrounding deliverance and the artefacts, the significance of these lies in taking seriously the daily concerns of believers, thus attracting a large clientele. I argue that the demonization of Makandiwa and Magaya by both the older Pentecostal churches and other churches (mainline and AICs) is due to the serious threat posed to their membership by the two men. The charismatic nature of the young and gifted duo seems to be more appealing to many people more than it is to older father figures such as Ezekiel Guti of ZAOGA who can no longer exude the zeal and energy to match these younger prophets.

I argue that the use of artefacts has attracted many people, including those who are not members of the church. Some clients come from mainline churches to access power and prosperity, while retaining their membership of these older churches. Another important factor in the two movements is how they have attracted committed intellectuals, leading politicians and professionals in Zimbabwe. This attraction has financial overtones and partly accounts for the financial stamina that these two churches have. The notion of 'seeding to the Man of God' is prominent in both churches. This means that attracting people from the elite class enables the financing of these movements. In turn, it explains their success in 'exporting' the gospel and social activism beyond Zimbabwe. The study of Pentecostalism is not complete without making reference to theologies of success, commonly known as dominion theology.

Prosperity messages

It is within the area of prosperity that further confirmation of the continued interaction of UFIC and PHD with the traditional beliefs can be found. The aspect of giving is biblical, but Magaya and Makandiwa carry prosperity further to horizons of serious contestation. In one of the sermons Makandiwa said, 'I understand that we have different destinies but I don't believe that the child of

God should die in the wilderness ... there are seasons but you should not die poor' (Sermon 4 May 2013).

The demonization of poverty and the attitude of unravelling a spiritual cause for poverty, hunger, marriage problems are examples of how Makandiwa and Magaya continue to operate within the traditional world view. The study construes this as resilience since the resilience takes many forms. This poses the need for a serious consideration of important issues. First, there is need to examine the status of ATR in postcolonial Zimbabwe where there has been a relentless effort by the Evangelical Fellowship of Zimbabwe (body of Pentecostals and Evangelicals) to declare Zimbabwe a Christian nation, although this has been heavily criticized given the multi-religious nature of the country. Second, it calls for theologians, particularly within the Christian fraternity, to revisit and re-evaluate theologies in the light of African existential realities, particularly on salvation.

Makandiwa has gone further to sell anointed bricks, drinks and fruits for higher prices than those on the market. While it is claimed by believers that they are anointed and enhance success, it appears that it is one way that leaders amass wealth and also use to finance the ever-expanding evangelistic missions. This is in line with the observations by Gifford (1990) when he points to an emerging form of business Christianity. However, members deny the accusation that their churches practise business Christianity and argue that this is done in order to finance and export the gospel. During the infancy days of the UFIC, there were months that members were encouraged to sow into 'the life of the Man of God and UFIC'. In addition, the concept of partnering in both churches is very significant and enhances the financial stamina of the two leaders. Believers partner with the prophets by giving specific sums of money regularly. PHD has partners beyond the borders, for example, in South Africa where members can pay R200 (on average, about US$ 20) to access the sermons of the prophet (*NewsDay* 6 November 2015).

Innovation in the United Family International Church and the Prophetic Healing and Deliverance Ministries

Both the UFIC and PHD subscribe to the use of religious icons. The study argues that these two churches have invented new types of practices, as well as symbolic opportunities for survival (Kalu 1998: 3–4), in advancing the dominion theology in order to encourage members to fit into the modern society and promote upward social mobility. However, as pointed out by Biri (2012) features sourced from the traditional spirituality are expressed in different ways and forms in Pentecostal churches. This expression of aspects of traditional beliefs and practices is what she calls the 'silent but echoing voice' that continues to inform and guide the Pentecostals in spite of the adversarial stance towards the indigenous beliefs and practices.

The two prophets have mobilized financial resources for the needy, in hospitals, children homes, rescuing the bankrupt national soccer team (Magaya), widows and orphans and many other things. This social activism has increased the visibility of Makandiwa and Magaya. However, some critics argue that most pastors have become God's finance ministers. The lavish lifestyle perhaps is the point of departure from the n'anga who did not profiteer from the people. However, that difference with the n'anga has made Makandiwa and Magaya assume the new role of a traditional chief. The properties of the churches bear names of the movement, and there is high centralization of power in the persons of the two prophets.

Other critics argue that there is serious lack of fiscal accountability in Pentecostalism which is worrisome because of exploitation and abuse of the contributions from the members of the church. What is significant is how Makandiwa and Magaya assume the role of the traditional chiefs who distribute *zunde ramambo* (traditional form of social security). Biri (2012) describes Makandiwa and Guti who assume the position of the traditional chief through *zunde ramambo*, a traditional practice where subjects contribute grain to the chief who later redistributes to the needy, the widows and orphans. The popularity of Makandiwa and Magaya in pioneering social projects is a direct result of accumulating money and resources from their congregants. It is important to note that while the two churches have been actively involved in community services through donating funds and resources, it is 'the Man of God' who directs the use of funds and resources. It also appears that in both movements while the needy are given attention through social activism, there is the danger that the prophets might access more resources than they need for their modest upkeep. Also, the emphasis of healing, prophecy and deliverance should be understood within the context of the African map of the universe.

Kalu (2008: xi) aptly captures this. He says:

> All forms of religious expression use the resources of the indigenous cultures. People appropriate the gospel from their cultural worldviews. Therefore, the cultural discourse foregrounds the fit of the Pentecostal movement into the indigenous worldviews as an explanation for the attraction and growth of Pentecostalism.

As has been noted throughout this chapter, the belief in witchcraft among Pentecostals is very strong and is an example of how members of the UFIC and PHD Ministries continue to operate within their traditional world view. This belief also accounts for how they seek deliverance and salvation. The mechanisms to deal with witchcraft vary and include fervent warfare prayers and sowing/seeding money for deliverance. In the UFIC, the phrase 'back to sender' is quite established. Sabastian Magacha, one of the UFIC musicians, also composed a song which captures the same phrase, 'back to sender'. The 'sender' refers to witches who are believed to cast spells on others. Adogame (2004) aptly captures the language of warfare that is deployed in prayers in order to combat the evil forces.

In Shona traditional religion and culture, the *n'anga* ascertains the causes of misfortunes, and the victims often asked the *n'anga* to revenge by causing the witch to suffer the negative consequences intended for the victim. This act captures the 'back to sender' slogan in the UFIC, PHD and other Pentecostal churches in Zimbabwe. Overall, it can be argued that the rise of Makandiwa and Magaya has encouraged religious vitality, as they have challenged the old established Pentecostal churches that seem to have been sapped of their Pentecostal vigour because of institutionalization and bureaucratization. But what is more important is how other churches ignore the three aspects of prophecy, deliverance and healing, which are central in African beliefs and practices. It suffices to say while Western-initiated churches in Zimbabwe insist on their adherence to Western-type theologies that denied and silenced witchcraft beliefs, Makandiwa and Magaya have publicly reaffirmed the reality of witchcraft in their churches through prophecy, healing and deliverance.

It is also important to point out the role and place of women in the two churches, which has a direct link with the traditional religions and cultures. In the deliverance sessions, common problems range from finances and marital problems particularly caused by the so-called spiritual forces. Women go to the sessions in numbers in search of marital solutions. I argue that the concept of spiritual husbands that is popularized is sourced more from the traditional understanding of the cause of lack of marriage among women. In the traditional religion, it is believed that a deceased person who died without a husband can hinder a young woman's marriage if she is chosen by the spirit as a wife. Apart from such spirits, bad luck (*munyama*) or witches can also prevent a young woman from getting married. Thus, a *n'anga* has to ascertain the cause and provide a solution to remedy such a crisis. The popularity of claiming solutions to such problems is one way that has seen the increased presence of women who seek marriage and marital solutions among many others.

Finally, it is vital to indicate that women constitute the majority of the members and clientele within these churches. Apart from their presence for deliverance, the success of PHD and UFIC is a result of prominent women, female preachers and organizers or administrators who have helped a lot in the establishment and spread of the churches. In spite of these contributions by women, it is the 'big man of a big God' that reaps the credit of founding, organizing and maintaining the welfare of the movement. Thus, this renders the names and efforts of women as appendices and footnotes in the movements.

Conclusion

This chapter has examined the UFIC and PHD and argued that the naming system and the use of artefacts show revitalization of the indigenous beliefs and practices. While the UFIC and PHD are modern in outlook, they continue to engage the indigenous spirituality in their churches. This has the effect of attracting a large clientele as opposed to Western-initiated churches in Zimbabwe. The UFIC and PHD churches have captured the imagination of many people by claiming to offer what is central to the lives of the people, namely peace of mind from dangerous spirits and prosperity in life's ventures. The question of the truth or falsity of those claims did not constitute a significant portion of this chapter. What is important is how the Pentecostal leaders creatively endeavour to penetrate the pulse of African spirituality in order to give meaning to life's existential realities and promote abundant life which many churches have either ignored or failed to address creatively. New religious concepts are used to renew older traditional concepts. Thus, these two newer Pentecostal churches have not cut ties with the traditional religions. Instead, they have engaged in a lot of innovation to appeal to the young and upwardly mobile professionals to present a new image of religion in contemporary Zimbabwe.

2

Miracles, *muti* and magic: An inquiry into the analogous nature of Pentecostal miracles and African traditional beliefs

Obert Bernard Mlambo and Clive Tendai Zimunya

Background

This chapter inquires into the nature of miracles: some Pentecostal churches in Zimbabwe exist against a background of an African belief system where beliefs in witchcraft and magic-related practices are rampant. In a context where miraculous occurrences are fast taking centre stage in Zimbabwe, the chapter analyses what miracles are and the source of the power behind their performance in Pentecostal churches. The chapter then looks into some practices in traditional African religion that can be paralleled with such miraculous occurrences in Pentecostal churches. This part of the investigation stems from anecdotes of people who were once part of the African traditional religions (ATRs) and later became well-known prophets in Pentecostal ministries. We then analyse whether getting power from an African traditional source and using such power to perform miracles in Pentecostal churches is an innovation that amounts to the same thing as being a 'modernized' version of a traditional African healer. We also analyse whether such innovations could be specially designed to outwit African traditional religious belief systems, with which the Pentecostal movements seem to be in a competition in the battle to get converts. This is important because often African traditional beliefs are usually deemed to be associated with malevolent activities and denounced in church as evil.

Introduction

On different worship days in Zimbabwe, churches are filling up with thousands of churchgoers who are hoping to get salvation in one form or the other. The new

Pentecostal movements, characterized by charismatic preachers, the gospel of prosperity and the occurrence of a host of 'miracle' deliverances from a number of problems, are perhaps the most popular. Many of these congregants have flocked from a number of other mainline churches such as the Roman Catholic Church and the United Methodist churches whose conservative doctrines have made their popularity dwindle over the past few years, in favour of the promise of miraculous deliverances. Others have also come from a background of African traditional religious beliefs, with many confessing in the churches that they were once part of a witchcraft cult or that they have had spells cast on them from those who practise such witchcraft activities.

The latter are perhaps the bulk of the congregants who are under the impression that most of their problems stem from witchcraft. The charismatic preachers in the new Pentecostal churches are believed to have special powers from God that can miraculously remove the curses on such people and make their lives better and more prosperous. Problems of any sort, such as not getting married, divorce, alcohol and substance abuse, and even medical conditions such as tuberculosis, are not viewed as normal parts of human life that the individuals themselves have control over, but as abnormalities that have to be removed by such specially gifted individuals. Interestingly, such churches are arising in a background of African traditional religious beliefs that also encompass specially gifted individuals who also claim to be able to remove the same curses and problems on their followers.

In fact, even some of the people who go to these new Pentecostal churches sometimes frequent these traditional gurus for assistance. The problem we pose is as follows: if the charismatic preachers and the traditional diviners have the same abilities, then what is the difference between them? Could it be that in the race for clients, one is just a Christianized, more appealing and modernized version of the other? Another problem is the source of the healing powers that the charismatic preachers have against a background of traditional diviners who can supply such powers. Could it also be that the charismatic pastors get their power from an African traditional religious source? These are the questions that the chapter seeks to address within the context of competition and innovation on the Zimbabwean religious market.

Defining terms

Our first port of call is perhaps to define terms. By charismatic preacher, we mean a preacher in the new Pentecostal churches who claims to possess supernatural gifts of speaking and healing. Someone deemed to be charismatic has the 'power of leadership or authority' over their followers. Such preachers, then, claim to have special gifts that they can offer to their followers and have an intelligence that the followers do not seem to possess.

A miracle can be defined as an occurrence of the extraordinary or the occurrence of something that defies the laws of nature. For instance, it is a law of nature that human beings die and stay dead. If a dead human being is raised from the dead, then this counts as a transgression of this particular law of nature. A miracle can be defined as a non-repeatable counter-instance of a law of nature. By non-repeatable it is meant that miracles are not rehearsed and no two miracles occur the same way. Perhaps the best example would be the miracles performed by Jesus in the Bible. In the biblical accounts, Jesus raised the dead (John 11:14-44), restored sight to the blind (Matthew 9:28-30), as well as restored hearing to the deaf (Mark7:32-35). In all these instances, the miraculous occurrences were not rehearsed such that an observer could repeat the miracle in the same way that a person could learn medicine from observing others doing it.

But miracles do not necessarily involve a transgression of a law of nature. According to Mark Corner (2005: 3), a miracle can be defined simply as a wonderful event. In ordinary usage people often use the word 'miracle' in a variety of ways that highlight this point. For example, when a baby is born, people often say that it is a miracle of life. In such cases there is no transgression of a law of nature. The emphasis is more upon the extraordinary impact of nature itself in its day-to-day working, whether nature is expressed in terms that are economic, technological or biological.

Our focus on miracles is informed by our interaction with members and clients of Pentecostal churches in Zimbabwe. Indeed, the dominant marketing approach adopted by the Pentecostal churches is to advertise their activities as being characterized by miracles and wonders. Members and clients visit the healing and deliverance services offered by the leading prophets, such as Emmanuel Makandiwa and Walter Magaya, expecting to witness or benefit from miracles. Consequently, it is important to invest in clarifying the meaning of miracles in order to appreciate the expectations of both those who venture in search of miracles and those who are expected to deliver such miracles.

Miracles and coincidence

In this section, we seek to draw a distinction between miracles and coincidence. This distinction is important as it enables one to appreciate the depth of the search for miracles. We begin with the following example: Suppose a person survives the collapse of a building and stays buried under the rubble for three weeks in the aftermath of an earthquake. This would be seen by some as 'miraculous'. But miraculous here does not imply that concrete became feather-light or that human beings suddenly developed a bodily frame with the resistance of steel. What is implied here is that the human body has strong natural powers of resistance under stress and that there are often pockets of air inside the debris. The result can be a welcome piece of good fortune when someone survives trapped for days. 'Miracle' here seems to mean something close to an 'extraordinary stroke of luck' and has elements of providential care rather than 'miraculous interference'.

R. F. Holland's (1965) definition offers an account of a 'miracle' as 'an extraordinary coincidence of a beneficial nature interpreted religiously' and appears closest to the providential examples. However, Holland offers an account of a miracle which does not necessitate any transgression of the law of nature. God must do something; God must somehow act in some special way. People think of the Deity acting in such a way that the workings of nature do not follow the course they would have followed had God not acted. In the case of the Red Sea parting, God does something nature could never do. In other instances, God does something nature could have done, but it is God, rather than nature, who does it.

God's actions and interventions

Philosophers such as Swinburne and Mackie use the term 'intervention' to describe a special act of God. Thus, according to Mackie, 'we can give a coherent definition of a miracle as a supernatural intrusion into the normally closed system that works in accordance with those laws' (1982: 22). However, this implies that human beings ordinarily inhabit a self-sufficient universe which they interpret and manage of their own accord. Occasionally, however, perhaps because of a particular threat to this universe or a particularly deserving victim within it, God will break it from outside and rearrange it. Those inside that universe might give up trying to sort their own lives out and simply summon God to solve their problems for them. The world, then, is like a children's playground with God on the outside keeping a watchful eye in case things went out of control. Ordinarily, the Deity will let things run their course. On occasion, however, the Divine being has to intervene. A problem with this account is that it implies that God ordinarily stands apart from it. Occasional presence implies ordinary absence. It suggests that the universe is a self-sustaining entity which is looked down upon by a divine observer 'from above'. It is therefore important to use the phrase 'special act of God' to define 'miracle' rather than an act of 'divine intervention'.

Taking the notion of creation, some interpretations of the world as God's creation move in the direction of imagery, which presents the universe as a self-sufficient entity which the Deity can interfere with (or not) in a miraculous way. God 'creates' something which is seen as 'good' and is then coaxed in the right direction by its Maker through a series of external interventions – messages, threats, acts of violent destruction or of assistance – all of them coming 'from beyond' as part of God's tireless efforts to guide humanity. A self-sufficient universe of this sort is presented in one of the most famous images of the world as God's creation, namely that of William Paley (1854) with his watchmaker analogy. Paley asks us to imagine someone who discovers a watch lying on the ground. They are unsure of what the object is, but from its intricate design they are clear that it is not a natural object. Such craftsmanship demands a craftsman.

Paley wants us to respond to the natural universe as the walker responds to the watch. The universe is too intricate 'just to be'; it must have a maker. Paley's way of seeing the universe is another example of viewing it as a thing 'outside God'. However, it is often pointed out that the better the quality of the watch, the less it needs service. A perfect watch would require no interference. Miracles, therefore, become evidence of God's imperfect craftsmanship. It is possible to describe miracles in such a way as to avoid this sense of a normally absent God who occasionally turns up to set things right or at least to help them along.

It could be emphasized that God is never apart from the world, that the Deity is, after all, described as 'omnipresent', and that this attribute must obviously entail a constant presence. The dependence of the created universe upon the Creator is a constant and absolute one, like that of a tune to its singer. Once the singer stops singing, then the tune stops too. Viewing God in this way means that God is always present, sustaining the universe in being. It would suffice to say that God's involvement takes different forms. Performing miracles may be one of those forms. From the standpoint of this chapter, God is not apart from the created universe but always present in it. For a miracle to have occurred, therefore, it appears the following things are necessary:

1. The event must be extraordinary,
2. A violation of a law of nature must take place,
3. It must be done in the name of the Deity,
4. It must have a religious significance and
5. It must be beneficial.

A look at the miracles performed in Zimbabwe by the charismatic preachers reveals that there is a host of consistencies as well as an equal share of inconsistencies in line with our characterization of miracles. It appears that the charismatic preachers possess special powers that they allegedly get from God. These powers enable them to perform miracles such as healing incurable diseases such as cancer (satisfying criteria 1 and 2), as well as other physiological disabilities. This is all done in the name of God (satisfying criteria 3 and 4), and it obviously benefits the healed (criteria 5). While these inconsistencies such as ordinary events being termed miracles, the names of the healers being invoked and the miracles benefitting the miracle worker, and these might be clear to one who is using the laws of logic and rationality. Their quest is a simple one: to receive miracles that transform their lives in fundamental ways. This is influenced by the indigenous spiritual beliefs.

The nature of African traditional beliefs

Now that an outline of what counts as a miracle has been given, it now remains the task of this chapter to outline some of the tenets of African traditional belief systems. In Africa, in Zimbabwe in particular, there exists an abundance of beliefs in a spiritual realm in which spirits of the deceased dwell. These spirits have a hierarchy up to the highest spirit, whom we can equate to God. In Shona this is *Musikavanhu* (Creator of human beings).

These spirits share a variety of relationships with the living, and among the most interesting relationship is that the spirits can be coaxed into helping an individual through a variety of incantations and ritual ceremonies. For instance, when the rainy season is approaching, various ceremonies that summon the help of the spirits to bring good rains are held in the form of *Doro remukwerera* (beer to honour the ancestors). Through offerings and sacrifices of beer and, usually, cows, the spirits can bring good rains, or so it is generally believed. If all necessary rituals and rites are performed and no rains come, blame is usually placed, not on the lack of faith on the part of the performers, but on some abnormal occurrences, such as two people of the same totem marrying each other (*makunakuna*) or some other activity either considered abnormal or unusual.

It is important also to note that members of the 'spiritual community' can also be coerced to bring both good and harm to an individual. An individual seeking to enhance or safeguard their wealth, for example (a good thing), can go to a traditional healer (*n'anga*) to ask for such a favour from the spiritual realm.

Depending on their previous relationship with the spiritual world (if they have been observing rituals and rites), or on their current offering (in the form of cows, goats and chickens), the applicant may be granted their wish and have their desires come true. At the same time, a person can consult such traditional specialists for harming another individuals. For instance, there are cases wherein a person consults a traditional specialist to harm their enemy or a person whom they deem to have done them wrong or treated them unfairly. In some cases, anecdotal evidence suggests that a person can even take the footprint of the intended victim (usually the sand on which the victim would have stepped on) to the traditional specialist, and this would suffice to have a harm of the sender's choice (even death) to the victim.

Traditional 'specialists'

The people who have a close connection to the spiritual realm are viewed with great esteem by believers. The traditional specialists are considered as powerful individuals with great powers that they source from the spiritual realm. Some are considered to have *shavi renjuzu* (literally mermaid spirit), which enables them to have special powers. According to this view, the individuals in question are 'kidnapped' by mermaids, usually at a water source, especially dams, and then go underwater on a spiritual journey where they are taught the art and craft of healing and consulting the living dead. Such stories are usually rife in places where there are dams nearby. In other places where there are no dams nearby (or even in those places where dams are present), the kidnapping does not occur, but the spirit comes in the form of making the person suffer from a mysterious disease. It is then later on revealed, through the consultation of a spiritual specialist, that a spirit wants to dwell within them. Various rites and rituals are performed and the person is ordained a bona fide traditional specialist. A variety of other spirits exist that transform people in this nature, such as the *mhondoro* (lion) spirit.

Anecdotal evidence also seems to buttress this point. In June 2016, a narrative circulated in South Africa and Zimbabwe that a thief who had stolen a wallet from a traditional specialist received the shock of his life when the wallet turned into a snake. In rural areas, the places where traditional specialists live are deemed to be 'thief-proof', with stories of people who have been caught trying to steal from the specialists in abundance. Some were reported to be found just loitering around the place where they would have committed the act (especially if the thief steals from the specialist's farm), or the stolen items may start to command the thief to return them from the place where they were stolen.

It is from such reports that the specialists have come to get a special and elevated status in the minds of followers. They are viewed as people with the ability to coerce the spiritual realm and do the extraordinary (in the sense described in our discussion of miracles). This then brings us to our problem which can be formulated hypothetically as follows: if the traditional specialist has the ability to perform acts out of the ordinary, then can these be adequately called 'miracles' in the sense described earlier? Furthermore, suppose a traditional specialist decided to turn into a charismatic preacher, would there be a difference between the extraordinary acts that they would perform as a traditional specialist and as a charismatic preacher? Or better still, would people be in a position to recognize the difference?

As argued by Zimunya and Gwara (2013), because of the difficult economic conditions that Zimbabweans are finding themselves in the twenty-first century, they are eager to have 'miraculous' events in their lives. In other words, the harsh economic conditions have had the tendency of making people gullible to the miraculous. It can be adequately argued then that for the ordinary person to recognize the difference between the traditional specialist turned charismatic preacher would be close to impossible. But why, one may ask, would a traditional specialist decide to transform themselves into a charismatic preacher? The answer is to be discussed in the following section.

Reasons for transformation: The competitive front

In contemporary Zimbabwe, the religious dichotomy between the traditional religious beliefs and the Christian (as well as other religion of a foreign nature) is very distinct. However, it should be noted that whereas people in Zimbabwe can readily identify themselves as Catholic, or belonging to one of the Christian denominations, such as the Apostolic Faith Mission in Zimbabwe (AFM), Zimbabwe Assemblies of God Africa (ZAOGA), Seventh-Day Adventists or United Methodist Church, it is hardly the case that one can come across anyone who readily identifies themselves as belonging to African traditional religion. Due to the impact of Islamophobia, some Muslims also hesitate to make their affiliation public. This explains why there was great outcry in May 2016 from some of the citizens of Zimbabwe when there were rumours spreading that there were going to be schools built by the Muslims (http://www.zimeye.net/remove-christianity-and-we-build-schools-for-you-muslims/).

This being the case, it is important to examine why this is the case. ATR, although belonging to our African heritage, is deemed by most Zimbabweans as backward. Because people generally want to be identified with something that is deemed modern or advanced, they would rather be identified as belonging to some religious movement which is deemed 'modern'. In this regard, colonization did a thorough job in identifying the 'modern' and the 'backward'. Christianity was considered to be 'modern', while African beliefs were considered primitive. For the African to be modernized or civilized, they had to embrace Christian beliefs and discard their own. As such, colonization was a 'success' in this regard, since most people in Zimbabwe today would rather identify themselves with Christianity than as radical ATR adherents.

Christianity demonized African traditional beliefs such that people who believed in them or practised some of its tenets were to be considered as 'possessed' by 'evil' spirits which needed to be removed by Christian pastors. In such a situation, to openly admit that one belongs to ATR is tantamount to admitting that one is possessed by an 'evil' spirit which will need to be removed. It is, therefore, common during testimony time in some of the Pentecostal churches to hear people testify that they once practised some of the tenets of ATR (such as healing using the spiritual realm) but now they have been 'saved', meaning that they have now become better people by leaving their ATR practices behind and embracing the Christian religion.

Interestingly, it is common practice in Zimbabwe that people have double standards towards their religious beliefs. For example, one will hear a person who identifies him-/herself as belonging to one of the mentioned Christian denominations acknowledging the existence of people with special powers in ATR. Some will be Christians by day, and if they have a serious problem, they will secretly consult traditional specialists by night. Cases of people who have gone to traditional specialists after having failed to get their hopes fulfilled in church abound. For example, it is commonplace to hear of people who have sent their infants to have their fontanels (*nhova*) 'cleaned' by traditional experts, usually elderly women who know how to get the job done. This will be done even after the child has been '*dedicated*'[1] at church. Or a couple failing to have children after years of marriage may be advised to consult a traditional specialist to have their fortunes changed after years of prayer would have failed. Obviously this will be done in secret, since the people involved would not want to be 'exposed' as having consulted a source considered 'evil'.

This being the case, it is possible that there are individuals who call themselves charismatic preachers today, making a living out of their huge number of followers but in reality are getting their 'powers' from an ATR source. This would make sense, since the competition for followers is intense between the Christian movements and ATR. ATR actually finds itself in a disadvantaged position. Because it is generally believed that its adherents possess evil capabilities and most people do not want to be identified as 'backward', most of its followers are secretive in their approach. In any extended family[2] in Zimbabwe, it is generally the case that if a particular family in the extension is known to consult ATR specialists, then this particular family becomes feared, with some refusing to allow their children to visit or even to accept food or any gifts from such people. This usually explains standing feuds between families in the extended family system in Zimbabwe, with a particular family being blamed for the failures of other families. Even at work places, if a particular person is known or even just rumoured to consult ATR specialists, for any reason whatsoever, then that person becomes feared. Other people may seek to 'protect' themselves from these individuals and seek such protection from either their church pastors[3] or other ATR specialists.

Christian movements, on the other hand, occupy a very advantaged position, with people openly going to church every worship day, singing church hymns in public and even putting stickers on their cars and in their living rooms that declare them to be 'children' of a particular church movement or particular pastor.[4] The same is not true for ATR.

Transformation possibilities: Rebranding

Because of this gloomy case for ATR, it now becomes apparent that room for transformation is to a greater extent possible. An analogy in business may explain this point. In business, companies are always competing to sell products to generally the same clients. If two companies are selling similar products, but one has a clear advantage over the other, perhaps it will be in the branding of their product, the disadvantaged company may adopt a branding strategy that will liken their product to the company in the advantage. Consumers are almost always struck by first impressions. The more appealing a product is on the outside, the more they are likely to buy it. The less attractive it is on the outside, the less likely that customers will buy it, even if the product inside is better than anything else on the market.

This analogy is also true of the religious situation. This has seen many Christian movements competing for converts by sprucing up their image and impressive technological renovations of their buildings. For example, most churches now have impressive sound systems, elegantly dressed 'praise and worship teams', catchy international hymns, as well as giant screens, where the preacher, lyrics for hymns and biblical verses are displayed for the congregants to see. A look at the ATR side looks rather gloomy. The place of consultation for the 'specialist' is usually a mud hut or a small room (in the urban setting) with an assortment of herbs and ointments. Together with the secretive nature of its clients, the brand of ATR is at a disadvantage.

Anecdotes exist of people who have rebranded themselves from being ATR specialists into Christian preachers. This is true of the Apostolic group known as *Mapostori enguwo tsvuku* (literally Apostles of the red cloth). According to widespread belief, this church is characterized by people who are ATR specialists but couched in Christian outfits. According to this belief, these people are actually traditional experts themselves with the abilities of bringing harm to anyone whom their followers wish. This being the case, there is a certain level of *rebranding* that occurs so that the ATR specialists become more appealing to potential 'clients'. From this, it is possible that this is a micro case that may represent the macro.

The case of charismatic preachers who consult West African 'Spiritual Fathers' brings a thought-provoking aspect. West African countries, just like Southern African countries such as Zimbabwe, are characterized by a rampant belief in the supernatural. Individuals can consult traditional experts to get medicines (*muti*) to have special healing or extraordinary powers. The take of this chapter is that if a calling into ministry is from God, then there would be no need to have a spiritual earthly father, since their authority would be coming directly from God. But this consultation of earthly fathers is problematic for some critics. This could be the rebranding that the chapter has been discussing. The ordinary person cannot tell whether the power a charismatic preacher possesses is from God or an ATR expert, leaving them vulnerable. The miracles performed in the charismatic churches can also be performed by the traditional specialist, which makes it difficult to tell the difference.

The bad economic situation in Zimbabwe worsens the situation. Previously, ATR specialists would charge chickens, goats and money as their fees for their services. They would then make a living out of their 'gifts'. With the coming of the Pentecostal movements and their charismatic preachers, together with their promise of wealth in their gospel of prosperity, the ATR specialists have found themselves almost *jobless*. Because of the bad economic situation, people are rushing to where they can get quick success. They flock to Pentecostal movements where problems of an economic nature are identified as having a spiritual cause that needs to be removed. The ATR specialists even become part (if not the chief) cause of the problem bedevilling many. The ATR specialists then find themselves at a disadvantage. In this situation, a rebranding of the *trade* becomes an obvious necessity. Instead of performing rituals and rites in the name of departed ancestral spirits, it becomes more lucrative to perform the miraculous in a 'modern' Christian setting (which is considered highly desirable by many). Because many people in the churches do not know (and can never fully know) the source of the power behind the performance of miracles, it is possible that many of the charismatic preachers that we are witnessing are rebranded ATR experts who have received their power from other ATR experts from various parts of Africa.

Conclusion

From the above analysis, it is apparent that the word 'miracle' is a highly complex term which involves a variety of meanings and assumptions. The task at hand was to analyse the concept of a miracle and determine whether what ATR experts do is the same thing as a miracle performed by charismatic Pentecostal preachers in the new Pentecostal churches. It was seen that both realms do more or less the same things. We then analysed whether it would make a difference if an ATR expert would rebrand themselves into becoming a charismatic Pentecostal preacher, and it was observed that in the case where this happens, there is no difference, since the ordinary person cannot tell the difference. Furthermore, it is really immaterial for the one seeking the miracle. Fundamentally, all they are interested in is for their situation to change for the better. Due to the formidable odds that they face, they regard such transformation as a 'breakthrough' or a miracle. This then led us to the conclusion that this rebranding has been necessitated by the bad economic situation in Zimbabwe which has seen the rise in the need for clients from both the Christian movements and the ATR experts. In a situation of serious competition and where a real battle for relevance and survival rages incessantly, sacred specialists of both ATR and Christianity have been forced to be creative and innovative in order to retain their share of the market. This challenges the notion that ATR is a relic from the past. It also confirms that competition forces religious actors to come up with more appealing religious beliefs and practices in order for them to remain relevant.

3

'The devil is on fire': Analysing Pentecostalism as a place of refuge amidst economic and political turmoil in Zimbabwe

Lovemore Ndlovu

Background

Mega prophets such as Emmanuel Makandiwa of the United Family International Church (UFIC) and Walter Magaya of the Prophetic Healing and Deliverance (PHD) Ministries did not emerge from a socio-economic or political vacuum. Instead, they emerged from within concrete socio-economic and political contexts. This chapter provides an overview of such a context by analysing how the general Pentecostal movement responded to these realities. Appreciating how the Pentecostal movement provided succour in a troubled economic context in this chapter facilitates an appreciation of the emergence and role of mega prophets in subsequent chapters.

From 2000, the citizens of Zimbabwe experienced difficulties as the country was plunged into the worst economic and political crisis of all time, resulting in, among others, food shortages and absolute poverty. Against this background, the chapter seeks to explore the role of religion during the unsettled times. Contemporary studies on Pentecostalism in Zimbabwe show Pentecostalism as a quintessentially popular religion that addresses existential problems and thus offers protection and security to the suffering. In order to contribute to this discourse, an empirical study was conducted. The data obtained showed that Pentecostalism provides a sanctuary to believers affected by abuse, violation and poverty.

Introduction and statement of the problem

From 2000, Zimbabwe has been experiencing major economic, political and social challenges. The economy has not been performing well, and this led to a dramatic decline in the living conditions of the people. Around 2008–9, the country had one of the highest inflation rates in the world. This triggered, among others, food shortages and the adoption of the United States dollar and South African rand as official currencies. Against this background, the chapter seeks to explore the role of religion during these unsettled times.

This study focused on Pentecostalism because of its popularity in the contemporary market of faiths in Zimbabwean society and in Africa as a whole. As is the case in other parts of the world, there is revival of religion, particularly among Pentecostals.[1] Pentecostals, according to scholars such as Barrett et al. (2001: 19), Cox (1996a: xv), Dayton (1987: 10), Droogers (2005: 258), Hunt (2003: 75) and Walker (1997: 27), are the fastest-growing contemporary branch of evangelical Christianity in Africa and many parts of the world. Zimbabweans of all walks of life, therefore, turn to Pentecostalism in search for solutions to their existential problems.

Sociologists of religion such as Hunt (2002: 14) have been preoccupied with the contentious theory – the secularization theory. The secularization theory is grounded on the notion that religion is soon going to decline and will be replaced by a post-religious secular order. With the advent of industrialization and growth in scientific thinking, some sociologists thought that religion will decline or even disappear. However, some sociologists of religion such as Cox (1996a: xv) have argued that the so-called decline of religion is something of a myth and cannot be substantiated by either historical or contemporary evidence.

Contributing to the secularization theory, Haralambos and Holborn (2004: 436) note that a major problem with the theory is that it is given different meanings by different sociologists. Problems, therefore, arise in evaluating the theory of secularization due to the absence of a general definition. Corroborating the above contestation by Haralambos and Holborn (2004: 436), Bruce (2002: 1–2) asserts that 'there is no one secularisation theory; rather, there are clusters of descriptions and explanations that cohere reasonably well'.

In light of the above remarks, this study sought to critique the secularization theory and subsequently contribute to the discourse on secularization while drawing empirical evidence from the Zimbabwe Assemblies of God Africa (ZAOGA). ZAOGA is one of the older Pentecostal churches in Zimbabwe (after the Apostolic Faith Mission (AFM)). Appreciating the dynamics in ZAOGA, therefore, assists one in understanding developments within the newer Pentecostal movements.

The problem that underlay this study centred on two issues: firstly, the role of religion during the unsettled times; secondly, the study sought to establish the impact of the economic and political turmoil on Pentecostal religiosity. Thus, it reflects on whether the economic and political conditions in Zimbabwe led to a resurgence or decline of Pentecostal religiosity.

Against the backdrop of the preceding discussion, the following research questions were formulated:

- What was the role of religion during the unsettled times in Zimbabwe?
- Did Pentecostalism as religion succeed in providing a sanctuary to believers affected by economic and political turmoil?
- Is there evidence of decline or resurgence of Pentecostal religiosity in Zimbabwe?
- What is the major attraction of Pentecostalism in Zimbabwe during the unsettled times?

Purpose of the study

With the above research questions in mind, the purpose of the chapter was, firstly, to contribute to the secularization theory whether the conditions in Zimbabwe point to a resurgence or decline of Pentecostal religiosity. Secondly, the chapter was aimed at analysing the role of religion during the unsettled times. Thirdly, the chapter looked at how religion, particularly how Pentecostalism, adapts to suit the interests of the believers during the unsettled times. Finally, the chapter looked at the major attraction of Pentecostalism in contemporary Zimbabwe society.

In order to achieve the purpose, the key concepts in the study were clarified; a review of literature pertaining to Pentecostalism was done; an empirical study for the Zimbabwe situation was undertaken; and conclusions and recommendations were put forward.

Clarification of key concepts

Pentecostalism

Pentecostalism refers to all the churches that consider themselves Pentecostal because of the emphasis they place on to the believer's access to the work and gifts – charismata – of the Holy Spirit (Droogers 2005: 258; Hunt et al. 1997: 2). According to Droogers (2005: 258), 'these charismata, such as speaking in tongues, prophecy, healing and exorcism, are part of the Pentecostal praxis'. However, the Pentecostal churches differ in size, style and organization. Pentecostalism as religion is not limited or confined to the aforementioned churches, certain churches which emphasize the presence of the Holy Spirit in the so-called charismatic movements in Protestant and Catholic churches could qualify to be included. These charismatic churches operate within the mainstream churches in order to 'renew' them without the intention of founding separate churches (Droogers 2005: 258). It is, hence, difficult to draw a clear distinction between Pentecostalism and other phenomena such as Evangelical churches or Christian fundamentalism because there could be significant overlap.

Hunt et al. (1997: 2) make a clear distinction between what they call classical Pentecostalism and neo-Pentecostalism. According to Hunt et al. (1997: 2), the earlier Pentecostal movement, with its alleged beginnings at Azusa street mission in California in 1906, is now typically referred to as classical Pentecostalism. On a global basis, classical Pentecostalism has produced its own variants or denominations which have come to take their rightful place alongside the other mainstream historical churches. These contemporary variants or denominations are now typically referred to as neo-Pentecostalism, otherwise known as the charismatic movement. The latter includes churches within the established denominations that have been open to charismatic renewal, along with itinerant ministries and para-church organizations outside of these structures (Hunt et al. 1997: 2).

Prosperity ministries

According to advocates of prosperity ministries in ZAOGA, Africans stay poor because of a spirit of poverty. Prosperity ministries thus aim at emancipating Africans from poverty. As noted by Maxwell (2006: 204), even though Africans are born again, only their soul has in fact been redeemed. The pernicious influence of ancestral spirits remains in the blood. The ancestors were social and economic failures during their own life times because they led lives of violence, indolence, drunkenness, polygamy, ancestor veneration and witchcraft – lives of waste and poverty rather than accumulation (Maxwell 2006: 204).

Zimbabwe

Zimbabwe is the African name for the former Rhodesia and was the official name of the country upon attainment of independence and majority rule in 1980. The name Zimbabwe is taken from the massive stone ruins of Great Zimbabwe, near Fort Victoria [now Masvingo], in the south-east part of the country. For many years, Great Zimbabwe was the centre of a thriving precolonial civilization, which extended over much of central and south-central Africa (International Defence and Aid Fund for Southern Africa 1977: 5).

Method of research

Literature review

According to Barrett et al. (2001: 19), Cox (1996a: xv) and Hunt (2003: 75), Pentecostalism represents the most significant movement of revival over the last hundred years, and today it constitutes the fastest-growing wing of Christianity and indeed of any expression of religiosity in the world other than Islam. Martin (1990: 163) identifies Pentecostalism as a new spiritual communication characterized by speaking in tongues and testimonies to 'blessings'. Pentecostal communication is, therefore, manifested in the healing touch, in ecstatic speech, in stories and testimonies, in music and also in an atmosphere of participation in which those hitherto voices, including women, make their voice heard (Martin 1990: 163).

Pentecostalism is defined by Droogers (2005: 259) as 'that form of Christianity in which the Holy Spirit occupies a central place'. Initially the core distinguishing features of Pentecostalism included the emphasis on speaking in tongues and the 'second baptism' in the Spirit; however, the entire Pentecostal movement is evolving so rapidly that the aforementioned aspects no longer hold. Furthermore, on a global scale, its ability to enculturate, which has led to its rapid growth, has seemingly transformed the movement out of all recognition (Hunt 2003: 78).

Martin (1990: 258) advocates that the appeal of contemporary Pentecostalism in the Third World is a result of its ability to offer a popularized form of Protestant Christianity which satisfies the requirements of the impoverished masses. As Martin (1990: 258) puts it:

> The very rapid growth of Pentecostalism occurs against this background. It offers participation, mutual support, emotional release, a sense of identity and dignity, and though authoritarian it does not offer authority to those who also have status in the outside world. Pentecostalism provides a substitute society, and within that society cares largely for its own.

Walker (1997: 28) notes that Pentecostalism as a religion has ministered to the poor and the disinherited in a culturally appropriate manner and in so doing has initiated them into the working processes and value systems of modernity. He explains in this respect:

> At the very least Pentecostalism throughout the world has not only provided meaning and succour to its adherents but it has also equipped many of them with the values of ascetic Protestantism so useful to the modern enterprise, and so essential for social mobility in a capitalist economy.
>
> (Walker 1997: 36)

Chalfant et al. (1981: 227) view Pentecostalism as a powerful form of fundamentalism. They argue that it demonstrates the appeal of a close relationship between evangelism, a literal interpretation of the Bible and a religious experience including tongues, healing, miracles and other paranormal experiences. Cox (1996a: 81–3) asserts that Pentecostalism is backward looking particularly when he speaks of 'primal spirituality'. According to Cox (1996a: 81–3), the movement attempts a restoration of the spiritual power which began the faith. It thus seeks to return to archetypal religious experiences exemplified by the emphasis put on the charismata. Hence, there is 'primal hope' that looks forward to the dawn of a new age, a millenarian heaven on earth.[2]

Scholars such as Droogers (2005: 265) allude to the fact that external conditions such as poverty and underdevelopment trigger revival and innovation in Pentecostal religiosity. Modernization does not lead to secularization but to sacralization. Droogers (2005: 265) confirms as follows:

> Though modernization seems identical with progress, to many people suffering is abundant, especially in the third world, but also in the urban margins of so-called developed countries. The wealth of the few is paid for by the poverty of the many. Because Pentecostalism applies the gifts of the Spirit to instant resolution of problems (especially through healing), the link with suffering and problem-solving is only natural. The Pentecostal church is one of the addresses where healing and health appear to be available. When modernisation has not produced an adequate medical infrastructure, despite the illusion of progress, such help is more than welcome.

Maxwell (2006: 184) carried out an in-depth study of the Zimbabwe Assemblies of God Africa. The study was carried out during the economic and political turmoil when Zimbabwe's health care and education deteriorated, unemployment increased, public sector wages were falling behind the rate of inflation and civil servants were forced to strike. Growing industrial unrest from the mid-1990s onwards reflected growing trade union militancy that eventually led to the formation of the MDC (Maxwell 2006: 184–5). As Maxwell (2006: 185) correctly states: 'Zimbabweans increasingly experienced their state as violent, bankrupt and immoral.' Maxwell (2006: 184) summarizes the conditions in Zimbabwe as follows: 'In Zimbabwe healthcare and education deteriorated, unemployment increased, while the population expanded with many young people migrating to towns and cities. By 1998 many Zimbabweans were only eating one meal a day.'

In Maxwell's (2006: 189) study, the Pentecostal church is a 'refugee camp'. According to Maxwell (2006: 192), the preponderance of images of refuge, security and protection in contemporary Pentecostal preaching in Zimbabwe does suggest that there is an element of escapism or flight from the world in this form of Christian religion.

With the information obtained from the above international literature, an empirical study, particular to the Zimbabwe situation, and which produced descriptive statistical data, was undertaken.

The empirical study

Questionnaire

To obtain data about the role of Pentecostalism during the unsettled times, a questionnaire was developed. The findings of Martin (1996: 45–6) and Maxwell (2006: 189) were used in planning the questionnaire. According to Martin (1996: 45–6), 'the message of redemption or "freedom from slavery", and the promise of healing resonate powerfully amongst people caught up in every kind of abuse, violation and indebtedness'.

The questionnaire comprised two sections. The purpose of Section A, firstly, was to establish the gender of the respondents in order to determine whether gender plays a role when respondents explain what they perceive to be the major attraction of Pentecostalism from their own view point. The respondents were requested to tick off their specific gender in the applicable block. Secondly, Section A aimed at finding out the length of membership of each respondent at the church – how long one has been a member of the church. This was meant to find out the period when one joined the church and also to establish whether Pentecostalism as religion was able to sustain and retain members for a long period or more than two years. If the member was able to remain within the church, the researcher would then proceed and find out the major attraction of Pentecostalism to that member. Thirdly, Section A aimed at finding out whether the respondents had a special role within the church.

The purpose of Section B of the questionnaire, firstly, was to identify the specific problems that the respondents experienced as a result of the economic and political conditions in Zimbabwe from 2000. Secondly, Section B aimed at finding out the specific role of the church in addressing the problems of the believers in terms of pastoral care. Thirdly, Section B aimed at finding out the opinions of the respondents on whether the church succeeded in providing a sanctuary to those who were emotionally and spiritually distressed. Fourthly, the aim of Section B was to find out the values that were imparted to the believers as a way of mitigating the problems of the past decade. Fifth, the section aimed at finding out whether the church propagated prosperity or instant riches. An open question was presented to the respondents in which they were requested to outline their understanding of the concept 'prosperity ministries'. Finally, Section B aimed at finding out what motivated the respondents to join the church. The initial draft of the questionnaire was discussed with an expert to determine the validity of the two sections. It resulted in a change of wording in an attempt to ensure that the respondents understood the gist of the two sections.

The respondents

Fifty respondents (five groups of ten) participated in the study. Three of the five groups (thirty) comprised ordinary church members who did not hold any leadership positions. The ordinary church members comprised twenty women and ten men. The average length of membership ranged from six months to thirty-five years. Two of the five groups (twenty) comprised senior church members who held positions of responsibility in the church such as pastors, deacons and evangelists. This group comprised thirteen men and seven women and their average length of membership at the church ranged from ten to fifty years.

Data collection

Three weeks prior to the administration of the questionnaires, permission was obtained from all participants. The questionnaires were administered during five sessions. It was responded to by the following ZAOGA assemblies in Harare: Msasa Park, Cranborne, Kuwadzana, Chitungwiza and Baines Avenue.

All the respondents from each of the five assemblies completed the questionnaires all at once supervised by the researcher himself. This was to avoid respondents discussing with fellow members and, therefore, influencing the outcomes of the survey. However, there was a possibility that pastors could possibly exchange notes from one assembly to another in their weekly meetings; for example, the Msasa Park Assembly was very close to the Cranborne Assembly, and the two pastors would often meet.

The procedure for both groups of respondents was identical. Prior to the completion of the questionnaires, the instructions were read out loud to the respondents. Difficult words were explained, as any misunderstanding could have influenced the results of the respondents. The respondents were encouraged to ask questions prior to and during the completion of the questionnaires and were assured that they could take all the time they needed to complete the questionnaires. Participants' anonymity was assured and voluntary participation in the research project was ascertained. Respondents were asked to write their responses as comprehensively as possible on the questionnaire paper itself. A 100 per cent response rate was obtained because the questionnaire was completed in the presence of the researcher and thus collected by the researcher himself. The collected data were then prepared for analysis. A system of coding the qualitative data was used to analyse the responses to the open-ended questions. The coding of qualitative data entailed assigning unique labels to responses that contained references to specific categories of information. The following procedures were followed with regard to the analysis of the responses to the closed questions: sorting, quality checking, data entering, data categorizing and checking the frequency (N =) counts for each of the variables.

Results

Table 1 Responses on the different types of problems that affected the respondents as a result of the economic and political turmoil of the past decade (2000–2010)

Variable	Groups			
	Pastors		Ordinary believers	
	N =	%	N =	%
Poverty	18	90	25	83.3
Low salaries	13	65	16	53.3
Lack of health care	14	70	10	33.3
Lack of social services	10	50	18	60
All forms of abuse	10	50	15	50

Analysis

Respondents were asked a question on the different types of problems that affected them as a result of the economic and political turmoil of the past decade (2000–2010).

Pastors

Pastors identified the following as the major problems that affected them as a result of the economic and political turmoil of the past decade (2000–2010): poverty (90%, N = 18), low salaries (65%, N = 13), lack of health care (70%, N = 14), lack of social services (50%, N = 10), all forms of abuse (50%, N = 10). Respondents explained that the collapse of the Zimbabwean economy rendered the state unable to discharge its social services such as education, and state obligations such as payment of meaningful civil servants' salaries were ignored. However, 50 per cent (N = 10) noted that the state became immoral and, therefore, resorted to violence which resulted in all types of abuse such as sexual abuse (women being raped) and physical abuse (rampant beatings of party supporters).

Ordinary believers

Respondents in this category identified the following as the major problems that affected them as a result of the economic and political turmoil of the past decade (2000–2010): poverty (83.3%, N = 25), low salaries (53.3%, N = 16), lack of health care (33.3%, N = 10), lack of social services (60%, N = 18), all forms of abuse (50%, N = 15). The ordinary believers viewed poverty as the prime evil and a direct result of the economic and political turmoil of the past decade.

Table 2 Responses on the different types of roles played by the church in mitigating the problems experienced by the believers in the past decade (2000–2010)

Variable	Groups			
	Pastors		Ordinary believers	
	N =	%	N =	%
Pastoral	20	100	30	100
Donations to the poor	10	50	23	76.6
Looking after orphans	12	60	15	50
Counselling	8	40	12	40
Empowerment	15	75	18	60

Other problems obviously centred on health and other social services as the government became bankrupt and unable to offer such services. The ordinary believers also noted that as the state became more desperate in holding on to power, it had to apply more unorthodox and 'dirty' tactics such as intimidation and violence.

Analysis

Respondents were asked a question on the different types of roles played by the church in mitigating the problems experienced by the believers in the past decade (2000–2010).

Pastors

Pastors identified the following roles that were played by the church in mitigating the problems of the believers: pastoral (100%, N = 20); donations to the poor (50%, N = 10); looking after orphans (60%, N = 12); counselling (40%, N = 8); empowerment (75%, N = 15). Pastors emphasized pastoral care – guiding the church to face the challenges and realities of the past decade. The biggest challenge, then, was to look after church members who were emotionally and spiritually distressed and coming with all sorts of problems.

Ordinary believers

Ordinary believers identified the following roles that were played by the church in mitigating their problems: pastoral (100%, N = 30); donations to the poor (76.6%, N = 23); looking after orphans (50%, N = 15); counselling (40%, N = 12); empowerment (60%, N = 18). Among the ordinary believers, the most notable roles were that of providing pastoral care, making donations to the poor and empowering members to survive on their own through imparting survival skills

Table 3 Responses on whether the church succeeded in providing a sanctuary to those who were emotionally and spiritually distressed

Groups							
Pastors				Ordinary believers			
Affirmative		Negative		Affirmative		Negative	
Yes = N	%	No = N	%	Yes = N	%	No = N	%
20	100	0	0	30	100	0	0

and strategies. Due to high levels of poverty, the church was instrumental in mobilizing food, blankets and clothing for the most disadvantaged members of the church including payment of fees for orphaned children. Other members such as those suffering from incurable diseases such as HIV/AIDS were very dependent on the church for their welfare and well-being. The latter could not afford to fend for themselves due to ill health and the harsh economic conditions that prevailed.

Analysis

Respondents were asked a question whether the church succeeded in providing a sanctuary to those who were emotionally and spiritually distressed.

Pastors

All the respondents (100%, N = 20) were affirmative in their response to the above-mentioned question. Respondents agreed that the church provided a sanctuary to all the believers who were emotionally and spiritually distressed. Furthermore, they explained that the church provided hope, refuge and security to many Zimbabweans who were suffering due to the harsh economic conditions that prevailed.

Ordinary believers

All the respondents (100%, N = 30) in this category agreed that the church provided a sanctuary to those who were emotionally and spiritually distressed.

Table 4 Responses on the different values imparted to respondents as a strategy to mitigate the problems that affected the believers in the past decade (2000–2010)

Variable	Groups			
	Pastors		Ordinary believers	
	N =	%	N =	%
Perseverance	18	90	25	83.3
Self-denial	8	40	12	40
Purity	12	60	16	53.3
Generosity	9	45	14	46
Faithfulness	14	70	18	60

The respondents noted that the economic and political environment could no longer give believers hope for the future and the only answer came from God. Consequently, biblical citations such as 2 Corinthians 5:7 gave them strength to face their daily challenges. It says, 'for we walk by faith, not sight'.

Analysis

Respondents were asked a question on the different values given to them as a strategy to mitigate the problems they encountered.

Pastors

Pastors noted the following values that emerged from their teachings during the weekly sermons and cell group meetings: perseverance (90%, N = 18), self-denial (40%, N = 8), purity (60%, N = 12), generosity (45%, N = 9), faithfulness (70%, N = 14). It was clear from the pastors that they focused on preparing believers for the new age; hence, emphasis was placed on primal hope. They encouraged believers to be fearless, righteous and to endure the present-day problems.

Ordinary believers

Ordinary believers noted the following values that were drawn from the weekly sermons and cell group meetings: perseverance (83.3%, N = 25), self-denial (40%, N = 12), purity (53.3%, N = 16), generosity (46%, N = 14), faithfulness (60%, N = 18). Respondents in this category pointed out that the values imparted by the church leadership gave them strength to face the challenges of the day and prepared them to focus on the 'spiritual' treasures and not the 'material' treasures. Pentecostalism, therefore, provided believers with a place of refuge where believers could access the 'spiritual blessings' and not the 'material blessings'.

Table 5 Responses of the respondents on whether the church advocated prosperity or instant riches

Groups							
Pastors				Ordinary believers			
Affirmative		Negative		Affirmative		Negative	
Yes = N	%	No = N	%	Yes = N	%	No = N	%
2	10	18	90	3	10	27	90

Analysis

Respondents were asked a question whether the church advocated prosperity or instant riches.

Pastors

Out of the twenty pastors 90 per cent (N = 18) of them disagreed that their church advocated prosperity. They indicated that the church puts more emphasis on 'heavenly riches' rather than 'earthly riches'. Instant riches were perceived as earthly and therefore of no gain to the church. However, 10 per cent (N = 2) of the respondents argued that the church advocates 'instant riches' as blessings or breakthroughs that strong believers should receive.

Ordinary believers

Out of the thirty ordinary believers 90 per cent (N = 27) of them disagreed that the church advocated prosperity. They indicated that prosperity is not at the core of the ZAOGA ministry. However, 10 per cent (N = 3) argued that the church advocates prosperity as part of its strategy to fight the spirit of poverty.

Discussion

The results of this study are reviewed in terms of the research findings of scholars such as Droogers (2005), Martin (1996) and Maxwell (2006). In a study conducted by Droogers (2005: 263) which was focused on Pentecostalism, he suggested that what happens in economic life is compensated for by a similar but inverted process in religious life. Those who have been dispossessed in economic terms and do not enjoy access to the economic means of production gain control over the religious means of production and become the owners of a religious product that – under current market conditions – sells well.

Martin (1990: 205–6) conducted similar research on the relationship between Pentecostalism and economic advancement. He asserted that Pentecostal religion and economic advancement do often go together and, when they do so, appear mutually to support and reinforce one another. Pentecostalism attracts converts because it combines material and spiritual improvement. According to Martin (1990: 219), during the period of acute social distress, the poor saw that the austere moral and economic rules of Pentecostalism offered enticing – and well-defined – route for upward mobility.

Maxwell (2006: 207) also conducted similar research on the impact of Pentecostalism on the post-independence Zimbabwe society that was affected by the 'spirit of poverty'. In his findings, Maxwell (2006: 207) explains as follows:

> Doubtless many ZAOGA members rushed for deliverance to 'get ahead', drawn by the images of material success, sophistication and modernity actively promoted by the leadership. But it is clear from the hundreds of letters Guti received from ordinary church members that the majority did not so much seek prosperity as security: 'to stay well at home' – *kugara zwakanaka kumusha*. They looked to the church, and to Guti in particular, for protection from ancestral curse and for fertility, healing, employment, good marriages.

The research findings of the above-mentioned scholars illuminate the findings of this study because Pentecostalism is revealed as a sanctuary and a place of refuge which offers security and protection to the suffering. As Maxwell (2006: 209) further states, '[C]ontemporary Pentecostalism is a highly successful popular religion: a set of ideas and practices that addresses adherents' existential concerns for wholeness, purity, meaning and empowerment.'

Although ZAOGA is facing stiff competition from the mega prophets such as Makandiwa and Magaya, there is a sense in which it serves as the paradigm for a successful model of prophetic Pentecostalism in Zimbabwe. In this regard, its competitors seek to draw lessons from its longevity and fierce loyalty of its members. Furthermore, they also appreciate how ZAOGA organizes its members at the local congregation, mobilizing of resources and putting up a spectacle whenever a major event is organized by the main church. To this end, therefore, understanding the impact of ZAOGA on the Zimbabwean religious scene is valuable. It enables one to appreciate the extent to which newer or younger Pentecostal churches and personalities such as Makandiwa and Magaya have entered a market that already had some players who were doing very well.

Conclusion

The Zimbabwe Assemblies of God Africa represents one of the oldest and the largest Pentecostal churches in Zimbabwe. On average, each assembly receives between five to ten new aspiring members a week and the church has been experiencing an unprecedented growth, both within and outside the country. The results of this study reveal that Pentecostalism in Zimbabwe is growing very rapidly. According to Cox (1996a: xv), current trends show that it is secularity, not spirituality, that is headed for extinction. Some prominent sociologists of religion suggested that the technological advancements and growth in scientific thinking would lead to a decline or even disappearance of religion. However, this is not likely to be seen in many parts of the world including Zimbabwe. Instead, a religious renaissance or resurgence is underway.

Pentecostalism in Zimbabwe is evolving, particularly as seen during the economic and political turmoil of the past decade. It is clear from the preaching of the pastors at ZAOGA that emphasis is on teaching members of the church to be fearless and to seek security from Jesus, particularly his blood. According to Maxwell (2006: 188), Pentecostals tend to focus on Christ's blood protection quality in their ongoing struggle with the devil and his emissaries in this world. The economic and political chaos in Zimbabwe was seen by believers in ZAOGA as the work and manifestation of the devil and ZAOGA thus aimed at fighting the devil and putting the *devil on fire*. The ongoing struggle with the devil was evident during the weekly sermons and praise and worship sessions. The expression *Phuma Sathani!* (Go Satan!), therefore, dominated much of ZAOGA teachings and practices.

As observed in this study, the genius of Pentecostalism lies in its representation as a place of refuge, a sanctuary that provides hope and security to believers who are suffering abuse and violation. Believers are instructed to seek God and fight the devil. In God they are offered refuge, security and protection. Innovation is seen in how the Pentecostal gospel becomes a vital weapon amidst economic and political turmoil in Zimbabwe. However, ZAOGA provides not only spiritual refuge, but welfare for the many disadvantaged members of the church. Believers in ZAOGA are guided by their primal hope and eagerly wait for the dawn of a new age, a millenarian heaven on earth. Younger Pentecostal churches have had to be creative when trying to get a share of the spiritual market which has been dominated by older Pentecostal churches such as ZAOGA. They have appreciated ZAOGA's organizational capacity and investment in creating loyalty.

4

Pentecostal Prophets Emmanuel Makandiwa and Walter Magaya: Masculinity, competition and the postcolonial state in Zimbabwe

Ezra Chitando

Introduction

There have only been limited studies addressing the theme of masculinity in Zimbabwe. This is because most of the studies on gender have tended to focus exclusively on women (as is the case elsewhere). Gender has often been used synonymously with 'women's issues'. In the context of religious studies, gender studies have focused mostly on the status of women in African traditional religions, the various forms of Christianity, Islam and new religious movements. As a result, very few studies have addressed the theme of religion and masculinity in Zimbabwe.

Although there are limited studies on religion and masculinity in Zimbabwe, there have been endeavours to examine the theme from the dominant literary perspectives (Muchemwa and Muponde 2007) and psychological perspectives (Chiroro et al. 2002). Gaidzanwa (2015) has analysed the later former president Robert Mugabe's masculinist politics in Zimbabwe. Given the massive exodus of Zimbabweans into the Diaspora, Pasura and Christou (2018) include the responses of Zimbabwean men regarding their adjusting to the new context of the UK. In addition, beyond the specific case of Zimbabwe, there have been efforts to understand masculinity in Pentecostal churches in general (e.g. Van Klinken 2014; Jeater 2016; Lindhardt 2015 and Maskens 2015) or in specific Pentecostal churches, such as the Zimbabwe Assemblies of God Africa (ZAOGA) Forward in Faith (Chitando 2007). These studies highlight how Pentecostalism has contributed to the shaping of masculinities in Zimbabwe. The quest has been to appreciate how men have been socialized and how they perform their masculinity in a given social context. It has become evident that men's leadership of religious movements can, to a large extent, be attributed to the position that they occupy in society. Since Zimbabwean society, in line with trends elsewhere, generally constructs men as leaders in different sectors, it has not been that difficult to embrace the emergence of young male Pentecostal mega prophets in Zimbabwe.

In this chapter, I seek to examine the emergence of two of the leading male Pentecostal mega prophets in Zimbabwe, Emmanuel Makandiwa of the United Family International Church (UFIC) and Walter Magaya of the Prophetic Healing and Deliverance (PHD) Ministries using the concept of masculinity. My central argument is that the emergence and popularity of these young prophets are linked to the struggles of the Zimbabwean state to deliver on the promises of prosperity and development. The young male Pentecostal prophets emerged at a time when the late former president Robert Mugabe's charisma was on the wane. Although Mugabe continued to dominate the political scene, a significant part of the population was now turning to these (and other) young prophets on the basis of their promises of prosperity. If Mugabe delivered Zimbabweans from the yoke of colonialism and imperialism, it would be left to the young prophets to deliver Zimbabweans from angry and persistent spirits.

I argue that although initially Mugabe, a charismatic leader, had 'skillful rhetoric and messianic qualities' that legitimized him as 'a mediator and a friend' (cf Gibson 2003: 5), by the time of the formation of the government of national unity (GNU) in 2009, his status had come under serious question. Although musical groups such as the Mbare Chimurenga Choir of the ruling ZANU-PF party continued to lionize him, the generality of the population had begun to critique his capacity to take the nation to the Promised Land. In the song, 'VaMugabe', the Mbare Chimurenga Choir sang:

VaMugabe, Honorific title for Mugabe
ndimi mega Baba You are the only one
Pakutonga In ruling/governing
Pakuronga In organising
Pakugona In excellence
Muri mukuru (x3) You are the topmost, topmost, topmost

The Mbare Chimurenga Choir celebrated Mugabe's leadership, ascribing excellence to him in the areas of ruling and organizing. However, Hosiah Chipanga, another musician, declared that most of the citizens had been reduced to vendors in the song, 'Vendor', released in 2016. It was in the wake of serious economic problems that there was a major shift from 'Baba Mugabe' (Father Mugabe) to Papa Makandiwa and Papa Magaya. This is not to imply that the prophets became politicians, but to draw attention to the fact that they became an alternative source of deliverance. As the Zimbabwean state reeled under multiple challenges after 2000, more citizens began to invest in the young prophets. Adherents and clients believed that these prophets and the movements that they led produced club goods – both spiritual and material (Iannaccone and Berman 2006). It is these goods that appealed to clients and led to the popularity of the two young prophets. Although critics such as Mahohoma (2017) tend to concentrate on the accumulation of wealth by individual prophets, there is need to adopt a less judgemental approach and appreciate the extent to which competition, marketing and brand enhanced the standing of Makandiwa and Magaya in Zimbabwe.

Masculinity, fatherhood and the Postcolonial state in Zimbabwe

In order to put the popularity of Makandiwa and Magaya into its proper historical context, it is important to appreciate how the nationalist movement that became significant in the 1960s and the subsequent armed liberation struggle of the 1970s placed emphasis on male personalities. Furthermore, it is informative to understand fatherhood in Zimbabwean society. Joshua Nkomo, a leading nationalist who was later to become vice-president of Zimbabwe, was celebrated as 'Father Zimbabwe'. Although women participated in the nationalist awakening and the armed liberation struggle, the dominant narrative was that of the 'sons of the soil' (that is, men) embarking on a mission to restore African spirituality, pride and dignity. This dominance of men in nationalism was carried over to the state after independence in 1980. Hegemonic masculinity, namely the version of masculinity that dominates other interpretations of what it means to be a man in a particular context (Connell 1995), places men at the centre. According to Joane Nagel (1998: 248–9):

> By definition, nationalism is political and linked to the state and its institutions. Like the military, most state institutions have been historically and remain dominated by men. It is therefore no surprise that the culture and ideology of hegemonic masculinity go hand in hand with the culture and ideology of hegemonic nationalism. Masculinity and nationalism articulate well with one another.

Alongside the emphasis on men and masculinity in nationalism, in Zimbabwean (and other) society men are socialized and projected as 'providers'. In pre-colonial times, the man was expected to be either an accomplished hunter or a farmer. The very concept of '*baba*' (father) is associated with the ability to meet the demands of the nuclear and extended family. However, with the changes wrought by colonialism, patriarchal power, initially based on the capacity to hunt, became associated with the ability to provide for the family. With the attainment of independence in 1980, the nationalists, particularly Mugabe, were projected as the 'ultimate providers'.

In the early years of independence, Mugabe was presented as the father of the nation who would defend it and protect it from threats, perceived or real. In the first instance, Mugabe was to be the ultimate arbiter of all 'family disputes'. Musician Thomas Mapfumo, later to become one of Mugabe's arch critics, maintained that Mugabe was the 'cockerel' of Zimbabwe. All the most demanding cases that needed settling would be referred to Mugabe. During periodic droughts, Mugabe would be presented as one with messianic qualities who would feed the starving masses (Machingura 2012).

Alongside defending Zimbabwe from those who were believed to want to make it a colony again, Mugabe was presented as one who protected the country's moral foundations. His rantings against homosexuality must be located within this patriarchal context. A good father stands for what he believes is right and does not hesitate to name what he believes is wrong. Mugabe became the leader who coached his fellow citizens against the evils of colonialism and neo-colonialism. He extended his defence of the vulnerable to the entire Global South. At United Nations fora, he stood up against the global powers and defended the Global South. Like a caring father, he spoke against the skewed global economy and challenged the powerful nations of the world to work for justice and equality.

Despite Mugabe's declared intention of being the loving father who cares for 'his' children, Zimbabwe experienced serious socio-economic challenges during his tenure. The Zimbabwean state struggled to provide its citizens with the desired quality of life. The postcolonial state struggled to fulfil its 'fatherly' role. In the traditional set-up, hungry children would seek food and sustenance at their next-door neighbours. Similarly, many citizens left the country in search of greener pastures. Thus, millions of Zimbabweans went into economic exile within the Southern African region and further afield.

After years of suffering, the inclusive government or government of national unity (GNU) of 2009–2013 provided some respite. The hyperinflationary environment was stabilized, salaries became worthwhile and the quality of life improved. However, this was short-lived, as Mugabe won the 2013 elections. The gains that had been made under the GNU were quickly lost and the uncertainty regarding the future returned. Mugabe's fatherhood and ability to look after his 'children' became heavily contested. As his body grew weary and his stature as the 'strong man' of Zimbabwe was challenged in his own party, young Pentecostal prophets emerged as alternative sources of power, influence and authority. I turn to a discussion of this development below.

'Papa' deliverers: Youthful Pentecostal male prophets in Zimbabwe

A longer study is required in order to do justice to the history of Pentecostalism in Zimbabwe. Extant studies (see e.g. Maxwell 2006; Machingura et al. 2018; Togarasei 2018) have highlighted the expansion of this brand of Christianity in the country. Whereas older Pentecostal churches, such as the Apostolic Faith Mission (AFM) and the Zimbabwe Assemblies of God Africa (ZAOGA), had been an integral part of the spiritual map of the country, new players emerged as the first decade of the 2000s was coming to an end.

Younger male Pentecostal prophets appeared on the scene and had an immediate impact. Emerging from the AFM in 2008, Makandiwa gathered tens of thousands of adherents and clients at the City Sports Centre in Harare. A gifted preacher, he was popular for his ability to deliver lively and captivating sermons. Equally important was his presentation as one who could also deliver individuals and families from curses and other oppressive spiritual forces. As a total package, Makandiwa's message and activities can be understood in the context of the prosperity gospel. This is the conviction that true believers of Christ must not be poor in material terms. Rather, they must lead full and rewarding lives, this side of the grave. Whereas the missionaries tended to preach a gospel that placed emphasis on the salvation of the soul after death, Makandiwa preaches a gospel that promotes health and wealth in this current life. According to Attanasi (2012: 4):

> Health and wealth teachings define prosperity as more than material well-being; prosperity includes emotional, physical, and spiritual health, although the material aspects are often disproportionately emphasized. Such teachings often equate prosperity with God's shalom, a Hebrew word usually rendered 'peace' but also entailing justice, equity, responsible governance, and righteous acts.

As Makandiwa was consolidating his position on Zimbabwe's spiritual market, another young male prophet, Magaya, emerged. Magaya appealed to exactly the same clientele as Makandiwa. His PHD Ministries majored in prophecy, healing and deliverance. As with Makandiwa, tens of thousands of members and those who were seeking miracles attended his weekly sessions. PHD emerged in 2012, at a time when the Government of National Unity (GNU) had managed to calm down the economy. However, many citizens were still traumatized by the economic and social breakdown of the earlier years. Furthermore, there was a lot of uncertainty regarding the country's economic trajectory and recovery prospects. Like Makandiwa, Magaya was a proponent of the prosperity gospel, reassuring his members and clients that their lives would be transformed in the immediate future.

Both Makandiwa and Magaya sought to assuage the fears of Zimbabweans regarding the future. At a time when the state was paralyzed, with Mugabe's leadership being fiercely contested both within his own party and by the opposition, young charismatic prophets emerged as viable substitutes. Although they did not have political power, the young prophets presented themselves as having spiritual power, which would in turn bring economic salvation to the desperate citizens.

Young male Pentecostal prophets such as Makandiwa and Magaya had, in a sense, taken over the role of providing for the citizens. Consequently, the term 'Papa' became popular, as it was used to refer to the young prophets who were now foster parents to the 'orphaned' Zimbabweans. As the combined effects of poor economic management, corruption and sanctions compromised the livelihoods of most citizens, 'Papa' became both a real person and a concept promising release, hope and abundance. As 'Baba' Mugabe's powers ebbed, the status of the two young 'Papas' was enhanced. As the state was failing to provide social security, the movements initiated by the two 'Papas' offered new places to feel at home. Thus, the declaration at the UFIC was '*ndiri Mwana womuProfita*' (I am a child of the Prophet). This is a loaded declaration, as it suggests that one was a child of the prophet. In the face of life's challenges, the prophet would act to assist his 'child'. The statement must be understood within the context of pressing socio-economic and political challenges that Zimbabwe was undergoing. In the face of unemployment, irregular payments of salaries, bleak employment opportunities for graduates and other challenges, the prophet would plead with God for those under his protection to flourish.

Makandiwa, Magaya and other youthful prophets stepped up to reassure their adherents and clients that God had not abandoned them. As the government struggled to provide basic social services, the young prophets offered an alternative support system. Their adherents and clients gathered together, worshipped together and were energized to face the challenges. At a practical level, some of their adherents and clients formed networks that enabled them to identify and pursue business opportunities. Furthermore, the young prophets provided healing services at a time when the health delivery system was facing major challenges.

The fatherhood of the young prophets must be understood in terms of their putative spiritual authority and higher status in the spiritual hierarchy. Whereas in indigenous categories, the term '*Baba*' (Father) is often restricted to older males in the family/clan, its appropriation and deployment by the young prophets was quite strategic. It increased their respectability and authority. As young 'Papas', the Pentecostal prophets could give counsel on various issues, give directives to older people and act as pillars of strength in a context where many things were falling apart.

Masculinity, competition and branding in Zimbabwean Pentecostalism

The young Pentecostal prophets found themselves competing for clientele in a heavily subscribed spiritual market in Zimbabwe. In order to attract and retain membership (and by extension, retain or expand tithes and offerings), Makandiwa and Magaya were involved in an intriguing 'battle for souls'. Although it is possible to focus on their assertions that they were complementing each other, there is also merit in examining how they effectively involved in competition. The competition between the two leading prophets (and other prophets) generated considerable innovation. As Maseno (2017) has demonstrated in the context of female Pentecostal-Charismatic Church leaders in Kenya, branding enables them to claim a share of the spiritual market.

Insights from scholars who have studied religions as economic systems are very helpful in understanding the competition between Makandiwa and Magaya as two of the leading prophets in Zimbabwe's spiritual market at the time of writing. Whereas in the early phase there had been a lot of fluidity in the membership of the two movements that they headed (with clients moving freely between them in search of 'breakthroughs'), gradually many people decided to settle for either movement. During fieldwork, it became clear that there were very few people who felt free to move between the UFIC and PHD Ministries.

These were two distinct brands, and consumers had to choose between one of them. These brands were associated with the two leading prophets, and members of the UFIC or PHD Ministries did their best to justify why their brand was superior.

Branding was critical for the success of both movements. Each prophet presented himself as a resource used by the Holy Spirit to deliver individuals, families and the whole nation from spiritual attacks and other forces that deepened poverty. However, since the services they provided were similar, there was need for each one of the prophets to emphasize his uniqueness. Although Makandiwa's initial entry on the spiritual market was built on miracles, this dimension of his ministry would soon be understated in favour of his status as an outstanding teacher of the Word of God. Many respondents, including those from mainline Protestant churches and the Catholic Church, were keen to identify effective preaching as Makandiwa's highest selling point. Thus, one of the recurrent statements during fieldwork was 'I do not accept the drama associated with the so-called miracles, but, Makandiwa is a great teacher of the Word.' This is expounded by Matandare and Mugomba when writing:

> A well-known example of the phenomena in Zimbabwe is Prophet Emmanuel Makandiwa, whose reputation as a visionary leader has been earned through his presentation of sermons characterised by use of storytelling, including the use of symbolism and metaphors. He has managed to establish credibility with his audience because he speaks with enthusiasm and competence and is able to grab and hold the attention of his followers. He is very persuasive and effectively uses body language as well as verbal language in his sermons.
>
> (Matandare and Mugomba 2015: 169)

Makandiwa's success as a teacher of the gospel could be attributed to the theological training that he received at the Apostolic Faith Mission's Living Water's Bible College. Makandiwa's self-presentation is consistent with the social construction of a successful young man as one with self-control, mastery of language and control over others (Stewart 2016). The UFIC television channel, Christ TV, tended to focus more on Makandiwa's sermons and presented him as a gifted and charismatic preacher. Although the miracles continued to receive coverage, there was more emphasis on Makandiwa's gift of teaching.

On the other hand, Magaya presented himself more distinctively as a master exorcist and philanthropist. The name of his church, PHD, expressed the emphasis on the 'prophetic, healing and deliverance' dimensions of his ministry. His television channel, Yadah TV, tended to place emphasis on Magaya's healing and deliverance. Furthermore, Magaya is represented as a generous giver. Alongside working miracles and teaching prosperity, Magaya is shown as a church leader who gives without counting the cost. Thus, he will be presented supporting different individuals and causes. These include providing support to the national soccer team, supporting orphans and mentally challenged individuals and other worthy causes.

The branding that Makandiwa and Magaya employed was consistent with masculinity and marketing. Masculinity thrives on competition and demonstrating that one is, indeed, the 'alpha male'. In this competition, however, the two prophets employed creative strategies. Each young prophet deliberately built a brand identity which they sought to protect and extend at all costs. Brand loyalty implied ensuring that membership remained stable or, better still, that it grew. According to Ghodeswar:

> A brand is a distinguishing name and/or symbol (such as logo, trademark, or package design) intended to identify the goods or services of either one seller or a group of sellers, and to differentiate those goods or services from those of competitors. A brand thus signals to the customer the source of the product, and protects both the customer and the producer from competitors who would attempt to provide products that appear to be identical …. Brands provide the basis upon which consumers can identify and bond with a product or service or a group of products or services.
>
> (2008: 4)

Makandiwa and Magaya created brands that attracted loyal followers, as well as clients seeking solutions to pressing problems. In turn, they sought to ensure that they met the socio-economic and spiritual needs of their clients. In a real sense, they both met the needs of their clients, as well as generated demand for healing and deliverance by their clients. For example, by giving elaborate descriptions of the 'principalities and powers' that sought to frustrate the elect of God, the two prophets placed their clients on high alert for these forces. In turn, they positioned themselves as well equipped to overcome the negative forces and to promote prosperity for those who sought their services.

One of the distinguishing features of masculinity is the ability to address pressing social and economic challenges. One critic, Dube (2015: 1), expressed the role of the prophets as follows: 'In the absence of a functioning health sector and economy, the prophets, mostly from an Afro-Pentecostal tradition, promised people instant healing and economic prosperity.' The young male prophets can be regarded as living up to their expected social role of delivering individuals, families, communities and the nation from pressing problems. It might even be argued that, despite the competition between them, they can be regarded as replacing/supplementing the state.

Masculinities, innovation and competition in a challenged state

As I have argued above, the success that Makandiwa and Magaya have enjoyed must be understood in the context of a challenged state. As the Zimbabwean state struggled to provide basic services to its citizens, the two young male prophets stepped in. In this section, I will outline some of the key dimensions that enabled the young prophets to increase their clientele base. First, the patriarchal dividend worked in their favour. The patriarchal dividend refers to the benefits that men enjoy on the basis of being men (Connell 1995). Although there are women prophetic leaders in Zimbabwe, Makandiwa and Magaya were able to attract many followers because of the pre-existing image of men as leaders. The two young men capitalized on the social construction of men as leaders to establish their movements and to attract followers. Women who establish similar ministries have had to endure many more frustrations due to the bias towards men. In this sense, therefore, Pentecostal masculinity, serves to 'strengthen, to support, to consolidate, to biblically legitimize male domination, the ascendancy of men over women, patriarchy, the primary power of the men in and outside the assembly'(Maskens 2015: 331).

Second, as noted earlier, the two prophets have developed specific masculine brands that they have promoted through various strategies. As the state's health delivery system was malfunctioning and senior government officials resorted to being treated in South Africa, or further afield, the two presented themselves as 'master healers'. Although the field of traditional healing is dominated by women, the most popular 'national deliverers' have tended to be men. Consequently, Makandiwa and Magaya stepped up as accomplished 'Men of God' who restored the nation's health by exorcizing evil spirits, banishing 'spiritual husbands', binding the spirit of poverty and promoting good health and prosperity. Both prophets were, therefore, engaging in the masculine task of protecting individuals, communities and the nation at a time when the nation was struggling on multiple fronts.

Third, the competition between the two leading prophets and movements generated considerable creativity as they sought to increase their market share.

For example, in response to the critique that the prophets are always taking resources from their clients, in 2018 Magaya decided to distribute groceries to thousands of people who attended services at his main centre in Waterfalls, Harare. It is crucial to bear in mind the fact that the state was struggling to cushion citizens from a highly volatile economic situation. In this regard, one could argue that Magaya was replacing the state. He was playing the role associated with a responsible father by providing basics for his 'children'. In turn, Magaya was enhancing his brand. Similarly, Makandiwa has been involved in charitable works, especially through the charity wing headed by his wife. Both prophets have endeavoured to challenge the image of prophets as individuals who only receive and never give. For Maskens (2015: 331), 'The Pentecostal man distinguishes himself from the "ordinary" man because he is projecting himself as sensitive, communicative and responsible, an exemplary father, whose concerns are concentrated on the well-being of his family.'

Fourth, the two prophets sought to project a positive image of masculinity. Whereas the discourse has tended to focus on the 'crisis of masculinity' (men's violence, boys and men being overtaken by girls and women in education, women becoming 'breadwinners' and others), Makandiwa and Magaya seek to recover and defend a brand of masculinity that is positive. Even as the state was experienced by many as aloof and uncaring, these two young male prophets sought to make themselves relevant to the struggles of the majority. For example, while former president Mugabe was often out of the country seeking medical help in Singapore, Makandiwa and Magaya strove to be available to their followers and clients as much as possible. Even when they were absent physically, they sought to be experienced as loving and caring. However, Magaya in particular had to contend with accusations of problematic interactions with women at the time that this study was conducted. This serves to confirm that the ideals of Pentecostal masculinity are difficult to live up to.

Fifth, the two young Pentecostal prophets were keen to embody the masculine value of resourcefulness. Whereas the state was struggling to provide for the citizens and was relying on the 'look East' policy for support from China, the prophets were demonstrating their resourcefulness by initiating and completing projects using local funds. Both the UFIC and PHD Ministries were conducting big building projects, supporting orphans and disadvantaged women using resources from within these movements. Embracing the masculine value of being resourceful under trying circumstances, Makandiwa and Magaya mobilized their followers to remain steadfast in the face of serious challenges in Zimbabwe.

Critiques and contestations: Summarizing criticisms against young male prophets

Despite the success that Makandiwa and Magaya enjoyed, a number of critiques emerged (see also the chapters by Musoni; Mapuranga; and Chitando and Chikonzo in this volume). In this section, I shall summarize some of the major critiques. To begin with, although in this chapter I have argued that it is possible to consider the two as emerging at a time when the Zimbabwean state was struggling, some critics charged that the two prophets were too close to the same state. Thus, they charged that there were 'patriarchal contracts' between politicians representing the state and the prophets. Indeed, both Makandiwa and Magaya were playing it safe in their interactions with the state. Where some leaders of mainline churches were openly critical of Mugabe and his party, the two prophets were more cautious in their dealings with the state. They avoided openly confronting the state, although, to be fair, the overall political climate made it dangerous for anyone who dared to criticize Mugabe.

Other critics charged that Pentecostal prophets such as Makandiwa and Magaya were now 'competing with Christ' (Magezi and Banda 2017). By seeking to fulfil patriarchal expectations, the two prophets were getting acknowledged and praised by their followers. Some critics felt that the two prophets were becoming the 'big men' (McCauley 2012). The two prophets were becoming very prominent and overshadowing other players within the Zimbabwean Pentecostal movement. This generated the critique that their members and clients were now placing them at the same level as the founder of Christianity himself.

There are others who also alleged that the strategies offered by Makandiwa and Magaya were not sustainable. For example, the emphasis on anointing oil was deemed inadequate as it did not direct citizens to engage in transformative actions (Banda 2018a). Therefore, they called on the two prophets to 'man up' and propose more effective strategies that would include challenging the abuse of power by politicians. They also encouraged the prophets to mobilize their members and clients to support active resistance of repression by citizens.

Another area of contestation related to the allegation that some prophets were abusing women due to their claims of spiritual power, as well as their better economic standing. Furthermore, it was contended that the prophets took advantage of their good relationship with the politicians to avoid prosecution. Thus, prophetic masculinity was portrayed as predatory. Manyonganise (2016a) observed that due to the power imbalance in church and society, some women have fallen prey to the prophets. Thus, there was a call for women to be vigilant when interacting with the young male prophets. To be fair, however, most of the rumours were not confirmed through concrete prosecution of the alleged offenders.

Mugabe, competing with the young prophets, had a number of stinging criticisms. On different occasions, Mugabe castigated the prophets for propagating the prosperity gospel and becoming too central to the lives of their congregants. According to him, they were creating the impression that other Christians could not say prayers that could reach God directly without passing through them. He challenged other Christians to break free from such a theology. He also felt that the emphasis on money was unfortunate, as it deepened poverty among the majority. Furthermore, Mugabe was not pleased that some young prophets were making declarations regarding certain politicians being primed to take up certain political positions in future (Gadzikwa, 2020).

Conclusion

Prophetic Pentecostalism has become an established phenomenon in many parts of Africa. In Zimbabwe, it has attracted a significant following. Through careful marketing, and attending to the felt needs of many citizens, the young prophets have captured a notable share of the spiritual market. Two main brands, Makandiwa and Magaya (and the movements which they front) have emerged. These two have been actively involved in innovation and competition in order to preserve and increase their market share. Although it is possible to refer to ecumenism and analyse collaboration between Makandiwa and Magaya, it is also helpful to examine the extent to which the two young prophets have been involved in a battle for influence and control of the spiritual market in Zimbabwe.

In this chapter, I have argued that the challenges that Mugabe and the state that he fronted experienced provided an opportunity for the emergence and thriving of the young prophets. As Mugabe and the state struggled to satisfy the demands of the citizens, the young prophets emerged as attractive alternatives. They claimed to have access to heaven and to plead with God to bring health and well-being to their members, clients and the entire citizenry. Thus, 'Baba Mugabe' (Father Mugabe) was being systematically replaced by the two young 'papas' years before the military officially and finally removed him from office. Even as the young Pentecostal prophets competed (between and among themselves, as there were numerous other players), they posed a joint front in their competition against Mugabe/the state/government. They had to be innovative as they sought to attract and retain followers and clients. Whereas in the 1980s many citizens could proudly proclaim, '*ndiri mwana waVaMugabe*' ('I am Mr/Cde Mugabe's child'), the collapse of the system led many to proclaim, following the emergence of dynamic young prophets in 2008 (Makandiwa) and 2012 (Magaya), '*ndiri mwana wemuprofita*' ('I am a child of the prophet').

5

Religion in a new era: Pentecostalism and innovation in the Prophetic Healing and Deliverance Ministries in Zimbabwe

Tabona Shoko

Introduction

The rise of Pentecostalism in Zimbabwe is indicative of the fact that there is an urgent need to meet the spiritual needs of the people of Zimbabwe. This dramatic rise is timely as Zimbabwe experiences a chain of economic challenges that ranges from economic hyperinflation in the 2000s to cash shortages at the time of writing. This has been largely attributed to non-performing industry that has triggered high rate of unemployment and suffering. In Zimbabwe today it is not uncommon to find phone messages, posters announcing Christian crusades, seminars, workshops and revivals, stuck on every tree and wall, which is evidence that many Zimbabweans are hungry for a message of hope that can deliver them from the tribulations in their homeland. Because the situation in the country has made them hungry for more of God's word in order to find peace and direction in their lives, many have turned to Pentecostal churches that emphasize healing and deliverance. In order to get the message of hope across to as many people as possible, many Christian evangelists are now beginning to compile their sermons and repackaging them to books and CDs and conveying as WhatsApp texts and car stickers. As a result, many newly formed Pentecostal churches such as the Emmanuel Makandiwa's United Family International Church (UFIC), Uebert Angel's Good News Church, Shepherd Bushiri's Enlightened Christian Gathering (from Malawi and with branches in South Africa) and Prophet Magaya's Prophetic Healing and Deliverance (PHD) Ministries have engaged in free enterprise to earn a huge following among the masses in Zimbabwe. What unites all these African (Pentecostal)-initiated churches is their fundamental belief in activities of the spirit, hence the designation, 'spiritual movements'

(Daneel 1970: 15). However some people are concerned over the various changes that are brought about in the religious landscape like prosperity gospel preachers walking on air, performing miracle babies, miracle money, availing miracle condoms and deliverance. This chapter explores Prophet Magaya's PHD Ministries' innovative skills of blending the traditional and Christian world views to survive the harsh economic and religious terrain in Zimbabwe.

Background

The Prophetic Healing and Deliverance Ministries is a Christian Pentecostal ministry that was founded by Prophet Walter Magaya in 2012 in Harare, Zimbabwe. Born on 6 November 1983 in Mhondoro Ngezi, Magaya was a member of the Catholic Church in Zimbabwe who grew up in Chitungwiza, Unit L, Seke, a dormitory town of Harare. The church's headquarters is at Zindoga Shopping Centre in Waterfalls, Harare. He is married to Tendai Katsiga-Magaya. Magaya is in fact the prophet and founder of the PHD Ministries. He claimed to have received his anointing in 2009 from Prophet Temitope Balogun Joshua (born 12 June 1963), commonly referred to as T. B. Joshua, a Nigerian prophet and televangelist, leader and founder of the Synagogue Church of All Nations (SCOAN), a religious organization that runs the Emmanuel television station from Lagos, Nigeria. Thereafter T. B. Joshua became Magaya's spiritual father (*Daily News* 6 November 2014). Magaya at one time conducted all-night service that was attended by more than 350,000 people in November 2014 and graced by musicians and dancers such as Tocky Vibes. The presence of musicians such as Alick Macheso, Nicholas Zacharia and dancers like Bev at all-night sessions by Magaya later became sweetener to attract crowds seeking contentment and peace of mind from the economic stress. In PHD Ministries there are important people such as Oscar Pambuka, ZTV anchor man; Psychology Maziwisa, former member of parliament, Highfields West; Nyasha Chikwinya, former ZANU-PF legislator and minister of women's affairs; Walter Muzembi, former MP, Masvingo, and minister of tourism, the ambassador of Mozambique to Zimbabwe; and others. In PHD Ministries there are people from all walks of life, vendors, industrial workers, politicians and business people. PHD membership is interesting in that there are also believers from the Catholic and Protestant churches, justifying the prophet's stance that PHD is not a church but a ministry. In his self-styled charismatic approach, Magaya has also appealed to traditional world views that have seen him attract more members to his ministry.

The genesis of Pentecostalism and PHD Ministries

Prophetic healing ministry is one of the newest religious movements in Southern Africa and in particular Zimbabwe. It is an undeniable fact that most new religious movements and AICs in Southern Africa originated from economic and political issues in South Africa. Magaya's PHD did not emerge as result of migrant labourers (like the older AICs of the 1930s), though it eclipsed other religious movements in size and influence. Also it did not arise because of schisms that characterized other movements. Rather, PHD revolves around the founder Walter Magaya and his wife Tendai, who assumed the title prophetess.

Zimbabwe's economic crisis that followed the land reform in 2000 reached its peak in 2008–2009, which generated economic hardships; shortages of commodities; fuel and electricity; shortages of foreign currency; and hyperinflation. The economic meltdown also resulted in political violence and the collapse of industry, removal of education and health subsidies, increased rural to urban migration and increased crime rates (Sachikonye 2011: 5). The imposition of sanctions by the West on Zimbabwe from 2002 worsened the economic situation in the country. All these factors helped in the precipitation and growth of Pentecostalism which gave birth to PHD Ministries.

In this context, many people flocked to PHD Ministries due to worsening of living conditions. This was in a context of increased homelessness and unemployment (Maxwell 2006: 6). Thus, Pentecostals were preaching the message, 'In our church God offers hope to the hopeless and the suffering, from the sense of personal objection created by the shattered hopes of independence and the elusive promise of modernity' (Maxwell 2006: 6). Magaya's ministry does this by focusing more on the contemporary needs of the society in which it operates. Also, traditional religion in its dynamic forms has also continued to exert influence on contemporary religious discourse.

Mentorship

One factor that makes PHD share similar views with African traditional religion is the idea of mentorship into the trade. In Shona traditional religion those who had to become spirit mediums had to go to someone who would tutor them on how to conduct their duties as practitioners (Moyo interview 12 May 2016). Similarly, Prophet Magaya was mentored in Nigeria by T. B. Joshua. He has revealed on several occasions that his secret powers of the gift of prophecy and healing grew phenomenally after he visited the Nigerian preacher after he initially consulted on business ventures (Magaya, sermon 8 November 2014). The same can be said of Prophets Makandiwa and Angel who were inducted by their spiritual father, Ghanaian Prophet Victor Kusi Boateng. This is reminiscent of traditional healers who visit specialist *n'anga* called *godobori* for spiritual strength (Shoko 2007: 25).

Spiritual father

Walter Magaya's spiritual father is T. B. Joshua of Nigeria. He has undertaken numerous trips to the West African country and some analysts think that probably his visits are meant to borrow some power from some foreign prophetic tradition so that he may use it to woo a lot of people to his own church. Some think that T. B. Joshua may be the actual source of power or otherwise he knows Magaya's source of power. Magaya announced; Rather, Shoko and Chiwara on 21 December 2015 that T. B. Joshua was his spiritual father and that he was proud of him since he wielded greater powers of anointing, deliverance, teaching and guidance. But according to *Sunday Mail* dated 6 March 2016, spiritual fathers receive honour as if they are demigods. Rather Shoko and Chiwara observe that in their culture traditional healers have spiritual powers whom they respect and consult for more powers (Shoko and Chiwara 2013: 223).

The teachings of the Prophetic Healing and Deliverance Ministries

Pentecostalism features as the fastest-growing stream of Christianity in the world today. African Pentecostalism emphasizes personal salvation in Christ, as a transformative experience wrought by the Holy Spirit. The thrust of PHD Ministries is miracles or mighty works of the Holy Spirit, one which the 'Man of God' is endowed with and that which he uses for prophecy, healing and delivering people from evil. The teachings of PHD state that in the world of spirits people are haunted or possessed but communication with the dead is prohibited. The dead are believed to haunt people to such an extent that they will not be able to accomplish anything in life like giving birth, getting employment, gaining wealth and prospering. So PHD teaches that their God is a God of prosperity and wealth. As such on the sidelines of his church's *crusade* called 'Miracle Night', in May 2016, Magaya urged the Zimbabweans to remain focused, saying the country would overcome the prevailing economic challenges.

Belief in spirits

Prophet Magaya's PHD Ministries challenges Zimbabweans to throw away their traditional resources of supernatural succour and turn towards the Living God of the Bible. He says, 'Your culture is full of demonic things and it is not responding to your cries, come to PHD Ministries and be born again, receive your salvation.' But close analysis shows that PHD Ministries does not reject the traditional past wholesomely but engages with it, refurnishing history and domesticating it. He uses the Bible as a resource for explaining the past and critiquing the present. PHD Ministries has embraced modernity and is thoroughly modern in its outlook. As such they pose a special attraction for youth, promote lay leadership and ecclesiastical office based on a person's charismatic gifts and innovative use of technologies (Asamoah-Gyadu 2007: 392). But despite all this innovation, they still draw a lot from tradition. Traditional African ideas about spirits have become Christianized by mapping them onto Christian ideas about the devil and demons. Meyer (1998) describes this as 'transplanting the devil,' by which she means the way in which African Pentecostals have redescribed the African world of spirits in terms of the Christian world of demons. It would appear the Christian discourse about the devil and demons allows Pentecostals to draw a sharp distinction between the world of traditional religion and the Christian world, while also acknowledging the reality of the spirit world. Such churches as PHD simply rename these spirits as demons and talk about the need to be delivered from their possession and influence.

Gospel of prosperity

Scholars in African Christianity have observed that many mainline churches are losing quite a number of their adherents to a new wave of spiritual movements under whose banner African Pentecostalism operates. Magaya's PHD Ministries has proved to be a crowd puller, with thousands of congregants attending their Sunday and midweek services. At the birth of PHD in 2012, the number of attendees was initially a moderate number of forty congregants, but at the time of writing the figure has ballooned to the average of 50,000 strong attendance at every service. In this context, the mass exodus of the religious adherents of mainline churches to Pentecostal churches such as PHD is best understood in terms of the Pentecostal main thrust on prosperity. Close scrutiny shows that some of the reasons behind the popularity of this new Pentecostal church include the very close link to the Shona traditional religion which believes in the idea of prosperity that is manifest in health, wealth and well-being. The indigenous religion is world affirming. Believers subscribe to life 'here and now' and that humans must enjoy their prosperity in hunting, success in agriculture and marriage here on earth (Platvoet 1988: 10). In fact, the religion prescribes that life in this world must be good and everything is done in view of the attainment of prosperity, in terms of health, wealth and social well-being. Therefore, the new Pentecostal movements have taken up some of the key concepts in African traditional religion and have recast them in Christian idiom, thereby confirming their innovation. It would appear many Zimbabweans are satisfied with such creativity as the emerging Pentecostal churches fill the void left by mainline churches.

Principle of giving and seeding

PHD encourages its membership to participate in giving and seeding as part of their practice. In the base religion, namely Shona traditional religion, individuals are encouraged to give in abundance and those who are mean are ridiculed. This concept of giving is largely embedded in the concept of *Ubuntu* which emphasizes good relations with one's neighbours through hospitality, friendship, togetherness, unity and solidarity. One who gives is called *mapavhurire* (a celebrated generous person who is to be admired), and the greedy person is mocked as being anti-social. However, the difference is that in PHD one should give in order to receive in abundance.

Payment for service

One researcher, Nyasha Mundondo (2015), observed that there is a lot of fundraising happening in the PHD church. There are anointed places and items one is expected to access, at a challenging cost for the majority of the adherents. In order for one to have a consultation with Prophet Magaya, one has to go to the Guest House at the cost of US$250. The anointed items are also quite expensive.

For example, the DVDs which come with the 'Resurrection Power' anointing oil bottle cost $10, badges and stickers cost a dollar each, plastic wristbands $5, T-shirts with the prophet's name $15, sewing garment $10, hats $5 and books which are published every week cost $1.There is a place called the Holy Ground which is believed to have healing powers, and one can only go there with an offering in their hands. Since people are in search of deliverance they end up giving all they have in order to enter the Holy Ground with the hope that everything will get better after stepping on that ground (Mundondo 2015: 34). This practice shows parallels with traditional healing practices where a healer requests 'gifts' of fowls, goats, cattle or money as payment for healing services.

Prophecy

PHD Ministries is associated with a special gift of prophecy. This concept of knowledge of the unknown is prevalent and called divination in traditional religion. In this case, Pentecostal prophecy seems to share common features with the *n'anga* practice. Our understanding of a prophet is '[o]ne who utters divinely inspired revelations, one gifted with more than ordinary spiritual and moral insight, one who foretells future events, predictor, and an effective or leading spokesman for a cause, doctrine or group' (Gelfand et al. 1985: 3). In most cases, prophets are called by the divine into the ministry although in some cases they pass through a prophetic initiation process. For instance, the call of the prophet Isaiah (6:1-9) in the Bible involves the divine who called and commissioned Isaiah to become a prophet. If Elisha the son of Shaphat is to be considered prophet, then his commissioning was through prophetic initiation by Elijah as his mentor (1 Kings 19:16-17). This same phenomenon of a prophetic call is also prevalent in the Shona traditional religion, especially the call of a *n'anga*. This may suggest appealing similarities between a prophet and *n'anga*. For example, many assistants of a *n'anga* (*makumbi*) eventually become *n'anga* themselves (Shoko and Chiwara 2013: 268). As such, Magaya's prophecy appears a modern Pentecostal innovation of tradition.

Healing

The theology of deliverance and healing dominates PHD Ministries. The need for healing and deliverance has led PHD to grow at such an impressive rate. The name of the church, Prophetic, Healing and Deliverance, itself portrays the major aim of the ministry. Its primary aim is to heal and deliver people from demoniac curses. Magaya putatively possesses the powers to heal many diseases such as cancer, diabetes and physically challenged people. Through the Holy Spirit, he is believed to have healed thousands of people all over the world. There are various methods which Pentecostals use to heal. These include the laying of hands, distant healing, using of anointing oil and healing by word of faith. All these correspond to what Magaya does in his ministry.

In PHD Ministries, the believers strive to integrate worship and healing, and in their services considerable attention is given to the cause of suffering and sickness. They ascribe an important role to the power of the Holy Spirit in their services marked by divine healing. This concern for the sick and healing has features that resemble traditional religion. In traditional religion, health is apparently one of the primary concerns of the Shona people. The traditional belief system has many causes of illness such as spirits, witchcraft and sorcery, as well as social and natural causes (Shoko 2009: 45). There are different types of spirits, but those usually associated with disease are ancestors, avenging spirits and alien spirits. While ancestors are positive and guard, protect and provide for the living, they can be malevolent when neglected and cause sickness, misfortune and death. If a spirit such as that of witchcraft (*shavi rokuroya*) desires to possess a family member and the member rejects it, a *n'anga* is called to exorcize (Shoko 2007: 35). Due to witchcraft beliefs that permeate PHD Ministries, some people, especially the youth and the middle aged, are now accusing their families' older members of being witches and wizards due to the prophecy they are getting from the church.

This Pentecostal gospel has created some elite people who believe they are better than anyone else and do not want to be associated with those practising traditional religion and those going to the white garment churches (Mapostori) as they label them 'primitive worshippers of ancestral and marine spirits'. But in a dramatic exchange of words, the *vapositori* have claimed that God had revealed to them that Magaya was not a Man of God but uses magic and other ungodly antics such as oil from snakes to lure people to his congregation. So they had approached their association for permission 'to destroy artefacts' which they claim Magaya uses to lure people to his church (*NewsDay* 9 February 2015). Here, it can be seen that innovation and competition go together.

Miracles

Miracles are another religious feature that characterizes Prophet Magaya and PHD Ministries. The miracles ostensibly performed by Magaya include healing and exorcism. His breathtaking miracles have made him one of the most prominent miracle workers among the Pentecostal prophets in Zimbabwe and even abroad. People flock in large numbers to his services to witness these miracles, as well as to receive them. According to him, the Bible authorizes his miracle working (Magaya Preaching 10 February 2016). PHD Ministries maintains that Magaya has notably prayed for the physically challenged and they get healed. This is evidenced by walking crutches and wheelchairs that are hung in his church at Waterfalls. Those who get healed leave their crutches behind (Mtethwa 2016: 29).

The prophet has made claims he can cure AIDS as testified by one client who reportedly tested positive but who changed status after visiting 'the Man of God' at the guest house (Client X, testimony Yadah TV 13 September 2014). This is also consistent with the traditional approach. Thus, 'Quite often especially where there are psychological problems, the traditional interpretation of disease attributed it to possessing spirits that need to be accommodated or exorcised' (Bourdillon 1993: 91). The same procedure is performed by n'anga in the Shona traditional religion. It seems many people would want to identify with miracle performers for their own security. As G. Parrinder states, '[M]agical practices occupy a large part of the thought and time of many people all over the world' (Parrinder 1961: 27). It follows that in both contexts, there is the general understanding that diseases are caused by possessing spirits that need to be exorcised. The healing miracles, therefore, take a central position in PHD Ministries as they do in the n'anga's ministry in the traditional religion (Shoko and Chiwara 2013: 274).

Exorcism of evil spirits

Exorcism of evil spirits is a form of healing 'miracle' which is common among men endowed with spiritual powers. These miracles in PHD Ministries are necessitated by the failure of the mainline churches to address the spiritual problems of people in their society. On the one hand, ministers of the mainline churches do not, on the whole, know how to deal with sickness related to social tension. On rare occasions such a minister who gets involved in healing or the exorcism of traditional evil spirits is likely to get into trouble with his or her church. It seems Magaya capitalized on this weakness of the mainline churches and demonstrated his miraculous healing and exorcism powers to advertise his church and lure thousands of people (Shoko and Chiwara 2013: 275). He used his own station, Yadah TV, as well as other visual and audio media to advertise his ministry at large and his healing and exorcism miracles in particular. It is also a common feature these days that a *n'anga* can advertise his or her expertise through the print media such as posters and electronic media; radio and television; social media such as WhatsApp, Facebook, Twitter and others.

The use of elements

The use of elements such as wristbands, car stickers, anointing oil, T-shirts, DVDs and candles is widespread in PHD. These items sell like hot cakes. The elements are believed to be anointed by the 'Holy Man' and can be used to ward off evil (Shumba interview 2 April 2015).

Towels and amulets

PHD Ministries has invented the use of towels and amulets to heal people and protect them from evil attacks. K. Biri (2012) noted that in the Bible the Apostles prayed for aprons and handkerchiefs, and they were believed to have healing powers (Acts 19:12). This same applies to PHD's use of towels. From the interviews conducted, PHD Ministries followers are given small anointed towels which they use to wipe everything they want to anoint and to offer breakthrough. Mrs Mashoko, one of the followers, said that they are given the towels to wipe the things they want to possess in life. This includes cars, kitchen utensils and any material things and they will be theirs through faith (Mashoko interview 20 December 2015).Others use the towels to wipe people who are sick and they are believed to get healed. Magaya has also initiated the use of amulets and reminder bracelets which are put on by the followers and are believed to have healing powers. Some manifest behaviour indicative of being under a spiritual attack if they wear these amulets and bracelets. The adherents believe that these amulets have the healing powers and can lead to all breakthroughs that one needs in life. Amulets have the protective powers and the adherents will be protected from all forms of evil (Mtethwa 2016: 26). These icons are believed to be protective and divinely anointed. People need these amulets to protect them against life's situations such as robbery, accidents, sickness and even death. They also believe that they can use them to secure promotion at work. They confirm the innovation in PHD as Shona traditional religion promotes the use of amulets.

Use of anointing oil

Prophet Magaya makes use of anointing oil which is said to have healing and anointing powers. This oil has its background in the Bible (I Sam 10:1ff and Ps 23:5). However, its use in PHD is now complicated. Some people from Zimbabwe and abroad have testified about the miracle of anointing oil. For instance, a student studying at Midlands State University said that after writing her assignment she applied anointing oil on the document and she got the highest mark, way above everyone (Tine interview 12 February 2016). However, other people argued that anointing oil works depending on one's faith. What matters most on the issue of anointing oil is that it is sold to the people, unlike in the Bible where it was given freely.

Singing and dancing

According to Shoko (2010: 227) singing and dancing are an important feature in Pentecostal ministries, and there are people who are responsible for leading praise and worshipping songs. Singing is of much importance since it evokes the Holy Spirit. Psalms 100:2 makes reference to singing and making joyful noise unto the Lord. They play instruments like keyboard and pianos, and with this, it is believed that people will easily feel the presence of God. People could be heard saying, '*nziyo iyi inondiswededza padhuze naMwari*' (this song makes me to feel the presence of the Lord). Singing is also used on certain occasions; for instance if the prophet is healing people, there are certain songs sung, and if when it is time they usually sing the one given below:

> *Zvibereko zvemunashe mamiriyoni* (fruits of spirits came in abundance)
> *Huyai tidyare mathousnds* (come let's seed our gifts, in thousands)
> *Aya ndiwo mamirion* (they come in abundance, in millions) (PHD praising songs)

These types of songs invoke the believers to give abundantly. Songs can also be sung when the prophet or pastor is about to preach so that they will enter into an ecstatic motion (Mtethwa 2016: 24). Similarly, traditional music is a way of life and not just a form of entertainment. It is used in vital aspects of life such as to communicate, pass information and welcome heroes among other ritual functions. There are diverse genres of music in Zimbabwe like hymns and dirges that create mood and feel for the occasion. Music is an integral part of the traditional culture, with various ceremonies being preceded by some sort of music.

Holy place

Prophet Magaya came up with the idea of the holy ground in his ministry. His headquarters at Zindoga is a marvellous warehouse that has been converted into holy place of worship. His guest house in Marlborough, Harare, is an *axis mundi* where all heath ailments are addressed. The place is exclusively holy. The idea of holy ground and holy place has its origins in the Bible; for instance, when Moses saw the burning bush, he had a voice which urged him to remove his shoes because he had stepped on a holy place (Exodus 3:1ff). The Jewish tradition also allows only the priests to enter into the holy of holies to give sacrifices because the place was deemed holy (Luke 1:8). The same applies to the PHD's holy ground which is believed to have the powers which cause people to manifest, be healed and all life's challenges to be solved. The prophet has stipulated the time at which people should get on to this ground. When people enter this sacred space they will remove their shoes; others will be holding papers where their problems are written so that they will leave them in the holy ground. Others will be vomiting from *kudyiswa* (given food by witches while unaware).

Social engagement

Magaya has come out on television and newspapers as someone whose ministry is characterized by frequent charity work. In 2015 Magaya bought a book worth US$50,000,000 by the then First Lady entitled 'Amai Dr Grace Mugabe at 50' as part of her fiftieth birthday anniversary. The initiative was in recognition of the work that the First Lady was doing to promote charity work in Zimbabwe (*The Herald* 27 July 2015). Magaya has constructed a state-of-the-art hotel and a stadium worth US$15 million. Furthermore, Magaya has supported the National Teams with thousands of dollars for their soccer initiatives and he is constructing a stadium in Waterfalls for sports tournaments. In August 2015 Magaya donated 1.2 million rand towards the construction of 2.5 megalitres reservoir at Parirenyatwa Group of hospitals (*The Herald* 21 August 2015).

All this charity work is in accordance with scripture. In the Christian context, the kings and chiefs welfare is the responsibility of the prophetic powers in their midst. For instance, the biblical prophet Isaiah acted as an advisor to the King (chs 7–9). Similarly Emmanuel Makandiwa, a fellow prophet, was broadcast on ZTV news handing over a beautiful house, which he constructed for his chief in his rural community. These acts of charity by Pentecostal prophets such as Magaya demonstrate their creativity and commitment to social transformation. However, critics contend that there is a calculative dimension that must be factored in.

Conclusion

It is largely noted that Magaya is instrumental in the growth and expansion of a particular brand of Pentecostalism in general and PHD Ministries in particular. His roles as a prophet, healer and miracle worker have attracted a large number of people. It is clear that PHD Ministries' influence and rapid growth are a result of its innovation and rebranding of traditional beliefs and practices to suit the spiritual needs of the indigenous people of Zimbabwe. Although there are some differences in the practices and approaches in PHD, the fundamental belief system derives from traditional religion. Innovation, competition and creativity are, therefore, valuable concepts when interpreting the place of PHD Ministries on the contemporary religious scene in Zimbabwe.

6

Rebranding Pentecostalism: An analysis of the United Family International Church and Prophetic Healing Deliverance Ministries

Molly Manyonganise

Introduction

This chapter is an analysis of the United Family International Church (UFIC) and Prophetic Healing Deliverance Church (PHD) founded by Emmanuel Makandiwa and Walter Magaya, respectively. What it seeks to do is to look at how the emergence of the above-mentioned churches has to a large extent altered the religious landscape in Zimbabwe. The chapter argues that Makandiwa and Magaya have not only rejuvenated the religious zeal within most Christians but have also 'rebranded' the Pentecostal Christian faith. In trying to sustain this argument, the chapter focuses on how Makandiwa and Magaya have brought within the Christian arena innovative ways of being Christian. It is important to note at this juncture that the study is aware of the contestations from both within and outside Pentecostal churches in Zimbabwe regarding the way Makandiwa and Magaya have conducted business within their churches. While some of these critiques may be genuine, the others are a result of the perceived threat that PHD and UFIC have posed to the existence and well-being of long-established churches in Zimbabwe. Since their formation, there has been an exodus of people joining PHD and UFIC. The fluidity of membership in these churches has also resulted in people crossing the floor to UFIC and vice versa. This has resulted in overt and covert religious competition among Christian leaders in Zimbabwe in general and between Makandiwa and Magaya in particular. As the chapter looks at how the two church founders have rebranded Pentecostalism within the Zimbabwean context, it also brings out the latent antagonism that exists between them and at times their followers.

New Pentecostal prophetic movements in Zimbabwe

Pentecostalism may be understood as 'that stream of Christianity that emphasizes personal salvation in Christ as a transformative experience wrought by the Holy Spirit; and in which such pneumatic phenomena as "speaking in tongues", prophecies, visions, healing, miracles, and signs and wonders in general, are sought, accepted, valued, and consciously encouraged among members as evidence of the active presence of God's Spirit' (Asamoah-Gyadu, 2007: 389). Pentecostal Christianity has been referred to as charismatic and sometimes as fundamentalist due to its insistence on the literal translation of the Bible (Maxwell 2008: 403). Mayrargue (2008: 3) views Pentecostalism as an expression of evangelical Christianity because of its insistence on personal conversion.

Commenting on global Pentecostalism, Miller (2003: 5) argues that 'since its inception in the first century, Christianity has been evolving as a social institution, changing its organizational shape, redefining its mission, and creating new expressions of worship'. Pentecostal movements are classified into various forms. For example, the *New International Dictionary of Pentecostal and Charismatic Movements* cited in Yong (2005: 18) identifies three types of Pentecostalisms in the twentieth century. These are (a) the classical Pentecostal movement connected to the Azusa Street revival in 1906–09; (b) the charismatic-renewal movement in the mainline Protestant, Orthodox and Roman Catholic churches beginning in the 1960s; and (c) a neo-charismatic 'catch all' category that comprises independent, indigenous, post-denominational groups that cannot be classified as either Pentecostal or charismatic but share a common emphasis on the Holy Spirit, spiritual gifts, Pentecostal-like experiences, signs and wonders, and power encounters. These types are well represented in Zimbabwe as confirmed by Togarasei (2018). Togarasei classifies Pentecostal churches especially in Zimbabwe into two types, namely classical and modern Pentecostal churches (MPCs). Togarasei distinguishes modern Pentecostalism from the classical version of the 1920s in that it attracts the urban middle class, the elite and the fairly educated into its fold.

However, to the typologies discussed above, there has emerged in Zimbabwe a typically new Pentecostal phenomenon which I have termed 'Prophetic Pentecostalism'. Chibango (2016: 58) also notes that Pentecostal churches that have emerged in Zimbabwe of late need to be classified under a new Pentecostal movement, distinguished from the classical or old Pentecostalism such as the Apostolic Faith Mission [and others that fall within this category]. Some scholars would classify these as new Pentecostal churches (NPCs). Zimbabwe has witnessed the mushrooming of newly formed Pentecostal prophetic ministries which are dubbed to be modern and sophisticated. According to Manyonganise,

> Prophetic Pentecostalism ... refers to a new form of Christianity currently sweeping across Zimbabwe which has its anchor on prophecy. Basing their argument on Joel 2:28, this kind of Pentecostalism believes that God is still speaking to his people today. Founders of these churches allege that traditional Pentecostalism stifled the voices of prophets.
>
> (2016a: 272)

Examples of these churches are United Family International Church (UFIC) which was founded by Emmanuel Makandiwa in 2008 who broke away from AFM in Zimbabwe, Spirit Embassy founded by Uebert Angel (2007) and Kingdom Embassy by Passion Java; Walter Magaya's Prophetic Healing and Deliverance (PHD) Ministries also broke away from the Roman Catholic's Charismatic arm in 2012. Most of the 'prophetic' Pentecostal churches emerged during Zimbabwe's socio-economic and political crises. From Manyonganise's point of view, the emergence of these churches needs to be understood as an attempt to offer people a way out of the cage of these crises. This view is shared by a number of scholars. For example, Marongwe and Maposa (2015: 10) aver that 'the Zimbabwe crisis which rocked the country from the 1990s and which reached its climax in 2008 helps significantly to account for the phenomenal spread of Pentecostalism in the country'. This view is also shared by Chitando (2013) and Chibango (2016). Thus, Ukpong (n.d.) is of the view that 'Pentecostal experience is bound to thrive in a context where people are deprived, disorganized and made defective', while Mayrargue (2008: 6) specifically notes that 'many Africans turn to Pentecostalism as a result of problems they face'.

In this regard, 'Prophets' Makandiwa, Uebert Angel, Passion Java, Magaya and many others have convinced their followers that they can predict their future, as well as diagnose the causes of their misfortune. We see in their activities a close affinity with the African Initiated Churches or *mapositori* as they are called in Zimbabwe in that while the classical Pentecostals rejected the foretelling and forth-telling by white garmented churches in Zimbabwe by viewing it as synonymous with the traditional practice of divination, these newly formed churches have embraced the practice and have added some sophistication to it. For example, while the prophets in AICs used African indigenous languages as a medium of communication, the prophets in the new Pentecostal churches use English. In addition, they adorn themselves in expensive suits which, from their perspectives, are evidence of how God has blessed them. They have also made sensational claims of performing miracles of raining gold and money. This is what has come to be commonly known as 'miracle' money, gold and children. Also central to their teachings is the doctrine of fatherhood. This doctrine stipulates that each of them should submit to a spiritual father (Chitando et al. 2013b: 161). In this case, Makandiwa and Angel have Ghanaian Victor Kusi Boateng as their spiritual father; Angel is the spiritual father to Java while Magaya's spiritual father is the famous Nigerian 'Prophet' T. B. Joshua. While the use of the term 'father' is not new in Christian churches, its use in these Pentecostal prophetic movements (PPMs) has taken on new forms.

For Chitando et al. (2013b: 161), this doctrine needs to be understood within the wider contestations in masculinities as the prophets seek domination in terms of both space and power. A critical analysis of the fatherhood doctrine reveals a certain pattern which is taking root within Pentecostalism in Africa in general and Zimbabwe in particular where famous religious figures who are mainly male are forming networks of 'sons' and 'fathers'. While scholars writing on gender have called on religious leaders to confront patriarchy within their institutions, it becomes worrisome to see the absence of women in these leagues of 'sons' and 'fathers'. It is, therefore, not wrong to assume that the new Pentecostal prophetic movements continue to ignore the persistent gender bias which ensures that women remain invisible as leaders. Women scholars of religion are noting with concern how the new PPMs have continued to treat women as carers and nurturers especially by relegating the wives of the founders of these movements to charity work. Gabaitse (2015: 3) notes of Pentecostalism in general that its theology propagates gender injustice and inequality by reinforcing male supremacy. Turning to the focus of this chapter, what is clear from the movement is how it is rebranding Pentecostalism in Zimbabwe in unique ways that have left people with more questions than answers.

Rebranding Christianity: Creating unique identities

The new Pentecostal prophetic movements have presented Christianity as a commodity which is not only personal but also packaged and sold the same way as other marketed goods and services. What UFIC and PHD have done is to turn their messages, personalities of founders as well as merchandise into distinctive brands. In their bid to present their brands to the public, the two Pentecostal personalities have shown their mutually exclusive identities within the new Pentecostal prophetic movement in Zimbabwe. Makandiwa has presented himself as a sophisticated, rich and smart 'man of God' while on the other hand, for a long period, Magaya presented himself as a simplistic and dishevelled preacher of the gospel. Most of their male members copy the way that they dress and present themselves in public. From this, we can see how the existence of UFIC and PHD revolves around their leaders. In fact, the leadership of both Makandiwa and Magaya has taken on a cultic form as their members constantly refer to God as the God of either 'prophet' and refer to these men as 'Papa', 'Prophet', '*Munhu waMwari*' (Man of God) (Manyonganise 2016a: 275).

In 2013, at one of the Tuesday Services at the City Sports Centre, in a question and answer session, one of the youth asked whether, after all the congregants had witnessed what Makandiwa did, it would be blasphemous to regard him as Jesus Christ or rather was it possible that Jesus had come back and was disguising himself as Makandiwa. In answering, Makandiwa did not outrightly refute the claim but said the youth may have been right though it is wrong to equate any human being with Christ. I found such an answer to be ambiguous. In order to buttress the sacrality of Makandiwa, his wife, on 19 June 2016 when celebrating Father's Day, claimed that 'our father is a spirit' to the applause of the congregation. To view him as such is to set him apart from the rest of the prophets. In other words, he is seen as operating in a different realm, thereby giving him an identity that is unique. In August 2016, Magaya was arrested for alleged rape. However, in response through social media, his followers perceived the allegations as part of the trials and tribulations that their prophet was facing. I have argued elsewhere that this is tantamount to creating a personality cult out of these leaders, while Ukah (2003b: 257) opines that 'the ownership of most Pentecostal churches as a personal enterprise which entitles the founder to unquestioned loyalty as well as privileged position in the allocation of power and wealth act as a galvanizer of intense struggle for social, symbolic and economic resources'. Commenting on what he termed 'booming gospreneurship,' Mataire (2015) notes that

> [t]he growth of Pentecostals is leaning around individuals and the creation of break-away or new movements, rather than strong associations or institutionalized forms. The main ambition of the majority of the pastors is to start their own ministries so that they can control, mainly the funds.

The above assessment is to a greater extent correct if one looks at how Makandiwa and Magaya are treated by their congregants. As alluded to earlier on regarding their titles, they are projected as father figures at whose appearance, the congregants kneel and pay homage. To this end, Ukpong cited in Manyonganise (2016a: 275) argues that

> Pentecostalism has involuntarily tightened personality cult in the contemporary Christianity. It has succeeded to turn attention of the faithful not simply to 'deceased saints' but to the 'living saints'. This attitude is creating what we may call 'spiritual titanism' among Christianity that is to say, those with spiritual gifts, exercise them in titanic manner, using their gift to lord it over others and to bring them to servitude.

In the UFIC and PHD, God becomes the 'God of Papa Makandiwa or Magaya'; he is often referred to as the 'God of the Man of God'. This is said almost always when the congregants are praying or just talking in general conversations. Basically, this is tantamount to congregants putting their faith in individuals rather than in God or rather thinking that for them to be heard by God, they have to pass through their church leaders. This observation is often denied by followers of Makandiwa and Magaya, as they argue that even in the Bible, God is identified as the God of Abraham, Isaac and Jacob. Pastor Shaky from the UFIC on 14 August 2016 while preaching at the Chitungwiza Church claimed that actually there was no need to refer to the God of Moses now because Moses is already dead, but to focus on Prophet Makandiwa, whom he regarded as the 'Prophet of our time' since he has rebranded what it means to be Christian in Zimbabwe. He said, '*baba vedu vakauya nezvinyowani*' ('Our father brought something new').

The gospel of prosperity that is central in both UFIC and PHD also centres around the 'prophets'. In Chitando's opinion, prosperity theology associates material prosperity with divine favour (2013: 96). When one looks at the activities that take place at these churches, one is bound to come to the conclusion that their meeting centres have become marketplaces where the founders conduct both their material as well as spiritual businesses. In Togarasei's opinion, 'the prosperity gospel becomes some form of entrepreneurship for the pastors' (2014: 120). In the UFIC and PHD, the selling of branded merchandise is very common. Among these are stickers, wristbands, posters and other paraphernalia. Both churches make use of branded 'anointing' oil. In fact, the anointing oil bottles have photographs of Makandiwa and Magaya. However, while in UFIC the oil is given for 'free', in PHD one should have bought some of the merchandise for them to receive the oil. According to Chibango (2016: 68), the oil is only given to those who would have bought a DVD which costs US$10. In one of his sermons, Makandiwa castigated the hypocrisy of some prophets who claimed to be giving the oil for free yet they force people to purchase some items first. For him, it is as good as the oil is being sold and going against the traditional Pentecostal view that takes the salvific act of the Cross of Jesus Christ as having been offered for free and therefore, which should also be given for free. Such attitudes reveal the contestations around prosperity theology within the Pentecostal movement itself (Chitando 2013: 96). Despite all this, Chibango (2016: 68), in his analysis of PHD, notes that 'the sales of various church products together with "seeding" money have also contributed towards the building of the empire'. While this may be true of the church leaders, Chibango may have failed to see the significance of merchandise to the believers themselves. For example, believers in UFIC and PHD do not take the objects they purchase as profane. While this is a new phenomenon in Zimbabwe's Pentecostal turf, the congregants appropriate special meaning to these objects. To this end, Golden (2006: 235) argues that

> [w]hen viewing the meaning making of individuals, that the commodification of religion simply involves individuals who are seeking to acquire and incorporate objects into their lives that will help them reach their idealized selves. It is felt that believers infuse meaning into the commodified religious objects that bring them to greater spiritual heights.

From the point of view of believers in UFIC and PHD, the artefacts remind them daily of their beliefs and their identity as 'sons and daughters of the prophets'. When the general public sees the stickers on cars and houses they know the church to which one belongs. Hence, some of the religious objects are a mark of loyalty and membership. Some believers also ascribe mythical powers to the objects. A general discussion with some members of both churches revealed that they are of the view that the objects offer them some kind of protection from harm which may be caused by enemies or evil powers. Testimonies were given in the UFIC to this effect. One woman testified that one day her young son climbed up a tree as he was playing with other kids. He later lost balance and was about to fall. However, as he was falling, the wristband that he was putting on got hooked on one of the tree branches. He was then taken down without any injuries. From the mother's perspective, it was because of the 'anointing' of the prophet that was in the wristband that eventually saved the child. She then encouraged members of the church who had not purchased the wristbands to do so because she said they were not ordinary.

Another congregant who is a police officer testified that a thief came to his house in a police camp and was trying to steal his car. However, the car had stickers from UFIC with the 'Prophet's' image. The thief just fell asleep and was found in the morning beside the car. On being questioned the thief indicated that when he touched the car, he started losing strength and did not know how he had fallen asleep. One of the pastors in the church then implored the congregants who owned cars to put stickers on their cars as a way of dealing with thieves. A PHD member who resides in Rugare (a high-density suburb in Harare) revealed how some soil which she had taken from the 'holy' ground (the place where Magaya performs deliverance sessions) had enabled her to see miraculous things happen in her home. She said she had sprinkled the soil around her homestead to ward off witches and that since then she lives peacefully. As such, we can see that for the believers, these objects are a medium through which not only the power of God is manifested, but also the great 'anointing' of the prophets.

The same goes for the use of the media in UFIC and PHD. UFIC owns Christ TV while PHD owns Yadah TV. UFIC also publishes a magazine called *The Family* at the end of each month. For non-members of these churches, these satellite television channels are there merely to advertise the ministries so that more people can come and increase the founders' income. The attitude of these non-members is that 'advertising religion in the same manner as products diminishes or trivializes faith and threatens to reduce it to the secular realm' (Kelso 2006: 3). However, for members of these churches, the TV channels are useful in a number of ways. First, they are a means to evangelize the world since they can be viewed from anywhere. Second, they are a medium for the deliverance of members and non-members alike. The TV channels enable the church leaders to 'project their religious activities to a distinct height where their adherents and other viewers could understand better and perceive the churches' dogmas as the ideal beyond any other denominations (Obayi and Edogor 2016: 16). For example, TV viewers on Yadah TV are asked to touch the screen when Magaya is praying for healing and deliverance. Testimonies are given on both Yadah and Christ TV by people coming from far and wide of how they were delivered and healed from ailments by simply touching the screen or believing what the 'Men of God' were preaching. The use of the media has enabled UFIC and PHD to have followers in other countries who are not necessarily Zimbabwean. To this end, Kay (2009: 245) views religious broadcasting as bringing religion to public notice among people who would never consider entering a church building. For UFIC and PHD, religious broadcasting has advertised the churches within and beyond the Zimbabwean borders. However, for Ukah (2003b: 257), 'the aggressive use of media technology and the doctrinal reorientations ... are strategies of competition'.

Competing or complementary brotherhood

The church in general is seen as a family of God such that relationships within Pentecostal movements in particular are coined around brotherhood and sisterhood. In traditional Pentecostal churches in Zimbabwe, it is common for church leaders to preach in one another's church. They view their roles in their respective churches as complementing each other. However, this seems not to be the case in the newly formed Pentecostal prophetic movements. The media in Zimbabwe has brought out the antagonistic relationship that exists between UFIC and PHD. I am of the opinion that this may be due to the fact that the church leaders, especially those of PHD and UFIC, are competing for recognition from their members. In fact, the issue of creating unique identities through the branding of messages, personalities and merchandise strongly borders on competition rather than complementarity. It, therefore, becomes critical for this chapter to theorize competition among religious organizations in general, as well as between UFIC and PHD in particular.

Competition, when used in a religious marketplace and the idea of comparing religious services to ordinary commodities, has a particularly relevant implication in explaining how religious institutions entrench their positions in society (Yidana and Issahaku 2014: 4). In this case, religious movements are seen as divine industries (Yidana and Issahaku 2014: 2) or religious markets (Miller 2002: 439) where religious products are in the form of not only a set of beliefs and principles, but also the practice of such beliefs in the form of worship or liturgy (Chesnut 2007: 82). In his analysis of pneumacentric religion in Latin America, Chesnut (2007) adopts the theoretical framework of religious economy to explain the growth of Pentecostalism, Charismatic Catholicism and African diasporan religions. From his perspective, the framework is useful in showing how faith-based organizations, like commercial firms, compete for religious consumers. His opinion is against the views of some scholars who have chosen to regard Pentecostal Christianity in particular as a brand of Christianity whose leaders are after financial and material gains and the congregants as people who are after getting rich quickly through faith and miracles. He argues,

> It is worth noting that an economic approach to understanding religious choices does not claim purely financial or material motivations on the part of religious producers or religious consumers. Religious producers may have multiple other goals alongside and beyond member retention. Religious consumers, on the demand side of the equation seek not only to find opportunities to solve

personal problems, but also to find faith communities, spiritual meaning, and other goals when they make their religious choices.

(Chestnut 2007: 76)

The fusion of what is deemed spiritual and that which is worldly has at times made it difficult for people to say with certainty whether the PPMs in Zimbabwe are pursuing a religious agenda or otherwise. We may need at this point to adopt Einstein's view that 'the sacred and the secular are not mutually exclusive, but rather aid each other in the furtherance of their goals' (2008: 74). For example, in the case of UFIC and PHD, the church founders gain financially through the church members' purchase of the church's merchandise, while congregants believe they benefit because of the spiritual significance they attach to the purchased artefacts.

The discussion above has shown how the performance of miracles is central in the new PPMs in general and UFIC and PHD in particular. In other words, UFIC and PHD have tried to show that the spiritual God is concerned with the spiritual well-being of Christians in as much as he is concerned with their physical being. The packaging of a message that endeavours to show that God is actively involved in the lives of Christians has to a large extent brought conflict between UFIC and PHD. The rivalry between the ministries needs to be understood within the context of competition for religious space and market forte. In his study of the Redeemed Christian Church of God (RCCG) in Nigeria, Ukah (2003b) notes that Pentecostal churches deliberately create ways of controlling interference from outsiders, as well as competing ideas and personalities.

It has largely been alleged that the two prophets (Makandiwa and Magaya) are at loggerheads. The media has been on the forefront of portraying the two as antagonistic towards each other. Ncube (2015) in the *Standard* claimed that Magaya and Makandiwa were on a silent war path, as they sought for supremacy and dominance in the new crop of Pentecostal churches in Zimbabwe. It was contended in this newspaper that the two were locked in a battle for popularity and attracting the largest congregations and that as a result of this, the two try by all means to outdo each other in virtually everything. In discussions with the congregants of both churches, varied perspectives emerged. Some UFIC members felt that Magaya had copied Makandiwa when he introduced Yadah TV because Makandiwa was the first to have brought in Christ TV. Some PHD members also felt Makandiwa had stolen Magaya's idea of having guest houses where he would meet with his followers one on one. This was confirmed by one UFIC member who said,

Apa mudhara akaona kuti vanhu hobho vakanga vave kuenda kumaguest house ePHD. Vamwe vacho vaibva vaenda zvachose mushure mekuonana nemunhu waMwari. Mudhara had to think fast. Saka akazovakawo Life Haven. Pamusoro pezvo, vafundisi vese vari pedyo nekwaZindoga kuchechi yePHD vakaudzwa kuti vanofanira kusangana nevatendi veUFIC kakawanda kuitira kuti vanhu vasatize kuenda kuPHD.

(Here the old man (Makandiwa) saw that a lot of people were now going to PHD guest houses. Some of them would not return after meeting the 'Man of God'. The old man had to think fast. So he built Life Haven. On top of that, pastors manning areas that are close to Zindoga were told to meet with congregants often so that people would not go to PHD.)

From this discussion, it becomes clear that UFIC pastors of zones close to the PHD centre in Waterfalls have been encouraged to closely interact with their members so that the members are not disenchanted. This brings to the fore the overtness of the rivalry between UFIC and PHD. What this means is that the rivalry goes on while most of the congregants are not even aware of it. Thus, Miller (2002: 439) notes very well that rivalry may be overt – as among proselytizing organizations – or take the more subtle form of simply trying to retain and generate higher commitment among existing adherents. Commenting on the prayer camps held by the RCCG in Nigeria which are similar to Magaya's guest houses and Makandiwa's Life Haven, Ukah says,

> [T]he camp is a significant feature of Pentecostal rivalry and virulent contest for spheres of influence. It is a self-contained world where a unique brand of religiosity is brewed, packaged and distributed. The camp localizes God. The narratives which emerge from it insist that deity answers to all human predicaments, hence, people are drawn from far and wide to the centre of sacredness.
>
> (2003b: 259)

Furthermore, the founders of UFIC and PHD have tried to openly outdo each other in the transnationalization of their ministries. Both of them have established churches beyond the Zimbabwean borders. Of interest is how they both have branches in South Africa. Though Van Djik (1997: 144) has argued that 'Pentecostalism is historically a transnational phenomenon, which in its modern forms is reproduced in its local diversity through a highly accelerated circulation of goods, ideas and people', I argue that for UFIC and PHD, it is a way of showing dominance over each other. In UFIC, announcements are constantly made to the fact that Makandiwa is not a 'prophet' only for Zimbabwe but has been called to the nations.

Rivalry between UFIC and PHD is also covert at times. It plays itself out in public. A case in point is the issue that happened between Magaya and a former UFIC couple. Magaya is alleged to have prophesied to the couple that they were going to own an airline within a given period of time and that they had to 'seed' in the life of the prophet for this to happen and they complied. When the prophecy failed to materialize, the couple took Magaya to court in order to recover the money they had given him. In one of the UFIC services, Makandiwa prophesied to the husband that he needed to be careful as his life and that of his children were in danger. In fact, he instructed the man to employ bodyguards who would guard his children when they would be going to and from school. Though Makandiwa did not mention Magaya by name, it was clear from the congregants that he was referring to him because the media had reported that Magaya had allegedly deployed the police to harass the man's family and had specifically issued threats to the man that he was going to deal with him. Though one cannot ascertain the truth of Makandiwa's prophecy, it may be true that he wanted to ensure that the particular family did not go back to PHD because of the perceived threat especially considering that he was a member of UFIC before. In another incident, on 10 April 2016, the UFIC leader explained to the congregants quite a number of prophecies he had made since 2010 which had come to pass. Due to this Makandiwa declared that he was not in competition with anyone, implying that no other prophet could match what he was doing. On 15 May 2016, while preaching, Makandiwa said, '[N]o matter how great a prophet you have become, sons will compare you with minor prophets. You see your sons dining with crooks.' In this case, Makandiwa is negative towards not only the status of other 'prophets' but also their moral conduct. He, in a way, is setting himself apart from the rest as he not only declares himself the greatest of them all, but also tries to show that his conduct is without reproach.

Despite all this overt and covert rivalry, the leadership of UFIC and PHD have denied that there is bad blood between Makandiwa and Magaya. On 13 December 2015, Magaya paid a courtesy call on Makandiwa in a bid to correct 'misconceptions' that the two were sworn enemies. Earlier on, Magaya had argued that while it was normal for people to perceive two prominent spiritual movements working in a country as antagonistic, the work he was carrying out was different from that of Makandiwa. He said,

> Whenever you are in a nation and there are two people that are doing the same thing it may sound like that there is a clash. But what we are doing is that I am

following my calling and the other prophet is following his calling and I tell you our lines are totally different. I do not see anywhere we clash.

(*The Herald* 9 November 2015)

We can see that the denial goes contrary to what goes on behind the scenes and at times publicly as discussed above.

Conclusion

The purpose of this chapter has been to show how UFIC and PHD have rebranded Pentecostalism in Zimbabwe. Hence, the chapter has shown that to a large extent, the new movements have brought in new ideas which may be regarded as innovative. For example, they have placed religion as a product to be competed for, thereby fulfilling Einstein's observation that 'religion has become a product; products have become religions' (2008: 78). It was also shown in the chapter how the two Pentecostal movements have used the personalities of the founders, as well as artefacts, in a bid to create unique identities. This then led to a discussion on how the desire to be different has brought UFIC and PHD to a place where they have to compete rather than complement each other. A critical analysis of the points of conflict between Makandiwa and Magaya shows that theirs is a battle for supremacy – a need to attract and maintain followers who are the founders' revenue base more than anything else.

7

Survival of the fittest: A comparative analysis of United Family International Church and Prophetic and Healing Deliverance Ministries

Fungai Chirongoma

Background

Christianity is characterized by division and it stands as one of the religions of the world grappling with the problem of factionalism. In the specific case of Zimbabwe, the mainline churches, the Apostolic churches and Pentecostal churches stand as three most popular divisions. However, within these divisions, one can also experience sub-divisions. It is this diversity that results in competition. This is because where there is division, groups tend to compete for survival. This chapter focuses on the competition within Pentecostalism in Zimbabwe, with particular reference to the United Family International Church (UFIC) and the Prophetic and Healing Deliverance (PHD) Ministries. The chapter argues that, like commercial businesses, these churches compete for consumers because of the stiff competition in religious market; they promote their brands at their highest selling points in a bid to get customers (believers). The chapter illustrates how the use of anointed mantles, music, guest houses and social innovations, among other elements, have been used as advertising and marketing strategies to attract and retain believers.

Introduction

Competition is a common characteristic between different groups, persons, companies or churches operating the same business. Competition naturally occurs between two or more groups or members that coexist within the same environment (Keddy 2001: 552). As is the case in secular business, competition can also be experienced within religious groups. Churches may compete for consumers within the religious market. The religious market has been characterized by stiff competition. In Zimbabwe, around 2008 to the time of writing there has been a remarkable rise of newer and younger Pentecostal churches. It is such sprouting of Pentecostal churches that caused the religious arena to become a competing ground. The United Family International Church led by Emmanuel Makandiwa came on to the scene when the marketplace (religious arena) was less competitive. However, a situation of survival of the fittest came into play around 2012 with the rise of rival 'companies' such as Prophetic and Healing Deliverance Ministries of Walter Magaya. It is such stiff competition that saw the latter (PHD) improvizing new insights to upgrade the product (faith) that had already been in existence.

For survival, the UFIC came up with what it deemed better marketing strategies in a bid to retain its customers (believers), as well as getting new clients. Although church leaders deny the contention of existence of competition on the basis that prophets are called to fulfil different missions, commonality in their beliefs and practices stirs competition. This chapter focuses on competition in UFIC and PHD as evidenced by their marketing strategies presented in religious aspects such as anointed mantles, music, branding, guest lodges, as well as healing and miracles among other elements. A comparative analysis of aspects within these two churches shall present survival strategies in a stiffly competitive religious environment.

Competition: A definition

The field of competition is broad, covering sports, academics, economics and religion, among other aspects. For Rosenau, competition refers to the process by which contest or rivalry yields ranking, result or relative excellence (2003: 8). Key to note on competition is that it produces conflicts at times. Competition can be either productive or destructive. Furthermore, competition often triggers innovation and creativity. Religions always perform at their highest religious selling point to thrive in a competitive religious space. In religious circles, competition is understood in three categories, namely inter-religious competition, intra-religious competition and intra-intra-religious competition.

Inter-religious competition

This is the competition that is experienced among different religions. For example, this can be Christianity versus Islam, Islam versus Hinduism, Hinduism versus Buddhism and so on. Yidana and Issahaku (2014: 4) also explain this as inter-religious competition. It is the existence of diverse religions that generates competition. Laguda (2013: 25) notes that pluralism suggests that more than one ideology is in competition with others. Religious pluralism suggests that more than one religious cosmology is in competition with another in a bid to occupy space. Competition is a common phenomenon in any proselytizing religion (that is, a religion that seeks converts).

Intra-religious competition

Intra means 'within'. It is contrary to 'inter', which means between. Intra-religious competition, thus, becomes the kind of competition experienced within the same religion. For example, this can be a Hindu-Hindu competition or a Christian-Christian type of competition. For instance, in Islam, a Muslim group can compete with another Muslim group. A good example is that of the Sunni and the Shiites. These Muslim groups can compete because of different ideologies, regardless of having the common ground on the fundamentals of Islam (the five pillars). The same scenario is common in Christianity. Christianity is characterized by divisions. There are three major divisions of Christianity in Zimbabwe, namely mainline churches, the Apostolic churches and Pentecostal churches. Pentecostal churches compete with mainline churches. Yidana and Issahaku (2014: 4) call this inter-divine industry competition. They argue (2014) that churches are divine industries; hence, competition between them is inter-divine industries competition. This study, however, views it as intra-religious competition because it is competition within the same religion.

Intra-intra-religious competition

There is yet another form of religious competition. This is the competition experienced within the same religious sect. For example, this can be competition between a Pentecostal church versus another Pentecostal church, or an Apostolic church versus another Apostolic church. The author of this article calls this type of competition intra-intra-religious competition. Christianity gives clear examples of this kind of competition. As is the case in economic market where companies compete with other companies that run exactly the same business as theirs, Pentecostal churches compete with fellow Pentecostal churches that have the same theologies and ideologies as theirs. In a study of Pentecostal churches, Yidana and Issahaku call this type of competition intra-Pentecostal competition (2014: 4). This study focuses on intra-Pentecostal competition between two popular churches in Zimbabwe that are contesting for space on the religious market (namely the UFIC and PHD). The next section gives a historical background of the UFIC and PHD before looking at how they contest for space.

United Family International Church and Prophetic Healing and Deliverance Ministries: A background summary

A study on how UFIC and PHD compete for religious space cannot be complete without looking into the background of these churches. Since other chapters in this volume address this theme, here I shall only highlight the key issues. The two churches came into religious space at different times. The UFIC was founded by Emmanuel Makandiwa in the years 2008–2010, a period characterized by an economic crisis in Zimbabwe (S. Moyo relzim.org). The UFIC became the church of the moment, given the gospel of hope it was offering. Although there were other churches, such as the Spirit Embassy of Uebert Angel and Heartfelt Ministries of Apostle Tavonga Vutawashe that emerged around the same period, they never gained the leverage that the UFIC gained. It had psychological effects in a society ravaged by economic hardships. People flocked from mainline churches and others from Pentecostal churches as this new Pentecostal church was offering much hope through the gospel of prosperity. It came as a threat to other Pentecostal churches that were already in existence on the religious market.

A church quite similar to UFIC came into existence in 2012. PHD Ministries founded by Walter Magaya (www.pindula.co.zw) came into existence four years after the birth of the UFIC. PHD Ministries came with services quite similar to those of the UFIC. Like the former, it became well known for prophecy, healing and deliverance. It is the coming of the latter that triggered stiff competition on the religious market. As is the case in the world of business, if a new company arises in the market it offers lucrative services to lure customers. The companies already in the trade respond by improving their standards to remain relevant in the market. The above scenario gives a clear analogy of how the two churches began competing for space. Stark and Finke (2002: 49) assert that 'religion is a social phenomenon, it is natural for it to be marked by competition'. This, therefore, justifies the existence of competition between the two churches. One can, therefore, conclude that the coming of the latter church resulted in competition which has persisted to present. Whereas the latter came with innovative ideas, the former responded by bettering its services to retain its customers (believers). The section to follow gives a detailed analysis of competition in UFIC and PHD.

Competing for space on the religious market: The UFIC and PHD

Churches do not operate in a vacuum, but in spaces characterized by stiff competition. Consequently, they market themselves in a lucrative manner in a bid to get more clients (believers). Berger asserts that

> [a]s a result, the religious tradition, which previously could be authoritatively imposed, now has to be marketed. It must be 'sold' to the clientele that is no longer constrained to 'buy'. The pluralistic situation is, above all, a market situation. In it, the religious institutions become marketing agencies and the religious traditions become consumer commodities. And at any rate a good deal of religious activity in this situation comes to be dominated by the logic of market economics.
>
> (Berger 1990: 244)

It is clear from Berger's assertion that a 'survival of the fittest' strategy is a reality, even in religious spaces. As businesses sell their commodities, so do the Pentecostal churches sell their beliefs and practices. According to the rational choice approach to religion, 'religious environments are economies in which religions and religious groups are firms competing for customers who make rational choices among available products' (Bankston 2002: 311). Unlike tangible goods, beliefs and practices are services. Thus, they ought to be marketed in a way that attracts religious consumers to follow them. Thriving in such a market, therefore, requires one to apply principles of economics, creativity and innovativeness. The more denominations compete, the harder rival leaders need to strive to maintain their congregation (Norris and Inglehart 2011: 8). Innovation and creativity in UFIC and PHD as a way of surviving stiff competition will be presented in the section to follow.

Competition: Creativity and innovation

To thrive in a competitive space, one has to be innovative and creative; such principles apply in any scenario where competition is a reality. Although leaders of UFIC and PHD deny the existence of competition between the two churches, it is clear from the acts of these churches that they are competing for survival in a challenging religious market. However, it is important to concede that the participants themselves do not accept that they are in competition. For example, Magaya denied the existence of competition:

> Whenever you are in a nation and there are two that are doing the same thing it may sound like there is a clash. But what I am doing is I am following my calling and the other prophet is following his and I tell you, our lives are totally different and I do not see where we clash.
>
> (*The Herald* 09 November 2015)

Regardless of Magaya's denial of competition, a critical analysis of the activities presents a situation of competition. As a business coming in the market with a business similar to the one already running, when PHD came onto the map, it came with an attractive package since it had a knowledge of the market, borrowing ideas from those that were in the business already. PHD applied the *continuity, discontinuity and apparent discontinuity* approach. On continuity, the church carried on with the practices of the UFIC. On matters of discontinuity, the church did not adopt some of the practices of prior established churches. As a way of apparent discontinuity, the church brought in new theories on the map. Applying the above theory, one can be convinced that PHD came with innovation so as to gain leverage in the religious market. As a way of response, the UFIC also had to be creative and innovative to remain relevant and keep its customers (believers). One can, thus, agree with Miller's contention that competition creates innovation and creativity, leading to change and development (Miller 2002: 439). Such can clearly be understood upon analysing religious elements that were brought about in these churches. These include branding, anointed mantles, music, guest houses, crusades, as well as social involvement through housing projects and business seminars.

Branding

Brands play a crucial role in marketing and advertising products and services (Yong 2007: 384). Brands promote or market products in a space characterized by competition. A company's brand represents who they are, what they do, as well as the kind of quality they produce. The brand name, the 'United Family International Church', marketed their church on the religious market. The brand name presented it as a church that is all-encompassing, accommodating people from different backgrounds and nationalities to come together. The brand name is also in line with the church's vision, which is to 'building a God's society of all people and of all nations' (www.ufiministries.org accessed 25 October 2016). Thus the brand name alongside with the prosperity and healing gospel attracted masses to follow the brand.

As a marketing strategy, the latter church PHD came with a competitive brand name that could attract more followers. As mentioned earlier, brand names represent what a company does; thus, the name of the church Prophetic Healing and Deliverance Ministries became 'catchy' to appeal to a nation faced with economic hardships, sicknesses and spiritual bondage. The church was found in a community seeking healing, deliverance and prophecies. One can conclude that Magaya's coming up with such a brand name was perhaps a strategy to capture the attention of prospective followers.

The above portrays the essence of branding in a competitive context. Research indicates that some members from UFIC would occasionally go to PHD services while still being members of UFIC. However, they eventually converted to PHD.

> At first we could just attend services at PHD, yet being members of the UFIC. With time we later became full members at PHD. I am not by any means saying Prophet Makandiwa is not a true prophet, he is a true man of God, but going to PHD was a turning point in my life. I began experiencing breakthrough when I started going to PHD. I received my healing and deliverance.
> (Anonymous 02 November 2016)

A critical analysis of this case depicts how confidence in the brand name lured him to become a full member. PHD therefore indirectly benefits from its brand name in a competitive religious market. Companies with 'catchy' brand names usually see off stiff competition. On his part, Makandiwa launched a brand in June 2016. This was brand 'Emmanuel Makandiwa' in which the brand promises new style of leadership and new approach to innovation and inspiration (Ndlovu *The Herald* 8 June 2016). Both movements also engaged in innovation, as discussed below.

Anointed mantles

Mantles are visible representation of a specific anointing of the spirit (Brooks 2013: 39). Anointed mantles have become so popular in new Pentecostal churches in Zimbabwe. These range from oil, wristbands, water and pens (sometimes anointed condoms). In UFIC and PHD the most common of these mantles are oil, wristbands and bracelets.

Anointing oil

According to Pentecostal belief, oil is the symbol of the Holy Spirit (Phillips 1987: 67). Pentecostal believers use the Bible (e.g. Psalms 23:5 and James 5:14) to justify the use of oil. Some study participants maintained that in the Bible, anointing oil influenced the election of priests and kings; hence, it would have the same effect in the lives of the believers. The founders of the two churches under study also value anointing oil as a powerful mantle. The researcher attended numerous sessions where the two prophets were preaching on the power of anointing oil. For Magaya, 'anointing oil is a physical symbolism of God's healing and deliverance power'. The oil is also seen as one of the major anointed mantles that has brought thousands of testimonies in his church (http://iharare.co.zw/magaya-introduces-new-range-of-anointing-oil/). In the same vein, Makandiwa also speaks of the power of anointing oil. According to him, 'The anointing oil unlocks all the doors of impossibilities in one's life. It will lubricate your lives and things will start moving smoothly' (http://www.herald.co.zw/thousands-queue-for-makandiwas-anointing-oil/). Makandiwa made this declaration as part of his marketing strategy while introducing his version of anointing oil.

In a sermon, Makandiwa spoke of how he got a vision of the oil four years before the year he launched it but did not launch it as he was waiting for God's time to release the oil. He spoke of the power associated with the oil that he had to release. 'I do not introduce a thing until I am sure ... this oil is not fake, oil can be faked but the power cannot be faked' (https://www.youtube.com/watch?v=OoLPlFj94Dc). The sermon was to teach on the power of the oil and how it is used. Makandiwa released the oil four months after his teaching on the oil. The media presented that Magaya released his own anointing oil a few weeks before Makandiwa's release of his oil. Rupapa and Shumba explained on how Magaya whom they call an arch rival of Makandiwa released his oil few weeks before Makandiwa's release in August 2014 (*The Herald* 11 August 2014). It is from Makandiwa's words on the day of release of the oil that one can conclude that the two religious leaders are in competition. For Makandiwa;

> People should not sell the oil because the moment money is involved, the anointing power is taken away ... If you come across fake oil being sold on the black market put it on, and you don't feel a thing then it is not holy oil ... I did not advertise it on media because of fear of stampede.
>
> (Rupapa and Shumba *The Herald* 11 August 2014)

One can sense a feeling of competition in the religious market. What Makandiwa condemned was what Magaya was doing. Magaya advertised his oil in the media and the oil was also taken at a fee (http://www.herald.co.zw/thousands-queue-for-makandiwas-anointing-oil/). Another element that presents competition between the two is how the anointing oil is continuing to be released in series. Magaya first introduced the white bottle of anointing oil, the blue bottle succeeded it, and then the red bottle which he claimed had the power to raise the dead, heal and solve any situation. In a video clip watched by the researcher, Magaya introduced another new anointing oil (2016 series) which he claimed has overflowing and abundant blessing:

> God has allowed me to release the new anointing oil for the whole world ... You are welcome to be anointed ... this is the gift of the Holy Spirit to everyone. Wait and see on this one! Wait and see on this one! Wait and see on this one!
>
> (https://www.youtube.com/watch?v=-3GB98quj0I)

One can liken how Magaya marketed the new anointing oil to how different companies in the secular industry market their products. Whereas Makandiwa spoke of the unbeatable power of the first anointing oil he released in 2014, he later introduced new anointing oil. According to the UFIC website, Makandiwa handed over the new oil to thousands at Harare City Sports Centre. For Makandiwa, great miracles were to be experienced through the use of the oil, and it was deemed that it would bring great testimonies. One can, therefore, agree with Iannaccone's assertion that religious producers make efforts to provide commodities at least as attractive as their competitor's (Iannaccone 1990).

Anointed wristbands and bracelets

Mantles such as bracelets also show the existence of competition between UFIC and PHD. One UFIC member confirmed that they began wearing wristbands in year 2012, which was declared as 'the Year of Results' (Interview 23 October 2016). PHD Ministries also introduced the concept of wristbands. Insiders from both churches confirmed the protection power in wristbands (Group interview 23 October 2016). PHD Ministries later modified its wristband to stylist bracelets. The new bracelet was introduced on 1 August 2015, and it was called a reminder bracelet. Thus, 'The reminder bracelet is anointed to deliver and protect, it also reminds one to pray' (Interview 23 September 2016). The UFIC also modified its wristband from the previous one. In the world of business such is deemed product modification. Product modification is value adding to enhance the appeal to customers. For Lyer and Soberman (2000: 223), value adding modification to existing products is a marketing strategy. The strategy is critical in cases where firms compete for market share. UFIC and PHD thus adopt product modification for survival.

Although this section has concentrated on the anointed oil and wristbands, a range of other anointed items are used in the two churches. For example, the UFIC speaks of anointed bricks which enable one to build his or her own house because of the anointing. Apart from bricks, UFIC believes in anointed fruits which, according to one insider interviewed, enabled many to receive the fruits of the womb (Interview 22 September 2016). PHD Ministries believes in voice anointing in which people manifest demons just by listening to the recorded voice of Magaya (https://www.youtube.com/watch?v=vaSKDo3LvZ4&t=789s). The PHD spokesperson indicated that just like Moses who used a rod to perform miracles, Prophet Magaya is using his voice for people to be delivered. Thus, PHD has used innovation in order to ensure that Magaya's physical absence is either not felt or that it is minimized in a profound way.

Music

Music is yet another phenomenon that highlights the innovation and creativity of UFIC and PHD in a competitive religious arena. The power of music should not be overlooked in influencing as well as attracting multitude of followers. Advertisers heavily depend on music to catch the attention of customers. Music has been used as a basis to draw more people to church. UFIC and PHD adopt the same approach to attract followers. Because of competition, the two have embraced innovative means to make their music more appealing. They have resorted to bringing in secular musicians to perform in church. At an all-night prayer dubbed Judgement Night 2 in 2014, UFIC brought in popular secular musician Leonard Zhakata (https://www.youtube.com/watch?v=vlJ2QA45r9w). Zhakata played one of his secular songs 'Zvichemo'. Zhakata also played 'Mugove', a popular secular song, during a church service in December 2015. The song is said to have driven the emotions of the congregants in church.

PHD Ministries adopted the same approach as a way of luring members. The case of bringing in secular musician is rampant in PHD. Musicians such as Alick Macheso, Freman, Tocky Vibes, Zacharia Zacharia and Jah Prayzah among other musicians have once performed at PHD Ministries. In response to performance of a secular musician Alick Macheso at his church (all-men night prayer), Magaya indicated that it was a way of bringing men to church since men are sceptical when it comes to going to church. He said, 'You need to place well your worm on a hook to catch fish and for me I used Macheso to attract men to church' (Chaya *Daily News* 4 May 2015). Freeman, a Zimbabwe dancehall artist (03 September 2016) performed his song 'Zvakaipa Dai Ndarega' (I Wish to Stop Doing Evil) at PHD Ministries, which left the congregants overwhelmed with joy (https://www.youtube.com/watch?v=UTkzK1STq2w). Such can be explained as the church's way of attracting dancehall fans, particularly the youth. It is from the performance of secular artists in both churches that one can sense the vibe of competition between UFIC and PHD. The PHD praise and worship team also borrows tunes and beat of their praise songs from secular musicians (Interview 23 October 2016).

Big nights! Judgement Night versus Night of Turn Around

There are certain nights that are revered in UFIC and PHD Ministries. The nights are dubbed 'Judgement Night' in UFIC and 'Night of Turn Around' in PHD. The chapter likens these all-night vigils to campaigns and roadshows in the world of industry that give an opportunity to advertise and market the churches. It is how these night prayers are continually coming in seasons that justify viewing these events as marketing and advertising strategies of two competing firms. A member of UFIC confirmed that she started off with a Miracle Night in 2011, where she maintains that she experienced the great works of God. The Miracle Night was followed by a series of Judgement Nights, with the first one coming in

2012. The second was in 2014, the third was in 2015 and the fourth Judgement Night was in 2016 (Interview 23 October 2016).

Similarly, in PHD the Nights of Turn Around were also coming in a series. The first was in 2012, the second in 2013, the third in 2014, the fourth was in 2015 (Interview 25 October 2016) and the fifth was in November 2016. Furthermore, as highlighted earlier, secular artists involved during these events also confirm the idea of the events being used as campaigning or marketing schemes. In 2014, a secular musician, Zhakata, performed at the Judgement Night 2 as a teaser. Secular musicians have performed at a number of Night of Turn Around; Shinsoman (dancehall artist) and Oliver Mtukudzi (jazz artist) performed at Night of Turn Around 4 (Kakore *The Herald* 13 November 2015).

Social innovations

The above discussion looked into how UFIC and PHD are innovating so as to compete more favourably on the religious front. However, their innovation has extended to social innovations, with the two churches being involved in social initiatives. It must be appreciated that churches sometimes can be involved in non-proselytizing activities, extending their work to humanitarian and social welfare of the community, as well as to the business sector. Such social innovativeness can be derived from their involvement in housing projects and business symposia, respectively.

Housing projects

The UFIC and PHD have been involved in housing projects. In 2012 Makandiwa launched a housing scheme dubbed 'The Promised Land' in which over 200 people took up stands in Nyatsime area (Bulawayo 24, 21 April 2012). UFIC has been heavily involved in a housing scheme named 'Operation Nehemiah' which started in 2015. According to one insider, this housing scheme is inspired by the story of Nehemiah 2:8 in the Bible, which refers to preparations to build. In a number of his Tuesday Partners' services, Makandiwa encouraged his followers to build houses. Makandiwa also spoke of the special anointing which was upon Nehemiah. This was an anointing to be involved in successful building which the UFIC would participate in and build their own houses.

Similarly, PHD has also been involved in housing projects. *The Herald* of 13 August 2016 indicated how Magaya embarked on a project to build 46,000 houses in Harare, Mutare, Midlands and Bulawayo. He declared, 'As a ministry we are saying this to all partners of the ministry ... this is your time to own land' (*The Herald* 13 August 2016). Nyoni and Ncube refer to how Magaya launched a housing project in Bulawayo; the project targeted to build 5,000 houses by year end. The project would benefit PHD members who would be discounted by up to 60 per cent. The project also included building schools and shopping malls. Magaya stated that the project would also create jobs. He said, 'If you have anything to do with construction please go to our offices and drop papers there. We are looking at getting our labour here so that we create employment' (*NewsDay* 18 August 2016).

The housing projects have been very strategic in marketing the two churches. The challenge of urban housing is a pressing one for most residents. Unlike the mainline churches that do not have such initiatives, the newer Pentecostal churches have made securing housing for their members a priority. Many people desperate for houses convert in the hope of benefitting from these schemes. An analysis of some of the online responses confirmed a lot of interest in such ventures. However, the fear that such schemes would collapse was also expressed.

Business seminars

Although the concept of business seminars was circulating among Pentecostals prior to the rise of the two churches, Makandiwa increased their popularity. In 2014 Makandiwa hosted 'The Billionaires Mindset Summit' where he invited some of the leading Zimbabwean businessmen (Ruzvidzo *The Herald* 06 November 2014). At the summit Makandiwa was deemed a leading advisor on business strategy. He spoke on the ability to create wealth, explaining the importance of an idea, capital and ability to market effectively. He declared to the participants, 'The grace to sell, power to convince and the anointing to market is coming upon you' (www.ufiministries.org accessed 25 October 2016). In 2015 UFIC hosted yet another seminar, entitled 'The Empowerment Summit'. Bulla indicated that the summit was about raising a generation of God-fearing entrepreneurs who would bring new ideas to the Zimbabwean market (Bulla *The Sunday Mail* 21 June 2015). The summit was an opportunity to equip one and his or her business for success (www.ufiministries.org, accessed 25 October 2016). Furthermore, Makandiwa conducted the 'Billionaires Mindset

2016 Summit' with the theme of 'unlocking individual value for success'. The summit was from 26 to 29 October and it was running concurrently with a business expo.

Magaya has also adopted an approach of hosting business seminars. A business seminar held on 29 September 2016 was advertised on the PHD Facebook page. It asserted, 'God has brought forth you and your business to be revitalized and transformed.' A critical analysis shows that UFIC and PHD are in competition. One can conclude that Magaya introduced a service of business symposia in a bid to meet his customers' needs, as they might have been attracted by business seminars run by a rival company.

Conclusion

The 'survival of the fittest' situation between the UFIC and PHD reveals the existence of competition on the religious market. Such has been evidenced by innovation and creativity in the divine industry to remain relevant and appeal to customers in a competitive religious landscape. The coming of the latter (PHD) resulted in a dynamic environment full of competition. Thus, the former (UFIC) had to be proactive to retain its share of the market. This was achieved through a number of innovative strategies, namely branding, product modification and social involvement, among others. PHD, as a new brand on the market, had to market and advertise itself in an appealing manner that attracted more followers. For example, it improvised by adopting the use of secular musicians as a way of pulling the crowds. PHD thus adopted the continuity, discontinuity and apparent discontinuity model. Operating in a highly competitive religious context, both Pentecostal movements had to invest in innovation and creativity.

8

Old wine in new wine skins: Continuities and discontinuities of African traditional anthropological beliefs in the DiVineyard Church of His Presence

Fortune Sibanda

Introduction

Today, Africa is home to different religions, which include African traditional religions (ATRs), Christianity, Islam, Hinduism, Judaism, Buddhism, the Baha'i Faith, Rastafari and others. The scenario of a multiple religious landscape is replicated in Zimbabwe where the constitution of the country is religiously neutral and promotes religious pluralism in principle (Chitando 2007: 122). Although African traditional religion(s) is deemed the oldest form of religious manifestation on the African continent in addition to being 'the matrix in which African people are born, brought up and die', today Africa is counted among the most Christianized continents in the world (Amanze 2014: 286). In Zimbabwe, Christianity in its various shades comprises Orthodox churches, the Roman Catholic churches, Protestant churches, African Independent churches and Pentecostal churches, which constitute the majority with over 80 per cent of the population (Sibanda and Madzokere 2013b). Amidst this diversity of Christianity in Zimbabwe, there is great innovation and competition. A lot of this is due to the 'Zimbabwe crisis', whose effects are still causing untold suffering, unemployment, high mortality rates and hopelessness. It is from this economic crisis that many Pentecostal churches have emerged and gained popularity through an appealing message of wealth, health, abundant life and hope. Of late, this Pentecostal wave has stormed the urban religious space, attracting a significant following among the youth, ahead of other Christian denominations in Zimbabwe.

This chapter focuses on the interface between the anthropological beliefs in ATRs and those in the DiVineyard Church of His Presence (DCOHP) in Harare, Zimbabwe. DCOHP has an origin that is very similar and close to the Prophetic Healing and Deliverance (PHD) Ministries of Walter Magaya. It is posited that there are continuities and discontinuities between African traditional beliefs and the beliefs in the DCOHP. The intricate relationships of the cosmological (regarding the nature of the world), numinological (spiritual), anthropological (regarding the status of humanity) and soteriological (relating to salvation) beliefs demand that the dynamics of spiritual production in ATRs and the DCOHP are tackled in the study to illustrate the types of spiritual goods delivered to the spiritual consumers in Zimbabwe. It will be asked: What are the main traits of religious innovation and competition between ATRs and the DCOHP in Zimbabwe? What roles do technology and media play in religious innovation and competition in the DCOHP in Zimbabwe? Apparently, in a competitive religious economy, it is creativity and innovation that mirror the tastes and preferences of religious consumers and largely determine the fate of any given religious enterprise (Chesnut 2003: 40). Therefore, although there has been a changing religiosity from ATRs to Pentecostalism, the chapter underscores some enduring traits of ATRs adapted in the DCOHP in Zimbabwe, which are epitomized by the metaphor of 'old wine in new wine skins'. At this point, we turn to the theoretical framework in order to understand the dynamics of religious change, innovation and competition.

Theoretical framework

The study was informed by the religious economy paradigm in order to understand the reality of religious competition and innovation between ATRs and African Pentecostalism in the form of the DCOHP in Zimbabwe. The religious economy paradigm is a fairly recent development in the sociology of religion. It is based on the application of microeconomic theory to the social scientific study of religion in which religious phenomenon is described and analysed in economic terms (Chesnut 2003: 6). Some of the precursors of the religious economy paradigm include Peter Berger, a North American sociologist, who applied microeconomic theory to analyse ecumenism in the 1960s. In addition, Rodney Stark and Roger Finke are also counted among the pioneering scholars of religious economy in society.

On the one hand, the religious economy is depicted as an 'arena' or 'field', but on the other hand, a 'market model' has also been employed to describe it and how it works (Chesnut 2003). The relationship between religion and consumer culture is shown. Traditionally, there was a monopolistic religious market that had state support, but it did not satisfy all the people and their spiritual tastes. This was challenged by the introduction of pluralistic spiritual/religious economies that brought great competition and innovation. There is a new role played by consumers and consumerism in the global religious life (Spickard 2015). In the context of Zimbabwe, the flood gates to an open spiritual market were accessible in the postcolonial period through the new constitution that guaranteed the right to a religion and freedom of worship (Moyo 1987: 64). Whereas some scholars considered religious developments from the demand side, yet others focused on the supply side. In a competitive religious economy, there is more religiosity, higher religious participation and the emergence of a variety of religious firms or brands in the religious market to meet the demands of the different segments in the populace (Zaleski and Zech 1995). Therefore, the tools of microeconomics are relevant to the analysis of the religious market for ATRs and the DCOHP in Zimbabwe. In the age of the market, the diverse religions are the spiritual firms competing to provide branded products through 'religious service', in the fashion of a producer supplying to a consumer, which are a source of meanings, values and identities among believers in society. Since spiritual products offered to consumers must be useful to the existential needs of the people, the rival spiritual firms across the religious and denominational divide are forced to offer goods that address the spiritual needs of the believers in order to remain competitive. In the final analysis, the religious economy provides a powerful theoretical paradigm for understanding the vitality of ATRs, on the one hand, and the popularity and growth of African Pentecostalism, instanced by the DCOHP, on the other hand, which are competing for space in Harare.

Research methodology

The research utilized a multidisciplinary approach. The study employed in-depth interviews, participant observation and documentary analysis in the collection of data. Interviews were held with information-rich participants linked to ATRs such as traditional healers, diviners, herbalists and those who patronize their services in Harare and its dormitory environs such as Chitungwiza. Along the same lines, interviews were held with adherents and those that also patronize the services held in the DCOHP in Stoneridge, Harare, as well as those who have attended the church services in Chiredzi. Participant observation was utilized in two of the church services held at a house of one of the adherents of the DCOHP in Mt Pleasant, Harare, before the Harare services were moved to Stoneridge. The researcher also used library research, utilizing books and journal articles. Documentary analysis of print and electronic media was also vital in data collection. Visual and audiovisual materials such as videos, DVDs and other digital recordings of the DCOHP were also utilized for documentary analysis. The digital materials were particularly important because the DCOHP has archival material published and available online on the church's website, including over thirty YouTube videos to date. A few of the YouTube videos were selected in the study for identifying the anthropological beliefs in the DCOHP. In the same manner, the study found some TV programmes from the Zimbabwe Broadcasting Corporation such as 'Spiritual High Way' and 'ChiKristu neTsika' ('Christianity and Culture') useful as a basis for analysing, on the one hand, and aspects of African traditional religious beliefs and practices and their interface with Christianity in Zimbabwe, on the other hand.

In order to analyse and describe data collected, the study used the phenomenological and the socio-historical approaches. The elements of phenomenology that were useful to the study include *epoche* (bracketing), empathy, comparison and *eidetic* intuition, in which the meaning and essence of religious phenomena such as rituals, sacrifices and myths may be established. These elements make the phenomenological method to be in sync with the 'insider' perspective, but at the same time calling for reflexivity on the part of the researcher (Mapuranga et al. 2013). Notwithstanding the weaknesses of the approach, phenomenology was useful in studying the continuities and discontinuities between ATR and the DCOHP in Harare. The socio-historical approach was also found useful in understanding the social and historical circumstances bedevilling people who patronize the services of African traditional practitioners and church services of the DCOHP. Therefore, the socio-historical approach was used in a complementary way to the phenomenological method.

Classification of beliefs at a glance

Religious beliefs are multiple in types. As part of a preamble to an exploration of various beliefs, it is important to briefly explore what they are. Beliefs occupy a unique place within the religious experience of humankind. In a way, beliefs are interpretations, expressions and thoughts about faith. They are 'cognitive, intellectual articulations of the reality found in the faith expression' (Chiwara and Taringa 2010: 75). Therefore, there is a close relationship between faith and belief, but the distinction is that beliefs may be changed through expansion or reinterpretation while faith endures (Cox 1993). On this basis, one can compare and contrast the beliefs and practices in ATRs and in the DCOHP in Zimbabwe.

Though special focus in this chapter is placed on the anthropological beliefs, it is vital to also highlight the various categories of beliefs among humanity because they are connected in one way or the other. So, besides the anthropological beliefs, there are also the cosmological beliefs, numinological beliefs and soteriological beliefs. As Netland (1991: 40) rightly observes, there are different basic beliefs about 'the nature of the cosmos, the religious ultimate, the place of the human person in the cosmos, the relation of the person to the religious ultimate, the human predicament, and the possibility of deliverance from this predicament'. The cosmological beliefs indicate the nature, order or patterns of significance that constitute the world or worlds known to humanity (Chiwara and Taringa 2010). This encompasses how humanity perceives the levels or dimensions of the world or universe, be it a dual or tripartite conception or not. The numinological beliefs pertain to the numinous or the transcendent mystery. These are beliefs about the nature of the 'focus of faith', the sacred, the holy or the divine identified by different names in various religious traditions (Cox 1996b; Chiwara and Taringa 2010), instanced by 'God' in Christianity and Mwari in ATRs.

Anthropological beliefs relate to the status or nature of humanity in the world. They focus on the origin of people, their nature and destiny. They also focus on humanity's position in relation to the sacred. Essentially, they identify the fundamental human problem, which is described and understood differently in various religious traditions. This element on the plight of humanity will be further explored in separated sections focusing on anthropological beliefs in ATRs and the DCOHP. Soteriological beliefs relate to a resolution regarding human problems. They indicate the means by which salvation, liberation, release or final human fulfilment is attained (Chiwara and Taringa 2010). It is important to note that soteriological beliefs encompass the nature of human suffering and plight and are postulated differently in various religions of the world. Cox (1996b) regards the beliefs as closely interrelated as they follow one another in a descending order. In the words of Cox (1996b: 120), 'the numinological belief determines the other two since the anthropological is derived from the numinological and the soteriological is obtained from the numinological through the anthropological'. This assumes the transcendental origin of religion in most traditions. Therefore, reference to other beliefs in the study is inevitable.

Anthropological beliefs in African traditional religions

In order to understand the anthropological beliefs in ATRs, it is useful to highlight their world view using one of the ethnic groups, the Shona people. The Shona people believe in a tripartite conception of the world consisting of corporeal and non-corporeal forces. The Supreme Being (generally associated with the world above as *Nyadenga* – owner of the skies), known as *Mwari*, is regarded as the creator of human and non-human elements. On this basis the Shona refer to the Supreme Being as *Musikavanhu* (the Creator of humanity), *Mudzimumukuru* (the great ancestor), among other praise names. Humanity was placed at the centre of the world and is expected to relate dynamically with the family, community, ancestors, God and nature (Maimela 1985: 66). Ancestral spirits (*vadzimu*) are very critical as intermediaries between the Supreme Being and humanity. As the 'living-dead', ancestors are associated with the underworld where they were buried and hence the concept of *Varipasi*, but they also belong to *Nyikadzimu* (land of ancestors) whose geographical location is not specified. The Shona also believe in the existence of benevolent forces (including those of ancestors) that bring success and malevolent forces (sometimes manipulated by witches and sorcerers) that cause illness, failure and misfortune (Maimela 1985: 67). There is a close relationship between the Shona world view highlighted here and their anthropological beliefs.

In line with the above exposition, there are problematic areas of human need among the Africans that constitute anthropological beliefs under Shona traditional religious experiences. The presence of one or several of the problematic elements weighs down the individual or community through despair, frustration, disappointment, failure, sickness or even death (Maimela 1985: 69). Along these lines, scholars such as Maimela (1985), Magesa (1997) and Shoko (2007, 2010) identified related problematic areas in ATRs. The first human predicaments are the oppressions and anxieties that emanate from the day-to-day problems of life such as harsh weather encompassing droughts and floods; problems of hunger and poverty that lead to a high infant mortality rate; lack of fertility and consecutive loss of children; unemployment, misfortunes and failure in life's ventures (Maimela 1985: 68).

The second problematic area in ATRs is the anxiety that emanates from fear of evil spirits and malicious people such as witches and sorcerers. Sorcery and witchcraft are antisocial, torment human life and destroy the communal interrelationships. The spirits that may cause anxiety are various. These include *vadzimu* (ancestor spirits), *ngozi* (avenging spirits) and *mashavi* (alien spirits). The ancestral spirits are believed to guard and protect family members but may allow evil to cause illness when neglected or forgotten. Therefore, the anger, curse and withdrawal of blessings and support by ancestors must be avoided at all costs. The avenging spirits are dreaded and may wipe out the blood relatives of the offender until they are fully compensated (Sibanda 2016). The alien spirits come from people who received no proper burial and death rituals. Some are good while others are bad. The good ones may empower the host with skills such as dancing, singing and hunting. The bad one is deemed an evil spirit and may cause the host to engage in witchcraft, stealing and prostitution (Shoko 2007, 2010: 88). The third problematic area is the possibility of losing vital power which subsists in the Supreme Being, supernatural spirits and people. Therefore, people strive to avoid socio-moral issues that would lead to personal defilement and uncleanliness resulting in impotency and misfortunes for the community. The failure to observe rules of respect including the social, religious and cultural taboos may incite the punishment of the living and the dead in society (Magesa 1997; Shoko 2010). All in all, the fundamental human problems in ATR are multiple and emanate from different sources, including the spiritual and non-spiritual. Before turning to the anthropological beliefs in African Pentecostal churches represented in this chapter by the DCOHP, a brief historical overview of this church is useful.

Historical background of DiVineyard Church of His Presence

The DiVineyard Church of His Presence was founded by Mr John Chibwe in 2012 as part of the local trend to the global charismatic and Pentecostal transformation of the spiritual and religious landscape in Zimbabwe. John Chibwe hails from a poor and humble family background, which taught him elementary truths of love from an early age (www.divineyardchurch.org/about/john-chibwe). From this same website, it is observed that John Chibwe, a financial director of conglomerate Hippo Valley Estate in Chiredzi, explains his call and ministry as follows: 'By His grace, I am who I am, the least of all His vessels in His Vineyard, yet I am comforted by his truth, God exalts the humble and strengthens the weak. For this I rejoice in my infirmities, knowing that when I am weak then I am strong.' Before he founded his own church, John Chibwe used to frequent the Synagogue Church of All Nations (SCOAN) founded by Prophet T. B. Joshua in Nigeria. Arguably, even to this day Chibwe still has connections of one kind or another to the SCOAN, and this has attracted a substantial number of Zimbabweans who seek the services of Prophet T. B. Joshua.

Unlike his contemporaries such as Prophet Walter Magaya of Prophetic Healing and Deliverance Ministries who claim that T. B. Joshua is his own spiritual father, John Chibwe says he does not have the same perception about his relations with the Nigerian 'Man of God'. However, what is certain is that Chibwe still watches Emmanuel TV and regards it as his favourite spiritual channel. Some congregants in the DCOHP use a similar salutation, 'Emmanuel' with a similar response 'God with Us', as in SCOAN, when they stand up to speak. Furthermore, Chibwe once served as a partner of SCOAN's Emmanuel TV in the distribution of charity goods to the needy in Zimbabwe. The close link between SCOAN and Chibwe's ministry in Zimbabwe made it difficult for people who flocked to attend the fortnightly weekend services to distinguish between the two ministries. Chibwe initially held his Harare services at a private homestead in the leafy suburb of Mount Pleasant. Later, Chibwe's DCOHP had a base in Chiredzi and another one in Harare's Stoneridge suburb, which is a high-density settlement.

Although the orientation of DCOHP is part of the popular crowd-puller waves of African Pentecostal movements, Chibwe, as the founder and leader, seeks to provide a different picture in some areas from other varieties in Zimbabwe. He claims to preach the gospel as he receives it from God. For instance, Chibwe's gospel is primarily against earthly riches acquired by dubious means and thereby is suspicious of the gospel of prosperity. According to him, the gospel of prosperity has turned many prophets from being 'Men of God' to 'Men of Gold' through stressing 'gospelneurship' and profits (Chitando et al. 2013c). Chibwe branded some church leaders who concentrate on the gospel of prosperity as 'fake prophets' who should be exposed for what they are (http://allafrica.com/stories/201509100669).

In addition, Chibwe says unlike other preachers, he has not been brainwashed at theological training centres in his vocation. In his words, Chibwe once said: 'I am happy I did not go to a Bible school, otherwise I would have been brainwashed like other preachers. Because of that, I speak the word of God as it is given to me. Many will not tell the truth because they will start asking themselves what their teachers at the Bible school would say' (http://allafrica.com/stories/201509100669). Perhaps he is opposed to the 'intellectualized gospel' that characterized most of the Western missionary-founded churches, sometimes deemed as superficial. In this way, there is an extent to which Chibwe assumes a non-sophisticated foundation to his ministry, as is the case with people like Prophet T. B. Joshua in contrast to Pastor Chris Oyakhilome of Christ Embassy. Therefore, Chibwe is somewhat a charismatic figure. Along the same lines, Chibwe defies the use of titles such as 'Man of God', 'priest' or 'prophet' to identify himself and prefers to be addressed merely as Mr John Chibwe.

The DCOHP is yet to establish full church structures as Chibwe is the sole preacher and healer who is just assisted by ushers during church services. Media and modern technology such as the public address system are exploited to convey the 'full gospel' anchored on the need to be 'born again', an occasion that is worth celebrating than one's actual birthday. Such messages are meant for broadcasting to a wider audience through ShekhinahGlory TV. The ShekhinahGlory TV and Shekhinah Home of Hope are nascent projects for the DCOHP expected to transform the world through the gospel and works of love and forgiveness that would touch lives spiritually and physically. Like other Pentecostal churches, the DCOHP is characterized by a theology of health, wealth, deliverance and healing. In fact, the church started uploading video clips on its website, www.divineyardchurch.org, developed on the internet featuring, inter alia, people possessed with demons confessing that they were agents of the devil sent to mislead the world (http://allafrica.com/stories/201509100669). One can like the DCOHP on Facebook, follow them on Twitter or watch videos through YouTube. These are some of the avenues through which one can understand the anthropological beliefs that the church and its congregants purport to resolve.

Anthropological beliefs in African Pentecostal churches

The anthropological beliefs in Christianity and particularly the African Pentecostal churches represented by the DiVineyard Church of His Presence are anchored on the Bible and the African sociocultural and historical contexts in which they exist. There is an extent to which the Pentecostal churches have contextualized their ministries to mirror local existential needs of the victims of witchcraft, misfortune and afflictions of life attributed to the devil and his cohorts. Therefore, African Pentecostalism engages with the underlying 'African map of the universe' (Kalu 2003: 224), with its strong beliefs in a myriad of spirits and powers (Chitando 2013: 98). Along these lines, the DCOHP in Zimbabwe refers to the problematic areas faced by humanity such as sickness, affliction, poverty, prostitution, malfunctioning businesses and broken relationships as emanating from evil forces, demons and principalities. From the testimonies and mass prayer sessions recorded on some of the DCOHP video clips and observed from other platforms, diverse evil spirits manifested in one of the victims claiming to be the agent of Satan/Lucifer and having over 300 spirits including marine spirits, ancestral spirits, spiritual husbands, spirits of lust, lion spirits and a marine snake. The evil spirits declared that they had destroyed everything good, such as the victim's career, family, relationship and marriage – everything (www.divineyardchurch.org). Thus, on the whole, people are said to be troubled and tormented by the grip of Satan, poverty, witchcraft, evil spirits and barrenness, which have increased the popularity of this 'born-again' movement in the country.

In African Pentecostal churches, the Bible has been given a central role to the extent of becoming an 'African book' in its own right (Chitando et al. 2013a: 13). The use of the Bible as the divine Word of God is strongly upheld in the DCOHP as a radar of their operations. The DCOHP also shares a dominant teaching by most Christian churches that the Adamic sin was the original sin, which marked the fall of humanity (Gen. 3 cf. Romans 3:23). Through the first Adam came death and humanity alienated itself from God, but through the second Adam (that is, Jesus), this estrangement from God is overcome through a promise for life to those who believe (Rom 5:12-21). For Chibwe, the world is an arena of problems for humanity and he compares it to a prison. In his words delivered when he was denouncing celebrating one's birthday as a 'pagan' practice, Chibwe once said, 'You celebrate coming into prison that the world is? (The Book of) Job chapter 14 verse 1 says a man born of a woman is of few days and full of trouble. Is that what you celebrate?' (http://allafrica.com/stories/201509100669). This shows the importance of the Bible in understanding the anthropological beliefs in the DCOHP. Life is depicted as a struggle where humanity's victory over evil is determined in the spirit not against flesh, but against principalities, powers, the rulers of the darkness of this world and spiritual wickedness in high places through Jesus Christ (Eph 6:12). Therefore, the hope for the healing of all kinds of illnesses as well as deliverance from all forms of evil forces, whether spiritual or social, has attracted many people in to the DCOHP in Zimbabwe. We now turn to an exploration of the continuities and discontinuities between the anthropological beliefs in ATRs and the DCOHP in Harare.

Old wine in new wine skins: Continuities and discontinuities in ATRs and DCOHP

This section provides an exploration of the continuities and discontinuities between the anthropological beliefs in ATRs and the DCOHP in Harare. As has been noted above, there is a strong relationship between the cosmological, numinological, anthropological and soteriological beliefs, which demand that the dynamics of spiritual production in ATRs and the DCOHP be understood in this light. At times it is inadequate to refer to the anthropological beliefs without relating them to other kinds of beliefs. This was also the case in this chapter. We begin with the element of continuity which is anchored on the assumption of similarity between anthropological beliefs in ATRs and those held in the DCOHP.

Cartography of continuities

In the cartography of continuities, it is important to note that ATRs and the DCOHP are spiritualized cosmologies. This suggests that there are lines of congruence between the two systems. There are good and bad spirits in the three-tier universe upheld in ATRs and pursued from a biblical perspective in the DCOHP. For instance, in some mass prayer and healing segments of some church services in the DCOHP, it is declared in the name of Jesus that 'every knee will bow' to Him, those who are in heaven (above) and earth (human world) or under the earth (under world/ancestral world) (cf Phil 2:10). Thus, the 'African map of the universe' persists as both affirm the link between manifest and unseen realities, such that 'things which are seen are made of things which are not seen' (cf Heb. 11:3b), and some problems in the human world are first decided in the spiritual world (Kalu 2003: 231). For instance, success or failure in life among people faced with existential socio-economic challenges for surviving in the 'urban jungle' of Harare, such as poverty, sickness, unemployment, robbery, rape, adultery, corruption, business failure, among others, is accorded spiritual explanations in both ATRs and the DCOHP. The solution is not to fight flesh, but the spirit behind corruption, theft, robbery, rape, adultery, poverty and economic turmoil (Eph 6:10-17). These aspects show an element of adaptation and continuity with ATRs where *mashavi* (alien spirits) can possess people just as demon-possession is the major culprit for havoc in society as perceived in the DCOHP.

In line with the above, there is also congruence between ATRs and the DCOHP basing on their understanding of human life and its problems with a spiritual foundation. The biblical world view, just as in ATRs, considered life as uncertain, full of sin and misery. In the DCOHP, Satan/Lucifer heads the kingdom of darkness and works with unregenerate men and women, as well as a host of other fallen angels in the spirit world, which is opposed to the Kingdom of God. Therefore, the foe that Christians face as soldiers of Christ is portrayed in a military guise as principalities, powers, rulers of darkness and wicked spirits in high places (Eph. 6:12). They also affirm alongside the Bible that there are demonic and unclean spirits, which caused havoc in people such as blindness (Matt 12:22), insanity (Luke 8:26, 36), personal injuries (Mark 9:18), physical defects and deformities (Luke 13:11-17). These evil spirits or demons can possess a person and may take total control of the victim at will. This is noted through documentary analysis of the video clip from the DCOHP in which a former Satanist agent and former prostitute was possessed by over 300 evil spirits (www.divineyardchurch.org). This case is further developed below to show the impact of the belief in the powers of darkness.

The story provides a typical illustration of possession of evil forces in the DCOHP. The individual said when she was still possessed by the evil spirit she had power on her forehead, eyes, hands, private parts and legs useful in seducing men in prostitution. In her words, she narrated in a testimony: 'Whenever I used to look at a person in the eyes, they would be drawn to me no matter who they are; even pastors ... Even if that person [was] prayerful, I would just look [at] them in the eye and it would be over' (www.divineyardchurch.org). This shows the belief in the effect of the spirit of seduction emanating from the kingdom of darkness. This resonates with the African understanding of evil spirits which are also believed to cause problems among the Shona people. Among the various spirits that may cause illness, African tradition identifies ancestor spirits (*vadzimu*) due to anger for being neglected by their descendants, the avenging spirit (*ngozi*) from a wronged/indebted person and alien spirits (*mashavi*), which could cause the host to engage in stealing, prostitution or witchcraft (Shoko 2010). The activity of evil spirits is acknowledged as real in both ATRs and the DCOHP. As Kalu (2003: 232) asserts, the 'Pentecostal goes through life (...) keenly aware of the presence of evil forces as the African [traditionalist] does'. This shows that there are elements of continuity given that affliction, poverty, prostitution, hunger and all wants are attributed to forces of evil.

Another common cause of problems among people in ATRs and the DCOHP in Harare is that of human beings who exercise control over individuals, families and communities through evil powers such as witchcraft and sorcery. The evil forces are the underlying factors in these spiritual and non-spiritual mazes. In ATRs, the reality of witchcraft and sorcery is seen in the various problems faced by people due to malicious human beings motivated by hatred and jealousy. Witchcraft (*uroyi*) may result in barrenness, sickness, madness or even death. Witches (*varoyi*) may use *zvidhoma*, *mamhepo* and witch-familiars like snakes and hyenas to do their nocturnal and nefarious activities. Therefore, these activities thrive under the cover of darkness. Sorcery, which may occur in day light, includes the use of poison applied in the food or drink of the victim, as well as the use of manipulation of body parts of the victim such as clothes, hair and nail clippings – symbolic objects used to effect harm. In sorcery, the use of *chitsinga* leads to physical disorder while *chikwinho* causes some form of paralysis of legs or hands (Shoko 2010: 89). Alongside these operations of witches and sorcerers, people can associate some of their dreams, which are symbolic beliefs, to activities of witches. For instance, in the study it was established that some people believed that when they dreamt being bitten by a dog eating meat or drinking milk, it meant that they were being bewitched or there was an impending sickness.

In the DCOHP, they also acknowledge the existence of witchcraft and sorcery which cause spiritual/soul-to-soul attack and a lot of misery in victims. Through documentary analysis of some video clips in the DCOHP, this belief is illustrated, showing an adaptation from African traditional beliefs. One of the video clips, entitled 'Witchcraft!!! Anointed ash saved a man from a vicious attack by a demon possessed cat', reveals the church's stance on the misery suffered by believers. From here, the churches' use of symbolic objects to heal is exemplified by use of anointing soil, ashes and water, which are regarded as items of God not to be sold unlike in other Pentecostal churches in Harare. In another video clip entitled 'Deliverance from familiar spirits and satanic forces', similar anthropological beliefs are expressed as noted in belief in marine snake, mermaids and lion spirits that manifest as evil spirits. The incident of being initiated into Satanism is comparable to initiation into witchcraft in ATRs. The devil acts like the witches in a dream. To initiate victims, the devil gives people what they desire in the dream, such as one's favourite food, but this will be a spiritual attack. Just as in ATRs where the victim of bewitchment through food (*kudyiswa*) is relieved by undergoing *kurutsiswa* (vomiting) by a *n'anga* (traditional healer), in the DCOHP, deliverance in the name of Jesus Christ may encompass vomiting of poisonous substances. In yet another video clip on 'Healing of a fractured wrist', the victim had this to say: 'I didn't fall, it was a spiritual attack. I only dreamt whilst I was falling but I didn't fall physically. The doctor told me I had a fracture.' This resonates with the use of *chitsinga* and *chikwinho* (mystical attacks) in ATRs. So there is resonance between the two traditions on the effect of spiritual attacks.

There is also a continuity that is found in the soteriological beliefs that are experienced in material and spiritual terms in ATRs, just as in the DCOHP. The elements of wealth, health, long life and the ability to have children are some of the tangible/this-worldly hallmarks of ancestral blessings in ATRs. This is paired by a spiritual and other-worldly view of salvation in ATRs. In a blessing and deliverance theology, there is a promise for wealth, hope and abundant life, which are also a present possibility and reality through Jesus Christ in the DCOHP. A hint on the appropriation of cultural patterns that were creatively adapted into Christian framework is aptly captured by Kalu (2008: 20) when he asseverates that '[i]n Africa, prosperity theology tapped into fertile ground already watered by the traditional concept of prosperity, which is understood as wealth, longevity, and fertility or procreativity'. One participant in the DCOHP remarked in this regard: 'The Holy Ghost fire is invoked to consume all corrupt satanic spirits that seek to deny them from enjoying the fruits and wealth in the DiVineyard (vineyard) facilitated by Christ's sacrificial death ... Let all stolen fruits be restored again by fire and resurrection power.'

In spite of this creativity, the leader of the church, Chibwe, is wary of false prophets and what he described as 'GMO miracles' that produced 'miracle money'. He also described the selling of anointed items from God as 'a fall from Grace', when referring to practices in other competing Pentecostal churches in Harare. In other words, Chibwe was against 'gospelneurship' (Chitando et al. 2013a). In the final analysis, given that Pentecostalism tends to accept the reality of the ontologies of spirits, witches and occult powers in local culture as equally problematic among Christians, therefore, the plight of humanity in Harare shows elements of continuity in ATRs and Pentecostal Christianity, since the new can be viewed through 'the prism of indigenous categories' (Robbins 2003: 230). We now turn to the elements of discontinuity.

Cartography of discontinuities

Apart from the continuities between anthropological beliefs in ATRs and those of the DCOHP, there are points of discontinuity. In general, Pentecostalism stresses the need to establish disjunctive discourses and practices geared towards making raptures with the past. Yet, paradoxically, Pentecostalism is at once extremely open to localization and utterly opposed to local culture (Robbins 2003). In line with the above observations, the first aspect of discontinuity upheld in the DCOHP is the issue of sin as the cause for the fall of humanity through the first Adam and resolved by God's grace through Jesus Christ. One participant in the DCOHP, basing on the biblical scriptures, said:

> [T]here is a radical distinction with ATRs in that Christ is my hope for glory, the way, the truth and the life, without whom, I would definitely fall as noted in John 14:1-6, 27 and Colossians 2:28. This is something missing in ATRs where the ancestors never died for my sins. They are dead but Christ died and resurrected to show his power over death – Jesus is Alive!

From this perspective, the participant was in a serious mode of breaking with the past. Alongside this negative stance on ancestors, the religious functionaries in African tradition such as traditional healers (*n'angas*) and spirit mediums (*masvikiro*) were demonized and portrayed as Satanic in the DCOHP. This is supported by documentary analysis of some video clips where among the evil spirits exorcised were ancestral spirits. In these video clips, misleading terminologies are used to refer to the *n'anga* as a 'witchdoctor', a label that is meant to associate this sacred practitioner in ATRs as responsible for causing misfortune.

Unlike adherents in ATRs who are born into the tradition and whose lives drink from the past in a cyclic pattern like a snake with a tail in its mouth, the members of the DCOHP stress a break with the past where one is 'born again' in spirit on the basis of conversion. Attachment to the African tradition would make the believer to be 'tainted' by generational curses and ancestral spirits that could destroy one's career, family and relationships. In fact, in some cases, the 'born again' would evangelize family and community members in order to be delivered from evil forces, once and for all. Many of Chibwe's family members and those of other adherents joined the DCOHP as a way of breaking with the past. They formed a new community of brothers and sisters in Christ for personal and communal support. Everyone was a 'demon destroyer' as notable through mass prayer when all shout to the devil in unison countless times: 'Out! Out!' and 'loosen your grip now!' Hence, each believer, clergy or laity, is a potential sales representative of the religious goods and services in the DCOHP. What Mashau (2016: 7) says about the church in general can be applied to the DCOHP. He observed that the 'healing ministry, together with preaching, witnessing, teaching, developing, and building up the church could be accommodated in the four rubrics of being a church, that is, *kerygma* (proclamation), *diakonia* (ministry of service), *koinonia* (communion or fellowship) and *leitourgia* (the public worship and service of God)'. In ATRs, the situation is different as the problems are usually presented by the elders through a laid-down channel of communication to ancestors and then the Supreme Being. The past is very important for the present in ATRs. Therefore, in the DCOHP, the power of the present can disempower one's African past. This is a point of discontinuity with ATRs anchored by an aggressive marketing strategy of the religious product of the church in Harare.

The missionary and evangelistic approach in the DCOHP is disjunctive to what obtains in ATRs. Since ATRs are secretive, there is no publicity that is common. As one elder of Chitungwiza asserted in an interview, '[I]t is not common for a person in ATRs to publicize healing from evil spirits lest one is further bewitched or attacked by enemies. Even good things like the success of a child in school may be kept a secret to the wider community for similar reasons.' The position is different in the DCOHP because evangelism is enhanced by the use of media and technology in publicity issues, beginning with testimonies about one's sinful past, to the present enjoyed under the glory of Christ. One of the watch phrases in the DCOHP captures Chibwe as saying: 'To God be all the Glory. It is well, in Jesus' name, in good and bad times alike.' On this basis, the testimonies made public are meant to expose the wicked spirits that caused affliction, misery and defeat. The individuals and communities across the gender, class and age divides appear on the media to show how destructive and lethal the forces of darkness are and how they can be overcome in the name of Jesus Christ.

In addition, through testimonies made in public worship, former agents of the evil spirits describe their horrific experiences during their years of bondage in serving the false spirits. These testimonial narratives are used in the DCOHP for spiritual edification of other believers and to break one's past for a new life. There is a clarion call for testimonies in the DCOHP where they encourage people who may have 'received a touch from heaven either through visiting DiVineyard Church of His Presence, through anointing soil/ashes or through watching ShekhinahGlory TV' to testify. For Kalu (2003: 233), the media facilitates publicity that allows 'individuals and groups to constitute historical agents, empowered to do battle with (…) principalities and powers and they incite public testimonies about the works and victory over the wicked forces'. This shows that the use of low- and high-tech media, marketing and advertising in the church enhances their success in the pluralistic religious economy in Harare ahead of ATRs and other denominations practising 'passive' religion.

Conclusion

The chapter has demonstrated that there are areas of continuity and discontinuity on the anthropological beliefs in ATRs and the DCOHP in Harare. The problem of causality in light of the plight of humanity is explained by the existence of evil forces in the African and biblical world views, which cause sickness, barrenness, divorce and death. The 'African map of the universe' provides a basis for arguing for the existence of continuity regarding the categories of spirits in ATRs world view and that of the DCOHP where the powers, principalities and demons are perceived as enemies of humanity and God alike. The spirit can cause generational curses, divorce, corruption, economic turmoil, poverty and prostitution. Therefore, the two systems operate on the same map of the universe but colour it differently, thereby justifying the argument advanced in the chapter that the anthropological beliefs in the DCOHP in Harare constitute 'new wine in old wine skins'. The adaptation and creativity of the church are meant to address local concerns and contextual existential realities in Harare. Therefore, there is an extent to which the DCOHP did not relinquish the traditional world view with respect to anthropological beliefs. Nevertheless, the DCOHP also castigated African spiritual heritage through a 'spiritual warfare' that is part of the global and African Pentecostal 'project of cultural discontinuity' with the African past. Though the anthropological beliefs in ATRs endure with the faith, it is through innovation, competition and the creative use of media and information technology that the DCOHP has adapted African religious heritage to develop new ways of being spiritual, thereby appealing to some people with pressing existential problems in the religious economy of Harare. In the final analysis, the chapter concludes that both continuities and discontinuities obtain in the fundamental human problems in ATRs and the DCOHP in Harare. Competing against ATRs and Pentecostal churches, the DCOHP has had to reframe traditional beliefs, modify others and reject others in order to stake a claim to a share of the spiritual market. The founder of the movement, Chibwe, recalibrates his relationship with T. B. Joshua, challenges some of the interpretations of prosperity by other prophets and seeks to provide an alternative soteriological system.

9

Competition and complementarity in newer Zimbabwean Pentecostal ministries

Tenson Muyambo

Introduction

Pentecostalism in general is a fast-growing movement which has changed the Christian religious landscape within the sub-Saharan region and beyond (Togarasei 2013; Vengeyi 2013). Many things have been said about Pentecostalism, especially Zimbabwean Pentecostalism. There is lack of consensus as to what exactly Zimbabwean Pentecostalism constitutes. Some scholars equate Zimbabwean Pentecostalism to charismatic churches, particularly African Initiated Churches (Anderson 2004), while others view it as a modern and new movement that emphasizes the gospel of prosperity, modernity and Spiritism (Gifford 2004). There are also those who perceive African Pentecostalism in general and Zimbabwean Pentecostalism in particular as having striking similarities with North American Pentecostalism, as rooted in the Azusa Street Revival of 1906 (Maxwell 2006; Togarasei 2013). However, there seems to be consensus that Pentecostalism is a distinct form of Christianity that is becoming not only the widest expression of the Christian faith (Anderson 2004; Togarasei 2013), but a source of socio-economic and political hope for many (Maxwell 2006). In this regard, Pentecostalism is a variant of African Christianity that has not only become a subject of interest in Zimbabwe socio-economically and religiously but has become a battlefield for winning converts. It is not surprising, therefore, to note that the ministries or rather churches are engaging in 'silent battles' (Stolz 2010) that have seen competition and innovation becoming permanent features of religious groupings as they fight for the squashed religious space.

Competition and innovation have been there from time immemorial in all facets of human life. In other words, life itself is a matter of competition and innovation. This competition and innovation have not spared the religious facet of human life. Religious entities have been competing for religious space and relevance, followers and, in the majority of cases in Zimbabwe, for fame, and the associated benefits therein. Innovation has been used as a pull factor in that regard. It is against this backdrop that this chapter compares two Pentecostal movements, namely Emmanuel Makandiwa's United Family International Church (UFIC) and Walter Magaya's Prophetic Healing and Healing (PHD), respectively, in Zimbabwe, with the aim of assessing the extent of the level of competition and innovation thereof. The chapter does this by conceptualizing religious competition, giving a brief historical background of Zimbabwean Pentecostalism before UFIC and PHD, which are of a recent origin, and UFIC's and PHD's impact on the Zimbabwean religious landscape. The chapter then compares the two Pentecostal movements in terms of their prophetic, healing and deliverance characteristics. The chapter concludes by acknowledging the efficacy of religious competition and innovation from Matthew's notion of 'the harvest is plentiful, but the laborers are few' perspective (Matt 9:37-38).

Theoretical framework

Given the truism that religion has failed to 'die' as earlier on envisioned by the secularization theorists, this chapter focuses on religious competition and innovation in contemporary Zimbabwe. Theoretically, the chapter is informed by the religious market theory. Having waited for the demise of religion with the advent of industrialization, urbanization and globalization, the last three or so decades, however, have witnessed an auspicious steady rise of religion. The secularization theory is currently experiencing the most sustained challenge in its long history. Critics point to multiple indicators of religious health and vitality today, ranging from the continued popularity of churchgoing in the United States to the emergence of New Age spirituality in Western Europe, the growth in fundamentalist movements and religious parties in the Muslim world, the evangelical revival sweeping through Latin America, and the upsurge of ethno-religious conflict in international affairs (Norris and Inglehart 2004). There is a growing acceptance that the secularization theory which held that as societies developed they would outgrow religion is mistaken.

Concomitantly, Rodney Stark and Roger Finke (2000: 79) suggest it is time to bury the secularization thesis: 'After nearly three centuries of utterly failed prophesies and misrepresentations of both present and past, it seems time to carry the secularization doctrine to the graveyard of failed theories, and there to whisper "requiescat in peace."

Religion's resurgence and its competition, inter-religiously, can be best explained by the religious market theory which is simply put as the 'market theory' (Stolz 2010). This is a theory where competing religious groups or 'religious firms' offer religious products (Stark and Iannaccone 1994; Stark and Finke 2000). This theory is premised on the fact that individuals strive for rewards. The rewards may be 'this-worldly' or 'other-worldly' (Stolz 2010: 256). 'This-worldly' refers to rewards such as money and social contacts, whereas 'other-worldly' refers to afterlife rewards which are non-empirical and are obtained posthumously (Stark and Finke 2000: 88). The religious market theory provides the most critical and sustained challenge to the traditional secularization thesis. The religious market theory postulates that intense competition between rival denominations (supply) generates a ferment of activity, explaining the vitality of churchgoing (Norris and Inglehart 2004: 72). Religious groups compete for congregations with different degrees of vigour. Competition is thought to generate certain benefits, producing diversity, stimulating innovation, and compelling recruitment by congregations.

It is from this theoretical framework that this chapter analyses competition and innovation between UFIC and PHD Ministries in Zimbabwe. The theory provides the lenses through which the two ministries, which are locked in mortal combat, scramble and stampede for religious space and relevance on the Zimbabwean religious arena. The next section of the chapter is a brief background of Pentecostalism as a new wave of Zimbabwean Christianity. The rationale for doing this is basically informed by the fact that UFIC and PHD are 'new' Pentecostal movements whose ethos derive from Pentecostalism in general.

Methodological underpinnings

This study used a poly-methodical approach in gathering data. While the phenomenological approach, where the principle of *epoche* was handy in soliciting data from the believer's perspective, was used, observations and discourse analysis were incorporated to minimize the excesses of the phenomenological method. Apart from interviewing members of UFIC and PHD, available literature on the two movements such as books, articles and newspapers were analysed (discourse analysis). Observations during Sunday services, as well as interfacing with services conducted on television were also used in gathering data for the study. Members of the movements were purposively selected, and this is what Patton (1990: 106) calls purposive sampling. Only members who were thought to possess the desired information were interviewed. The views of the selected members could also be the views of the whole generality of the membership of the movements, UFIC and PHD. The views of the few interviewed were generalized to be representative of the views and attitudes of the churches' members.

'New wave' of Pentecostalism in Zimbabwe

In spite of the secularization threats on religion in the West (Elphick 1997: 347–69; Marongwe and Maposa 2015), religion in Zimbabwe is becoming a force to reckon with. Zimbabwe has become what Marongwe and Maposa (2015:10) call the 'epicentre' of the new Pentecostal wave. This is an acknowledgement by these scholars that religion, Pentecostal Christianity in particular, to which UFIC and PHD belong, is evidently demonstrating that religion is central to private and public lives of the Zimbabwean people. The proliferation of Pentecostal movements in Zimbabwe cannot be explicated without a survey of the socio-economic milieu the Zimbabwean society has been and still is experiencing from the mid-1990s.

An upsurge of Pentecostalism in Zimbabwe: The context

A plethora of problems, which the Zimbabwean government prefers to call 'challenges', accounts for the recent rise of Pentecostal movements. During the early 1990s, the Zimbabwe government introduced Economic Structural Adjustment Programme (ESAP) at the behest of Bretton Woods Institutions, namely the International Monetary Fund (IMF) and the World Bank. The programme was initiated with the intention of liberalizing the market (free market) and cutting down on government expenditure. The outcome of ESAP was a trail of suffering for the majority of the Zimbabwean populace. Workers were retrenched en masse, resulting in family breadwinners losing jobs. Mutsagondo et al. (2016: 4) agree that ESAP resulted in massive retrenchments, worsening unemployment and the crumbling of the Zimbabwean dollar. This was the beginning of the socio-economic crisis that reached its lowest depths around 2008. This period was marked by high inflation, with the Zimbabwean dollar taking an unprecedented tumble against major currencies. Earlier, the infamous operation *Murambatsvina* (coded Restore Order) of 2005 had already left many people homeless after their 'unlawful houses' were brought down. This left many people not only hopeless, but in unprecedented spiritual insecurity. Mutsagondo et al. (2016: 4) reported from their research on 'Ndau women, Informal Cross-Border Trade and the changing socio-economic dispensation in Zimbabwe' that Operation *Murambatsvina* of 2005 resulted in many informal sector traders being pushed out of business. Under such vulnerability, religion, especially Pentecostal Christianity, seemed, and still seems, to offer the 'bruised' and down-spirited masses the necessary refuge.

Pentecostal Christianity's promise of invincibility amidst people's suffering provides for the congregants a sense of resilience in the hope that their suffering is the work of the devil which needs nothing but exorcism. People's poverty is explained in terms of the work of demons that entrap people to perpetual suffering and bondage. This understanding and explanation of poverty and illness have seen many Pentecostal-oriented religious movements attracting large numbers of people. People flock to these movements with the hope that their socio-economic, as well as spiritual, conditions may improve. As more people come, the religious movements begin to compete for congregants and clients. In some instances, the competition is subtle, while in others it has become so explicit that battle lines are drawn. In order to outsmart each other, the movements innovate their teaching, preaching, prophecy, healing and deliverance sessions. Before the chapter looks at the competition between the two ministries, UFIC and PHD, it is prudent to briefly discuss their emergence and rise on the Zimbabwean religious arena.

The UFIC in Zimbabwe: A short historical background

What started as a lunch-hour fellowship at the Anglican Cathedral in Harare ended up as one of the biggest Pentecostal churches in Zimbabwe. The church was founded by Emmanuel Makandiwa in 2008. The lunch-hour fellowship became so popular with people such that the Anglican Cathedral could not accommodate the followers. Makandiwa moved to State Lottery Hall, which again became too small for the people. He then moved to the City Sports Centre (Mapuranga et al. 2013: 301–2).

Owing to the ever-increasing number of people coming to the lunch-hour fellowship, Makandiwa's initial church, the Apostolic Faith Mission in Zimbabwe (AFM), where he was a pastor, felt he was no longer in line with the AFM's doctrine. The church (AFM) thought Makandiwa was to be whipped into line. He was ordered to choose between AFM and his new brand United Family International Ministries. The growing tension between him and AFM ended into the split where Makandiwa formed his UFIC. This is how UFIC came into existence.

Putting the study into context

Of interest in the emergence of UFIC is the period. The year 2008 was and still is a year that many Zimbabweans would have at the back of their minds for some time. This is a year in which the Zimbabwean economy suffered severe reverses during the first decade of the twenty-first century (Mutsagondo and Makanga 2014). This is the year where Zimbabwe had an annual gross domestic product (GDP) of US$3.2 billion in 2008, down from around US$7 billion of 1980. It had a negative growth rate of -14.1 per cent, down from 3.9 per cent of 1980 and inflation rate of 231.1 million per cent in July 2008. The unemployment rate was 90 per cent (Mutsagondo et al. 2016: 10). This was a year of Zimbabwe's unprecedented socio-economic meltdown which resulted in spiritual insecurity for most Zimbabweans. Makandiwa's lunch-hour fellowship was a rallying point for people who were not only desperate, but hopeless as well. His fellowship sessions seemed to provide the spiritual answers that people were searching for. The spiritual as well as the socio-economic voids were being addressed, hence the ever-increasing crowds that could not fit in the Anglican Cathedral and State Lottery Hall. Having looked at the circumstances that saw the birth of UFIC, it is also important to briefly trace the development of PHD by Walter Magaya, before a comparison of the two major Pentecostal movements in Zimbabwe is made.

An overview of the Prophetic Healing and Deliverance Ministries

There are different and conflicting narratives relating to the origins of the Prophetic Healing and Deliverance (PHD) Ministries. This is due to the scanty documentation of the ministry's history. Study participants made it clear that Magaya himself says his is not a church, but ministries in prophecy, healing and deliverance, rose to prominence around 2012. The ministry was formed on the backdrop of the apparent working of miracles by its founder. Magaya is said to have founded the ministry after having visited Nigeria's Synagogue Church of All Nations, whose leader is Temitope Balogun Joshua (commonly known as T. B. Joshua). Magaya is said to have claimed that T. B. Joshua advised him that he (Magaya) had a lot of work to do in Zimbabwe (Chitando and Biri 2016).

Once again, the birth of the church or ministry coincides with the protracted period of Zimbabwe's deterioration in all facets of life. By 2012, Zimbabwe's socio-economic fortunes had not made any tremendous gains from the socio-economic malaise of 2008. The period from 2010 to the time of the study and writing was one of political polarity, job losses and continued socio-economic meltdown. Most citizens struggled to attain the basics of life and suffered from insecurity. Cornered and with no alternatives on the offing, Zimbabweans from all walks of life turned to religion. It was religion which seemed to remain the only secure place of refuge. Thus, the UFIC and PHD Ministries became known as crowd-pullers. The people who would go to these ministries became either permanent members or did so on a temporary basis. Those who were there on a temporary basis would go for specific needs such as the need for healing or deliverance. Once these needs were met, they reverted to their original churches, most of which were the mainline churches (also called mission churches). Having discussed the circumstances of the emergence of the two movements from around 2008 to 2012, the next section of the chapter is a comparison of UFIC and PHD in terms of their prophecies, healing and deliverance sessions.

UFIC versus PHD Ministries: A contest for superiority?

Given the circumstances under which the two ministries emerged, it is clear that their coming on to the Zimbabwean religious arena changed the religious landscape of Zimbabwe. The two ministries were game changers from a Pentecostal religious perspective. They changed how Pentecostals were doing business by bringing in innovation to the 'traditional' Pentecostal movements that came before them. For example, Makandiwa seemed to have manipulated the weaknesses inherent in the AFM, where he had been a pastor for some time. His introduction of the lunch-hour fellowship, which received huge responses, seems to have come as an answer to the urbanites' spiritual void during weekdays. Life was so burdensome such that the lunch-hour fellowship became the spiritual security for many people. In order to illustrate the 'silent battle' between Makandiwa and Magaya, the chapter compares how prophecy, healing and deliverance, the three cornerstones of Zimbabwe's Pentecostal churches (Marongwe and Maposa 2015:13), have become the battlefields for the two competing ministries.

Prophecy as an arena for superiority

Prophecy has been defined in Pentecostal circles as the ability to foresee and foretell the future, the ability to interpret dreams and other events in one's life, as well as the ability to diagnose problems in an individual's life (Marongwe and Maposa 2015). This is an area where the demonstration of power (what Marongwe and Maposa (2015) call mystical power) is evident in the two ministries. Having congregants who are eager to know what the future holds for them in these trying times, the two ministries have taken prophecy as an essential ministry within their organizations. Because of the stiff competition to lure more people than the other, Makandiwa and Magaya have gone beyond the 'normal' prophecy that has been dominating the market. Different religions have their own ways of foreseeing and foretelling, as well as interpreting dreams and any other mishaps within families and communities. Even African traditional religion, which has been dismissed as no religion at all by overzealous missionaries, had and still has its own way of prophesying through its own diviner-healers (Bourdillon 1986).

The two leaders of the respective ministries have taken prophecy to another level and have used it to outsmart each other. For example, Makandiwa is said to have predicted people's cell phone numbers, personal identity card numbers and many other accomplishments, all in the name of prophecy. When such secretive personal details are given by a 'Man of God' then there is no reason to doubt that one is a prophet par excellence. Not to be outdone, Magaya, on the other hand, is said to have prophesied of civil unrest in a Southern African state and is said to have urged the political leaders of that state to exercise high levels of restraint in dealing with the people. The prophesy is said to have been fulfilled in Zimbabwe where the general populace was taking to the streets protesting against the Zimbabwe African National Union Patriotic Front (ZANU PF)'s misrule, heavy handedness in dealing with people and a host of other complaints such as the need to reform the electoral policies and statutes in Zimbabwe. Whether this prophecy has come to pass during the lifespan of the prophet is beyond the purview of this discussion, but we should bear in mind that what could pass as prophecy could be the ability to deductively interpret the trend of events and be able to predict the possible outcome. Is this prophecy or deductive logic? Having assessed the situation simmering politically one could come up with a possible conclusion. The Zimbabwean political situation needs no prophecies for everyone whether a 'Man of God' or not can logically predict the future.

Healing for wellness

Healing in UFIC and PHD Ministries is a contested dimension that has attracted a lot of attention from academics and the generality of the Zimbabwean populace. It is at this point that I feel an attempt at definition of healing is prudent in order to guard against being vague, for the term 'healing' may mean different things to different people.

Togarasei (2013: 40) cautions that in defining healing, one needs to consider the meaning of curing also. He says so when referring to healing in the context of HIV and AIDS. It is interesting to note that medical anthropologists have made distinctions between healing and curing. While Wilson (1966) cited in Togarasei (2013: 40) understands curing as a restoration (of the physical body) to function in society, healing is a restoration to purposeful living in society. Given this thin line between curing and healing, I thought it was necessary to unpack the two words so as to clearly talk of healing without unwittingly referring to curing as practised in UFIC and PHD Ministries. Healing is more than just curing. Wilkinson (1998: 2) makes this clear by saying that healing extends to all areas of human life and being. It is making the individual 'whole' and be able to function in his/her society (Togarasei 2013: 40). For him healing can, therefore, be understood as the restoration or the promotion of a condition of well-being physically, spiritually and emotionally.

Having put healing into context, I now compare healing in UFIC and PHD. Both UFIC and PHD have used healing as an expression to restore health and well-being. Both believe in healing, but they compete on the methods for healing. In an effort to outsmart each other, the two leaders have brought some innovations into their healing sessions. Anointing oil has been used extensively by the two churches. Having seen that Makandiwa has used anointing oil to his advantage, Magaya followed suit and testimonies celebrating the anointing oil have been actively promoted. In interviews with one UFIC congregant, one discovers that there is stiff competition between Magaya and Makandiwa. The congregant had this to say:

> Magaya's church is simply a copycat of ours. Look at what he does. When prophet Makandiwa used anointing oil, Magaya followed suit. When Makandiwa introduced the concept of Judgement Nights, Magaya introduced the concept of Nights of Turn Around and we are convinced that he is copying us.
> (Interviewee 10 May 2016)

The above submissions are a clear demonstration that UFIC and PHD are in stiff competition. The competition is so stiff that the members of the two churches at times speak ill of each other. One interviewee from PHD Ministries said,

> Look at our building in Harare opposite Zindoga shops! It is a state of the art building as compared to theirs in Chitungwiza, which has been under construction for a long time. In comparative terms, the buildings are an illustration of who is who in terms of the gospel of prosperity. We are young, but look at the properties we have acquired in a short space of time through the grace of the prophet's (Magaya) God.

If this is the reasoning in the ordinary members of the ministries, then there must be subtle and under-the-carpet machinations by the powers that be in order to outdo one another. It was reported in the newspapers that Magaya clandestinely appears at Makandiwa's Sunday service (*NewsDay* 15 December 2015). Though the reporter purports that the visit was meant to demystify the myths that the two charismatic leaders were sworn enemies, the use of the word 'rival' in the article means more than what the visit is said to mean. In any case, why would the title of the article be 'Magaya in surprise visit at Makandiwa church service'? If it was 'Men of God' visiting each other, why is the visit described as a *surprise*? This poses quite a number of unanswered questions in terms of the relations between the two leaders and their respective churches.

In order to outdo each other, the two churches' congregants engage in activities or rather miracles that demonstrate an attempt to outsmart each other. For example, Makandiwa is alleged to have raised the dead and enabled a barren woman to conceive and deliver within three days (Mapuranga et al. 2013: 302). Similarly, Magaya is also said to have been visited by barren women for assistance. Some influential members of the society are alleged to have approached Magaya with their social problems that range from barrenness, demon possession and misfortunes in life.

To demonstrate that people have faith in what Magaya can do for them, I will refer to one case that I came across during my research. It is that of a medical doctor whose young brother was complaining of his eyesight. The young brother's left eye could no longer distinguish colours. During practical examinations in the sciences like chemistry and biology at school, the young brother could no longer notice colour changes when certain substances were mixed. The medical doctor took the young brother to Magaya's guest house for healing. Asked whether the young brother was taken to eye specialists, the medical doctor indicated that the way it happened was beyond medical explanation. She suspected foul play on the young brother's eyes. For her, it was a case of witchcraft.

From the above, one can discern that Magaya is regarded a healer who does not only remove bad spells cast on individuals. The same can be said of Makandiwa. During his 'Judgement Night 4' activity, Makandiwa 'took time to give prophecies to individuals. He prayed for hundreds of congregants. Scores of people with various ailments claimed to have received healing' (Chitemba 2016: 2). To illustrate the mystical powers, the two church leaders use wristbands. The congregants have the bands wherever they are. The bands are not given for free. They cost some money, but because the congregants have been made to believe that without the bands their life is prone to the devil's attack any time, the congregants ensure they protect themselves from the devil by putting on the wristbands.

Another area where the two church leaders have demonstrated their fierce competition is through the nights they have coded 'Judgement Nights' for Makandiwa and 'Night of Turn Around' for Magaya. At the time of writing, for Makandiwa, there had been four Judgement Nights (Judgement Nights 1–4) and Magaya also had four Nights of Turn Around.

Judgement Nights (1–4) versus Nights of Turn Around (1–4)

To spice up their prophecies, Makandiwa and Magaya have embarked on a number of activities. For Magaya, in addition to the concept of a guest house, where the 'spiritual patients' wait for the 'Man of God' to see them one on one, he also has Nights of Turn Around 1–4. At the time of writing this chapter he was yet to have Night of Turn Around number 5 at his headquarters in Waterfalls, Harare, Zimbabwe. Similarly, Makandiwa had been holding what he calls Judgement Nights 1–4. This night phenomenon is used to help people, but I contend that it has become the launch pad for the two ministries to lure congregants. The nights are used to demonstrate 'God at work', where prophecies, healing and deliverance punctuate the proceedings. While the 'Judgement Nights' by Makandiwa and 'Nights of Turn Around' by Magaya may be well-intentioned nights, one is reminded of the contest at Mt Carmel (1 Kgs 18:20-40) where Elijah engaged in a combat competition with the Baal prophets. The nights are meant to demonstrate the prophets' (Makandiwa and Magaya) spiritual powers. What happens at these nights is testimony that the two churches are locked in mortal combat.

Makandiwa's 'Judgement Night 4' was held at Mt Hampden headquarters on 26 August 2016 where he disclosed the 'mysterious tale' of his birth and mission. He sounded like the second biblical Jeremiah when he said that 'his father was visited by an angel and was shown a vision of the prophet's (Makandiwa) body structure, height and how he was to be born' (Chitemba 2016: 2). He boastfully said to his congregants, 'Before I was born, I was announced.' This mimics Jesus himself. The night was punctuated by prophecies to individuals, prayers for congregants and healing of various ailments. This 'Judgement Night 4' was well published in both electronic and print media. It is at this event where he declared that he was commissioned to 'break poverty so don't tell me to preach something else which is not prosperity … my mission is clear, to deal with poverty' (Chitemba 2016: 2). For this reason Makandiwa is reported to have caused the miraculous appearance of diamonds and gold in congregants' pockets (Mapuranga et al. 2013: 302).

Similarly, Magaya's Nights of Turn Around 5 in 2016 and 6 in 2017 received a lot of publicity. Wonders and miracles were anticipated and reported. For example, the 2016 event was being touted the 'biggest Christian event in the country' (Religion Writer 2016: 2), with congregants coming from countries such as Australia, Botswana, the DRC, Ethiopia, Malawi, Namibia, Nigeria, South Africa, South Sudan, the UK and Zambia, among others. The use of the superlative 'biggest' by the writer confirms that comparison was at play here. Even the enumeration of the countries from which members would come was meant to give the event an international flavour and was for the purpose of comparison. Emphasis is on who commands the larger crowd and who has a more international flair than the other. To extend their reach, the two prophets also held activities within the Southern African region and beyond.

From the foregoing, it is clear that the two churches' activities are presented hyperbolically with the intent to make them more than ordinary. Huge crowds are characteristic of these Judgement Nights and Night of Turn Around phenomena. The often inflated records of the number of people who would have attended the gatherings are made public, with the intention to illustrate who has managed to gather more people than the other. The competition has also been taken to technology where both churches have television channels – Yadah TV for Magaya and Christ TV for Makandiwa. Furthermore, during services, highly sophisticated technology is used such as state-of-the-art public address systems, wireless microphones and earphones. All this is done in a bid to 'move with the times'; no wonder the churches are coded twenty-first-century churches. Use of state-of-the-art technology is understood as a sign of sophistication. It has been used as a pooling resource for more members for the churches.

'That they may be one': Critical reflections

From a theological perspective, Matthew 9:37-38 reminds us of the need to understand that while the harvest is plentiful, the labourers to do the work are few. This reminder resonates with the idea that what observers may perceive as competition in the negative may be positive competition to enlarge the membership for the Kingdom of God. The verse cited means that there is a lot of work to be done, but few are the ones to do the work. While the two churches, UFIC and PHD, seem to compete for congregants, religious space, relevance and above all wanting to be *the church*, the underlying issue is that although UFIC and PHD are in competition, they have a unified goal, that is, to attract converts to Christianity. They complement each other, hence the axiom 'That they all be one' in the execution of their diverse but unified mandate. The visit by Magaya to Makandiwa Sunday service cited earlier can be argued to be a gesture of goodwill, not meant to spy Makandiwa. Magaya plainly made it clear that he had to plea with Makandiwa to ensure that he arrived on time. He (Magaya) has demonstrated that he is more than ready and prepared to work hand in glove with his counterpart, not rival, Makandiwa.

Arguably, Magaya and Makandiwa have been made to be rivals not by what they do and say, but by onlookers. The media is major culprit in this regard. Every newspaper article on the two tends to play up the perceived rivalry. The media always sets them against each other. They are made to appear as being in competition. This has affected their respective members who are then bent on wanting to prove to one another that their 'Man of God' is better and smarter than the other in the ministries of prophecy, healing and deliverance. But a closer look at the two leaders themselves suggests that they act and behave in the spirit of collaboration rather than competition.

Conclusion

From the foregoing, it has come out that religious competition for congregants, fame and relevance has been there in different contexts. UFIC and PHD have come at a time when the religious arena is inundated by a spiritual void created by the harsh socio-economic conditions bedevilling Zimbabwe. From a cursory examination of the two churches one is tempted to conclude that UFIC and PHD are engaged in a fierce competition, especially when we compare their 'Judgement Nights' and 'Nights of Turn Around'. They seem to be doing things to demonstrate who wields more mystical power (through prophecy, healing and deliverance) than the other. After a closer look at their activities one is persuaded to think that the two churches are a case of labourers in a plentiful field. They are enlarging the Kingdom of God. Thus, the competition that ensues between them is a matter of addressing the challenges that confront people in contemporary society. Whereas many want to see the two movements as being engaged in fierce competition for space, there is also the underlying argument raised by this chapter that clients who utilize their services stand to benefit from the innovation and competition. Through the introduction of innovation, church members and clients tend to benefit from the prophecies, healings and deliverances. The two movements' case is a demonstration that, indeed, the harvest is plenty and the labourers are few. It is a case of wanting to demonstrate that there is unity in diversity (Dunn 1990). The UFIC and PHD Ministries are united in ministering to the people of God, while their approaches are marked by subtle differences. Through innovation and competition, they have revitalized Zimbabwean Pentecostalism.

10

The quest for a unique identity: The case of Prophetic Healing and Deliverance Ministries in Zimbabwe

Martin Mujinga

Introduction

The quest for unique identity in the prophetic ministry in general and Zimbabwe in particular has led to serious enterprising by the practitioners with the aim of luring more members. This religious innovation has led some members of the traditional/older mainline churches to practise a 'limping dance' in their membership, with many moving back and forth and others migrating completely to prophetic ministries. The justification for these movements is varied, but chief among them is the prophet's quest for unique identity. Chitando et al. (2013a: 15) maintain that the current discourse around prophets and prophecy in Zimbabwe is largely inspired by a brand of Pentecostal prophets also known as the megachurch prophets. These churches include the United Family International Church (UFIC) led by Emmanuel Makandiwa and the Spirit Embassy (later rebranded as the Good News Church) founded by Uebert Angel (Vengeyi 2013). The latest prophet to join this arena is Walter Magaya, the founder of Prophetic Healing and Deliverance Ministries (PHD). Zimbabwean print and electronic media have been inundated with the names of Magaya and Makandiwa in particular and how they have influenced the religious landscape of Zimbabwe.

Magaya's stature has generated a lot of controversy, with some claiming that he was one of the most influential figures under the age of forty in Zimbabwe and he was counted third on the most influential people in Zimbabwe (eNCA 11 April 2015). His PHD Ministries has also been ranked one of the fastest-growing churches in Zimbabwe (eNCA 11 April 2015), with Magaya being presented as one of Zimbabwe's most sought-after 'super high preacher' (*The Chronicle* 1 July 2015). Research has demonstrated that Makandiwa, Tavonga Vutabwashe and Angel attract more than 45,000 followers every Sunday (Vengeyi 2013: 29; Chitando and Biri 2016: 73). Kamhungira and Chaya (2014) hold that by 2014, Magaya had doubled the number to 80,000 followers every Sunday.

This study was prompted by the T-shirts that were worn by Magaya's followers for his maiden Pretoria crusade in October 2015. The T-shirts brazenly declared: '*I am not ordinary with Magaya*'. The researcher met the followers on their way from South Africa. This encounter prompted some questions that demanded scholarly engagements. During the study, some of the members were interviewed, but their names were kept confidential. Although the researcher did not get hold of Magaya himself because of the church's procedures and protocols, the T-shirts' message alone raised some critical questions such as who is Walter Magaya? What makes his followers feel extraordinary? Is he unique from other prophets in Harare or is he an extension of the ministry with another face? This chapter wrestles with these and other related questions.

The emergence of Walter Magaya and the birth of Prophetic Healing and Deliverance Ministries

In spite of the popularity of Walter Magaya on the religious arena, not much scholarly attention has been paid to the man who has brought another flavour of Christianity to Harare (Chitando and Biri 2016). Walter Magaya's life story, like the stories of many founders of religions and movements, is not very clear. Kamhungira (2014) highlights that he was born on 14 November 1983 in Mhondoro-Ngezi and is married to Tendai Katsiga-Magaya, a banker by profession. According to Chitando and Biri (2016: 77), Magaya has a Catholic and Pentecostal background. Although Magaya claims that he received his call in 1998 when he was a member of Roman Catholic Church, his ministry, ethos and theology derive from Pentecostalism. Indeed, he was a member of the Catholic charismatic movement which has a Pentecostal outlook. Critics charge that the formation of many Pentecostal churches, including PHD Ministries, can be argued to be the quest by many people who leave mainline churches with the motive of forming their own brand of Christianity where they will not only be chief executives, but also controllers of large crowds of followers (Diara and Onah 2014: 395).

Magaya claimed to have received gift of prophecy in 2003 (Kamhungira 2014). However, he could not pursue this gift but decided to venture into business. His efforts in business enterprise led him to Nigeria in 2009 to visit Temitope Balogun Joshua (T. B. Joshua), a Nigerian prophet and televangelist. Since T. B. Joshua had many followers in Zimbabwe, Magaya became his agent in Zimbabwe, thereby attracting many people who visited T. B. Joshua in Nigeria to receive healing and deliverance (Kamhungira 2014; Chitando and Biri 2016: 77). Magaya claimed that he had over eighty business proposals and the reason for going to Nigeria was to seek recourse from Joshua as to which business to take (Kamhungira 2014). Magaya further remarks that he had tried a number of businesses that included commuter omnibuses, butcheries and running retail shops without success. In an interview with e-NCA 360, Magaya claimed that during his discussion with T. B. Joshua (who was later to become his 'spiritual father'), he was advised that he was going the wrong direction. His right route was that of being a prophet (eNCA 11 April 2015).

In order to begin his ministry, Magaya was furnished with anointing oil by T. B. Joshua and PHD Ministries was born in 2012 (although some followers had been assembled in 2011). The ministry started with forty congregants in 2011. In 2012, the ministry grew to five hundred followers. Since Magaya was practising his ministry within the Catholic Church, he was then advised by his friends from the Blood of the Lamb Christian Community to move to a spacious venue to grow his ministry (Kamhungira 2014). By 2013, PHD had over 5000 followers and in 2014 the ministry had grown to 80,000 followers every Sunday. By 2015, PHD Ministries followership had grown to more than 250,000 congregants weekly (Matsilele 2015). Magaya attributes this growth to people who come to his church as doubters and then go back home as followers and evangelists of PHD Ministries. Magaya claimed that 98 per cent of his followers came as doubters (Matsilele 2015).

At the time of writing, the PHD headquarters were in Waterfalls in Harare, opposite Zindoga Night Club. Magaya asserts that the mandate of his ministry is 100 per cent prophecy, 100 per cent healing and 100 per cent deliverance (phdministries.org/about_phd.html). He further claims that although ecclesia might refer to any gathering in the name of Jesus; however, his is a ministry and not a church (*NewsDay* 4 June 2015). For Magaya, a ministry can focus on singing or just preaching and PHD focuses on healing, deliverance and prophecy (phdministries.org/about_phd.html). During his trip to Botswana for a crusade, Magaya asserted that PHD was not yet a church and that God had not yet told him to start a church (*NewsDay* 4 June 2015). Although Magaya refutes that his ministry is not a church, however, its characteristics fit within the newer Pentecostal churches which are also known as prophetic ministries (Vengeyi 2013: 29). This might be part of his innovation to attract clients who are members of other denominations. Calling his movement a 'ministry' would suggest that it is ecumenical and members of other denominations would be free to attend his services, while they retain their membership elsewhere. In practice, this is what has been happening.

The ecumenical space of PHD Ministries in Zimbabwean ecclesiology

The church in Zimbabwe is divided into three major strands, namely missionary/mainline, African indigenous churches and Pentecostal churches. Missionary churches refer to those denominations that came with the advent of Europeans and Americans in Africa during the eighteenth and nineteenth centuries. These churches are identified with colonialism, the building of hospitals and schools, and they share the origins, history, faith, spirituality and practice, whether ethical or liturgical, with global partners (Ukah 2007: 6). The second grouping is the African indigenous churches (AICs). These churches were born in Africa at the beginning of the twentieth century. They either broke away from the missionary churches or they founded their churches independent of European missionary activities (Mapuranga 2013c: 303). Pentecostal churches constitute the third category. These are fast-expanding sectors of Christianity in Africa (Togarasei 2005: 305). They are divided into the classical/mission Pentecostal churches, indigenous Pentecostal churches and the 'newer' Pentecostal churches (Anderson 2002: 167).

Pentecostalism is a struggle for African identity through religious power (Kalu 2008: 63) and this theme features prominently in PHD Ministries. This struggle is what is prevailing in Harare, as the charismatic churches continue to come out with means of expanding their space. Older Pentecostal churches in Zimbabwe, such as the Apostolic Faith Mission (AFM) and the Zimbabwe Assemblies of God Africa (ZAOGA), are some of the largest denominations. However, within the last decades they have been overtaken by neo-Pentecostal churches which are more charismatic in nature (Asamoah-Gyadu 2010). The developments of charismatic movements led to the present Christian growth in Africa and they are reshaping Christian ministry, mission, spirituality, worship and theology in most parts of Africa (Kalu 2008: 26). The past twenty or thirty years in the history of Zimbabwe, Christianity has witnessed the emergence of the new breed of Pentecostalism that tends to attract the middle- and the upper-class urban residents (Togarasei 2005: 349; Taru and Settler 2015). Having been formed by reasonably well-educated urban youth, the churches remain elitist and modernist movement, although it is true that not everyone in the church is rich or educated. The churches attract those who are seeking both success and prosperity in life (Togarasei 2005: 355).

Pentecostal churches are identified by seven tenets, with the first being faith healing. This characteristic includes aspects of prophecy, exorcism, speaking in tongues, spontaneous prayers, exuberant liturgical expression and the emphasis on dreams and visions which are common (Ukah 2007: 14). These characteristics are not unique to PHD Ministries. Although Magaya feels that his church is 100 per cent prophetic, healing and deliverance, a closer look at how he runs his ministry shows that Magaya is not different from his contemporaries. In view of this, the only difference that can be noted is the name, but not the ecclesiastical tenets.

The second tenet is 'prosperity Christianity' or health and wealth gospel or name-it and claim-it gospel (Price 2005; Kalu 2008: 256). 'Prosperity Christianity' suggests that Jesus is only/mostly known in the context of health and wealth. In this, charismatic churches attract most of Africa's upwardly mobile youth. They are also identified with a penchant for mega-sized urban-centred congregations, internationalism, English as the medium of expression, a relaxed and fashioned conscious dress code for members, innovative appropriation of modern media technologies, a well-educated leader, not necessarily in theology, and a very modern outlook (Asamoah-Gyadu 2010). The prosperity gospel in general is divided into militant/radical and diffused (Masvotore 2016: 25). Militant prosperity advocates that God's will for every Christian is wealth, health, happiness and success, while the diffused form of prosperity is motivational. It creates the impression of a world with limitless possibilities and victories and without suffering (Masvotore 2016: 25). The two forms of prosperity describe Magaya's approach. The prosperity gospel in Africa is the fertile ground of Pentecostalism because in an African society, being well is an expression of prosperity (Shoko 2015). In order to promise people wellness, Magaya claims to heal all forms of aliments (PHD website). As such, many who throng to his shrine are people looking for prosperity. In one of Magaya's sermons, he preached:

> You are poor ... not yourself, only but also [for] your children. This is a demon which focuses on attacking the father, son and the grandchildren ... I want you to move in riches, not in poverty. (Yadah TV Programme accessed on 15 March 2015)

Magaya is not in conflict with those who came before him on his message of the gospel of prosperity. He maintains that prosperity is the eternal and universal gospel. He argues that the gospel of Jesus Christ was that of prosperity. Citing Luke 4:16, he insists that Jesus came to preach to the poor and empower those who have not been empowered (Magaya 15 March 2015). Magaya further taught that one should pay temple monies before anything else (Magaya 15 March 2015). In his interpretation of Jesus when teaching on Caeser, Magaya says that God is the owner of gold and silver and anyone who is the founder of the church has the right to be rich (Magaya 15 March 2015).

Two contradicting incidents are worth analysing. When Magaya went to Botswana, he announced that he had not come to make money (Magaya 4 June 2015). He further asserted that he did not take offering during crusades because he was already rich, with money coming from the international partners who wanted to remain anonymous (Magaya 4 June 2015). On the other hand, Magaya had a partners' meeting in Bulawayo (Zimbabwe's second capital) on 1 April 2015, two months before the Botswana trip. According to Bepete and Gagare (2015), Magaya disappointed hundreds of his followers who were turned away by his men after failing to pay US$20 to attend a fundraising event. Members of Magaya's security also barred those who did not have partner cards. One of the guards was heard shouting, '[I]t is of no use for people to crowd the place when they are not members and worse, without money' (Bepete and Gagare 2015). According to Masvotore (2016: 25), Makandiwa also has partners. Partnership with Makandiwa is a spiritual covenant. It means one is partaking of the calling and commissioning of the 'Man of God' who represents God in Zimbabwe, Africa and beyond. Masvotore quotes one UFIC congregant claiming that 'Prophet Makandiwa loves and cherishes one's commitment and one's partnership will not go without reward' (Masvotore 2016: 25). There are many benefits that one will enjoy as a partner, which include special conferences with Makandiwa and an opportunity to be with him personally ('one on one' in prophetic Pentecostal parlance). In this partnership, individual families and various entities count themselves to support the ministry financially or materially on a regular basis (Masvotore 2016: 25). This is the same concept of partnership that Magaya employs in PHD Ministries, and this confirms that there are patterns of similarity within the Zimbabwean prophetic Pentecostal movement.

It is not easy to separate Magaya from his contemporaries. A case in point is Magaya's predictions of 2016 as a year of abundance and great economic fortunes for the country (Nehanda Radio 4 January 2016). His counterpart, Makandiwa, also predicted a better life for Zimbabweans (Nehanda Radio 4

January 2016; Shoko 2015). Makandiwa had declared 2012 as a 'Year of Results' and some members of his church were convinced that they were already enjoying the declared results of 2012, as shown by posters and stickers seen on many vehicles in town and other properties which read, 'This is a result' (Shoko 2015: 33). Magaya made the same claim in his Waterfalls shrine. Before making the pronouncement, he told his followers that he had travelled to Nigeria to confirm with his spiritual father, T. B. Joshua, on Africa's economic fortunes. In his statement, Magaya stated that in 2015 he had prophesied that Zimbabwe was going back to its position as the bread basket of Africa (Nehanda Radio 4 January 2016).

Magaya led his followers in a prosperity mood as he rhetorically stated: '[A]sk your neighbour how big their house is, wardrobe, garage ... this is a year of overflowing'. David Maxwell (2006) confirms the background of such claims when he points out that in newer Pentecostal churches, people are taught to expect and seek change and to expect an experience of the sacred. Basing on the argument of prosperity, it is not immediately clear as to what extent is Magaya unique among his competitors and contemporaries.

The third characteristic is the economic dimension. Newer Pentecostal churches produce a huge array of videos, magazines, CDs, DVDs, books, keyholders and other religious memorabilia or ritual paraphernalia like handkerchiefs and olive oil (Ukah 2007: 16). They also use therapeutic substances, including the blessed water for their healing ministries (Ukah 2007: 17). Anointing oil is common in PHD Ministries because it is a symbol of God's healing and deliverance power (PHD website). For Magaya, anointing oil is a point of contact in spiritual warfare and is a symbol of the Holy Spirit. The oil protects the followers from the deadly dangers and traps. It does the cleansing and purification (PHD website). For PHD, anointing oil destroys or breaks the bondage, burden and oppression caused by the devil because the enemy's yoke connects and binds people with sin, poverty, diseases and limitations (PHD website). In addition, oil is claimed to break the yoke that is used to steal the promise of God made to his children (PHD website). One of the PHD members confirmed that anointing oil was one of the major mantles of the ministry that had brought thousands to testimonies. The oil is applied to all the affected parts of the body, for example, the forehead, head, ears or the eyes. One can also apply it to the affected parts of life such as documents or business wares (PHD Ministries member interview 2016).

Makandiwa also uses anointing oil (Shoko 2015: 31). Shoko states that the way Makandiwa uses a variety of methods and elements to heal is similar to the traditional healers (Shoko 2015: 31). This statement shows that Magaya shares much in common with other charismatic preachers and that they are influenced by African traditional healers (Biri 2012). Magaya wrote a book entitled *Marine Spirits: Mweya Yemumvura* (Water spirits). In this book, he attacked the African Initiated Churches in Zimbabwe as agents of the evil spirits with the propensity to threaten congregants to death (Zuze 2016). In retaliation, members of the AICs attacked Magaya stating that God has revealed to them that he is not a 'Man of God' because he uses magic and other ungodly antics to lure people to his congregation. Some AIC members also accused Magaya of having snakes that live in his anointing oil and the same oils are given to people as anointing oil (Mushava 2015). This highlights the extent to which religious competition does become intense at times in Zimbabwe.

Magaya also has a place that he calls the 'holy ground'. This represents his innovation and creativity. This is a fenced place at the church premises full of sand where people are claimed to be delivered. On one occasion, a man who could not get a chance to get into the space begged the woman who was inside to give him some sand. The *H-Metro* of 12 October 2015 reported that some prayer partners of PHD Ministries thronged the historic house belonging to Prophet Magaya's parents and took with them soil and guava tree leaves. One partner was heard saying '*zvangu zvaita na Prophet Magaya*' (it is well for me with Prophet Magaya). Such a sense of conviction confirms that Magaya's followers have confidence in his prophetic powers.

Biri (2012: 2) draws attention to the persistence of traditional beliefs and practices in Zimbabwean Pentecostalism (see also Chapter 1 in this volume). The rural background of many Pentecostal leaders is important because these spaces are constructed as the haven of African traditional religion (ATR). Many people flock to rural areas during holidays and moments of crises in their lives in order to carry out traditional rituals (Biri 2012: 2). It is interesting to note that although Magaya spent most of his time in an urban area (Chitungwiza), his rural home of Mhondoro is also counted among the areas where witchcraft beliefs remain very active in Zimbabwe (Moyo 2013; Moyo and Muhwati 2013; Moyo and Mine 2016: 81). The action of taking soil from Magaya's home is a common action in ATR especially when someone dies from a faraway place, people perform some rituals before they take the soil for reburial. Magaya's movement successfully adapts an indigenous practice into a Pentecostal one.

The fourth characteristic of the newer Pentecostal churches is religious advertising. These churches use posters, branded vests, caps, television channels and also make use of both electronic and print media (Ukah 2007: 17). Whenever

Magaya will be having a gathering, big posters are seen in most public places. Unlike the mainline churches that do not have aggressive marketing strategies, Magaya is quite creative in his advertising. He utilizes diverse platforms to sensitize clients and promote his activities.

Fifth, newer Pentecostal churches are fond of big religious camps. They buy very expensive large pieces of land (Ukah 2007:17). On these lands, the founders construct a range of facilities such as auditoriums, schools, guest houses, dormitories and presidential villas for VIP guests such as politicians. Politicians frequently visit these places to demonstrate their religiosity. Sometimes, they solicit votes or public sympathy (Ukah 2007: 18). In a number of Magaya's all-night programmes, some prominent politicians are screened on live televisions. On 13 November 2015, Magaya conducted a 'Night of Turn Around' in Harare that was attended by ten political figures from across the political divide, eight of whom were government ministers in former president Robert Mugabe's government (Online Correspondents 13 November 2015; *NewsDay* 4 July 2015).

Magaya was invited to the State House during the fiftieth birthday gala and fundraising dinner celebrations of the former First Lady Grace Mugabe (Mugabe 2015). This visit was a fulfilment of Magaya's vision and joy during his Botswana trip in June 2015 of meeting Mugabe, whom he described as a highly blessed and ranked man (Magaya 3 July 2015). According to Vengeyi, some commentators maintain that pro-status quo prophets are false prophets, while anti-status quo are deemed true prophets. For example, Makandiwa, Paul Mwazha, Wimbo and Noah Taguta who involved themselves in Zimbabwean politics particularly supporting the ruling party were labelled false prophets (Vengeyi 2013: 44). During the fundraising, Magaya bought a pictorial biography of Grace Mugabe at US$50,000 (Mugabe 2015).

Sixth, women receive a great deal of visibility and are integrated in the decision-making process in the newer Pentecostal churches and they end being prophetess (Biri and Togarasei 2013: 82). One of their major tasks is to protect the family estate and control other financial dealings. Couple ministry is also common with Magaya since he ministers with his wife, Tendai (Kamhungira 2014). Given the accounting background of Tendai Magaya, she is strategically placed in the family business in terms of doing the accounts of the ministry.

Seventh, is the firm-like structured organization of Pentecostal churches. The churches are founded and owned by one person. The owner claims to have a special divine authorization with the specific mandate with global ramification and is a special bridge between God and the people (Ukah 2007: 79). This person is referred to as 'the bank of grace' (Ukah 2007: 79). The founder also controls both charisma and cash and his word is law to his followers. Magaya fits into this mould.

Quest for healing in Prophetic Healing and Deliverance Ministries

The promise of healing is everywhere and the church has never existed without healing (Klassen 2011: ix). Healing has many descriptions, namely natural healing which comes through the body's intrinsic and environmental resources, medical healing which comes through preventive and therapeutic actions, the healing of the memories or inner healing which is used in the sense of psychology and emotional damage and lastly miraculous healing which comes through spectacular divine intervention which sets aside and speeds up natural and medical processes. The last type of healing is common in both the Old and New Testaments.

Magaya claims that he can heal all kinds of ailments, including HIV and AIDS and cancer (phdministries.org/about_phd.html). The same claim was uttered by Pastor Chris Oyakhilome of Nigeria, adding that his faith can heal cancer, heart diseases and HIV and AIDS (eTV 20 October 2010). One woman who was diagnosed as suffering from breast cancer in 2011 was said to have been healed by Magaya (Zimdiaspora 29 July 2013). In 2014, Magaya supported a Studio 263 actress who had the same ailment (Chese 2014). He gave her US$80,000 to travel to India to be treated. However, the cancer ailment could not be contained and the lady died in India (Zimdiaspora 7 December 2014). Magaya further claimed that one woman who visited him in December 2014 with a low CD4 count started to use anointing oil and barely three months later she was cured of HIV (eNCA 11 April 2015). For Magaya, it is these televised testimonies that draw people to PHD Ministries. In addition, Magaya is said to have cured a mentally challenged individual and constructed a house for him (YouTube 2016). Such activities show that Magaya operates with an innovative and expanded sense of mission.

The magnetic force of PHD Ministries

Since Zimbabwean economy has been experiencing serious problems, most of the young people both educated and uneducated, the jobless and those with jobs, flock to charismatic churches (Taru and Settler 2015: 116). One of the reasons why neo-Pentecostal churches attract youth is the lack of flexibility and innovation in the traditional churches (Counted 2012: 3). Most of these youth share many things in common which include residence, school, occupation, studentship, class, communication preference and jargon (Counted 2012: 3). In newer Pentecostal churches, programmes are created to help the youth to display their projects with pastors calling for meetings to encourage youth to join the various ministries departments in the church and even sponsor them to express their talents (Counted 2012: 3). Magaya did the same to one of his female congregants. He gave US$4300 and promised to build her a shop, a house and to buy her a car (YouTube.com). Magaya also did the same to one of the most controversial musicians whom he sponsored to open a boutique as a way of helping her to earn a decent living, since she was no longer a pole dancer. The musician later ditched the prophet, accusing him of hypocrisy (*The Herald* 20 May 2014).

The majority of the membership of megachurches are from high-density suburbs (Togarasei 2005: 355). The location of PHD Ministries makes it easier for people from Glen Norah A, B and C, Old and New Highfield, Mbare and Chitungwiza to either come on foot or take commuter omnibuses at a minimum fee. A number of commuter omnibuses change route to go to PHD Ministries, especially on Sundays. Some public transport conductors could be heard shouting '*kwaMagaya, kwaMagaya*', literally meaning 'let's go to Magaya's church'. Most of the people who come to PHD are attracted by the teaching on prosperity although it remains more of an aspiration than a reality for many (see Togarasei 2005: 355).

Magaya also attracts musicians during his all-night prayers which are usually a conglomerate of entertainment and prayer. The 'Night of Turn Around' that was held on 13 November 2013 had a variety of musicians performing. Many people thus came to the event in order to listen to the musicians of their choice more than the gospel. These musicians range from secular to gospel singers. Secular musicians included Zimbabwe dancehall singers (which is the most favourite music style of most Zimbabwe youth) such as Obey Makamure also known as Tocky Vibes, Wallace Chirimiko aka Winky D, rapper Alithias Musimbe (Maskiri) and Tinashe Romeo Antony also known as Shinsoman. These musicians could be heard changing some of the lyrics saying '*kuti PHD ndokuti church*' (PHD is the church of choice) (Online Correspondents 13 November 2014).

The second category of secular musicians was made up of the sungura singers who include popular musicians, Oliver Mutukudzi and Alick Macheso.

In justifying why he invited secular musicians to perform in the church, Magaya argued that Macheso's followers who have seen him perform at the beerhall could now follow him to church (Chaya 2015). Magaya added that he had no intention of bringing Macheso to PHD, but to let him attract and bring people who have never been to church. Macheso composed songs on the stage to shower praise to Magaya. For example, 'Magaya *rova bhora rechinamato hwai dzedu dzione kupona*' (Magaya never stop praying for our people to be saved). Macheso also composed a song on stage called 'Magaya is unconquerable'. The hitmaker Mukudzei Mukombe (Jah Prayzah) changed words of one of his songs '*Kumbumura mhute*' to '*KwaMagaya*' as a way of narrating how people are saved by Magaya (Chaya 2015). This highlights Magaya's creativity in attracting people to his movement, although conservative members of society have challenged this approach.

The third group are the gospel musicians such as Pastor Charles and Olivia Charamba, Sebastian (sometimes spelt as Sabastian) Magacha, Mathias Mhere, Agatha Murudza and Benjamin Dube, one of the celebrated musicians from South Africa. All these were part of the performance (Online Correspondents 13 November 2014). Magaya arrived at midnight when people had been socked in gig to preach to them about the Kingdom of God. From these submissions, Magaya is making all efforts to be unique, thereby secularizing the gospel in order to pull the crowds. In his effort to present himself uniquely, Magaya has been willing to extend the frontiers of mission and to experiment with new initiatives and ideas.

Conclusion

In a highly competitive religious environment, Magaya has sought to present PHD Ministries as a unique and leading spiritual movement. By focusing on prophecy, healing and deliverance, Magaya endeavours to meet the felt needs of the people in his context. Although he stretches the point by insisting on his uniqueness (since he shares many similarities with other newer Pentecostal prophets), Magaya has been highly creative. He has engaged the services of secular musicians and pole dancers, owns a football club, mobilizes politicians to his events, engages in publicity stunts and claims to heal even the most complicated of diseases. While this upsets members of mainline churches who accuse him of misleading the public, it is important to highlight that the highly competitive environment has pushed him to be creative and innovative. While sharing a lot in common with other prophets, Magaya nuances his uniqueness in order to create and maintain brand loyalty. As a 'father' to his congregants and clients, Magaya demands loyalty and promises to provide guidance towards the attainment of prosperity. When his clients and members begin to doubt, he reassures them creatively by resorting to motivational speeches and declaring, 'Delay is not denial.'

11

'Serve God full time and overtime': Pentecostalism in Zimbabwe and the reconfiguration of the gospel of prosperity

Kudzai Biri

Background

The gospel of prosperity under its several nomenclatures has attracted widespread attention and criticism, both in the public space and in academia. This chapter is a critical examination of the gospel of prosperity in Zimbabwe. It endeavours to counter some of the extreme claims by critics who claim that Pentecostal gospel of prosperity has become a 'cross less' Christianity. Utilizing mainly Zimbabwe Assemblies of God Africa (ZAOGA) of Ezekiel Guti, the United Family International Church (UFIC) and the Evangelical Fellowship of Zimbabwe (EFZ), I argue that critics often gloss over the totality of Pentecostal gospel of prosperity. This has served to perpetuate myths about Pentecostalism that portray the movement negatively. Yet there is evidence that Pentecostal discourses of prosperity are both multidimensional and rooted in both the biblical and Shona traditional milieux. While there might be areas that attract and justify criticism, it appears there is a failure to do justice when scholars critique the gospel of prosperity in its totality.

Introduction

The gospel of prosperity is one of the most controversial subjects in the academic study of religion. I need to point out that there is a lot of contestation over the label 'gospel'. Often, critics argue that it is rather a 'message', not gospel, because the gospel is in the Bible and that the gospel represents the good news of salvation. On the other hand, others maintain that prosperity teachings are central to the gospel, if not the gospel themselves. Other scholars like Gifford (2009) use the term 'dominion theology'.

This chapter is not concerned about the terminology relating to this controversial concept in Pentecostalism. This is because the significance of these variations shows that scholars have been at liberty to coin terms that describe Pentecostal teachings on prosperity. However, by virtue of its popularity, this chapter uses the term 'gospel of prosperity'. Also, in spite of these variations, scholars are at pains to retain a semblance of neutrality, as they debate the gospel of prosperity in the light of the historical teachings of Christianity. Many scholars have acknowledged the power and influence of Pentecostal spirituality in shaping the African and global religious landscapes (see e.g. Attanasi and Yong 2012, Freeman 2012; Wariboko 2014). Other scholars debate African Pentecostals' political activism through the prism of the gospel of prosperity (Afolayan et al. 2018). In spite of this influence, many studies have also criticized the gospel of prosperity as 'crossless Christianity' (Achunike 2004), impoverishing believers (Anderson 2004), encouraging penny capitalism (Maxwell 2002) and being churches of the rich (Togarasei 2010). However, others see the socio-economic significance of the movement in alleviating poverty (Togarasei 2011) and empowering the people, especially the marginalized, including women (Mapuranga 2018).

This chapter navigates through these criticisms against Pentecostals in Zimbabwe to argue that it appears Pentecostals have often balanced their teachings on prosperity. However, several factors such as the socio-economic and political crisis that Zimbabwe continues to experience have blurred the balance. For example, the crisis heightened messages on prosperity as leaders sought to empower their congregations against the ills of the economic crisis. This emphasis on prosperity during the crisis proved to be functional, as emphasis on prosperity became 'the durawall' (see Maxwell 1995) that was said to protect the believers. Many critics of the gospel of prosperity have often missed the contexts surrounding teachings on prosperity. It is not surprising that ZAOGA reconfigure the gospel of prosperity by emphasizing purity and not only the accumulation of wealth.[1]

I also argue that the background of the critics is significant, as there is a lot of contestation among Pentecostals in Zimbabwe. For example, one notes that hardcore critics of Makandiwa are often from the Apostolic Faith Mission (AFM) church where Makandiwa broke from. Because the breakaway was not condoned by the AFM leaders, some members of the AFM often castigate Makandiwa's healing claims and miracles, and some have even predicted doom for the UFIC. Some circles in ZAOGA have also castigated

Makandiwa's miracles and teachings on prosperity. It appears likely to get critics from ZAOGA and the AFM because Makandiwa appears to be the first talented young man to pose challenges to old established Pentecostals such as ZAOGA and the AFM. Although Guti of ZAOGA has a history of popularity, it appears his charisma has been usurped by age. The two churches suffered loss of membership to UFIC such that in one of ZAOGA Pastors' Deeper Life Conferences, Guti fumed over why his pastors could not do the same that Makandiwa was doing to prevent people from going to UFIC (Interview 30 October 2011).

These insights are significant because they unravel the diversity and complexity within Pentecostalism in Zimbabwe and also serve as an eye-opener when critiquing the gospel of prosperity in order to guard against myths and stereotypes of movements and figures. I, therefore, focus considerably on ZAOGA and UFIC because of the wealth of information that they provide on prosperity and also their (sometimes) contradictory messages which give weight to my claim that the critique of Pentecostal gospel of prosperity has not benefitted from a more balanced analysis.

Below, I set out the methods of data collection and analysis of the gospel of prosperity.

Methodology

The chapter utilizes general literature on Pentecostalism and the sermons by the Pentecostal leaders. Some of the leaders have written material for their congregations. Special attention is given to Guti because he has become a spiritual father of many Pentecostal leaders in Zimbabwe. Furthermore, many of the sprouting Pentecostals have been influenced by ZAOGA (Biri 2013b). The chapter pays attention to various dimensions of prosperity that include healing and financial success. Also through participant observation in EFZ's interdenominational conferences and ZAOGA services, I examine the teachings on prosperity. The following section examines some of the major criticisms against the prosperity gospel.

Criticisms often levelled against the prosperity gospel

Above, I pointed out that the teachings on prosperity are popular in Pentecostal circles but have attracted widespread criticism. One of the major criticisms is that there has been a wide gap in terms of material possession between founders of churches/ministries and their congregations. The theology of sowing and reaping (teachings encouraging believers to give) has enriched leaders while the masses became poor. The lavish lifestyles of Pentecostal leaders vis-à-vis the poverty that members of their churches (who are always encouraged to 'sow' into the life of the Men/Women of God or into the ministry) are a cause of concern. Other scholars identify the need for continued fundraising in Pentecostal churches as the basis of the success of these transnational movements. ZAOGA and UFIC have established healing centres such that the upkeep of these centres requires believers to meet the cost of maintaining the centres. Anderson (2004: 59) comments on fundraising, healing and the lavish styles of leaders. He says:

> Sometimes the emphasis on the miraculous has led to shameful showmanship and moral decadence, exaggerated and unsubstantiated claims of healing and a triumphalism that betrays the cross.

From the above citation, it is clear that healing claims have also been controversial, alongside the extreme wealth of leaders and poverty of believers. These healing claims also go hand in hand with the criticisms that Pentecostals teach a 'cross less' Christianity that does not accept suffering (symbolized by the cross). This was one of the major criticisms levelled against Makandiwa. However, critics were often loyal to the AFM, where Makandiwa broke from; hence, I argue that such criticism should be taken with caution. Also, I need to point out that in the whole package of the gospel of prosperity, Pentecostals cite biblical scriptures to justify their teachings. One major weakness in critics of the gospel of prosperity is the failure to provide concrete biblical passages in order to challenge or dismiss the Pentecostals. This is because in most instances, the Pentecostals who promote prosperity have utilized the scriptures to validate their teachings. In fact, in 1998 Guti gave his church the theme of the year 'Understanding the doctrine of my church by searching the scriptures'. Guti taught that everything that the church has to do should be grounded in the Bible. Thus, to argue that the Pentecostals do not quote from the Bible in the teachings on prosperity becomes suspect.[2] There is, therefore, need to engage the sermonic discourses in detail in order to establish how Pentecostal leaders encourage members to 'serve God full time and overtime' (which the chapter has adopted as title) which calls for uncompromised commitment to God and not only material wealth.

The church versus the 'world': God and material wealth

According to Guti, the world is putting God last and seeking after material wealth. Hence the church should be distinguished from this attitude by setting time for God first and then do other things later. Guti has also written a book (n.d.) where he teaches that material prosperity is not salvation. Real salvation is spiritual salvation. Guti also teaches and writes that Jesus died for the souls; hence, every member of ZAOGA should preach to at least one person every year. Guti has impacted his pastors in ZAOGA, and most of his pastors and other leaders have embraced his teachings. He claims that he had an encounter with the divine in his rural home and was commanded to 'fear not sin not' (1999). ZAOGA teachings revolve around 'fear not sin not'. The 'fear not sin not' concept has become the church's motto and 'fear not' is explained in terms of encouraging ZAOGA members to pursue after material wealth without fear. 'Sin not' is the basis of denouncing sin and encouraging both physical and spiritual purity. One notes that ZAOGA sources from the Bible and focuses both on the material and the spiritual.

During the ZAOGA anniversary celebrations, a ZAOGA elder from Ngaone (the founder's rural home) claimed that God had spoken to him and given him a message to teach ZAOGA to focus more on serving God than acquiring riches (sermon April 2013). This is in line with the encouragement that a ZAOGA pastor at Grange Christian Church said when he exhorted his congregation: 'Do not forget to serve God when you are blessed' (5 May 2013). This is because Guti (n.d.) has written and taught that

> [d]efinition of prosperity will only come when you are prospering spiritually by putting God first in your life ... When you are saved spiritually, true blessings always start from inside reflecting outside ... true blessing is having enough to eat, it is not money all the time. The key is peace of mind, peace in heart, peace in the family and good health. To be rich in material [sic] only is not good.
> (Guti n. d., 3-5)

The above quotation serves to indicate that the accusation that Pentecostals in Zimbabwe only focus on prosperity to the detriment of spiritual issues is not grounded on facts, but on rumours and stereotypes. The foregoing message shows sensitivity to the Bible, the needs of the people and encouraging salvation from evil. To add on this, during one of the Bible studies at the Grange church, a member asked the pastor why on tithes ZAOGA insisted on cash and not beasts or grain as in the Old Testament. In response, the pastor convinced his congregation by pointing out that ZAOGA used to take beasts and grain as tithes but the challenge was where to put/store the beasts and grain. Therefore, members of the church were encouraged to sell their beasts and grain and then bring cash to the church. In another Pentecostal church, namely the Celebration Church, the emphasis is on 'building people, building dreams, and, ultimately, building a nation' (Deuschle 2003).

Critics might argue that Pentecostals are reconfiguring the gospel of prosperity. Whether or not they are configuring the gospel of prosperity, I highlight that there appears to be lack of balanced criticism of Pentecostal gospel of prosperity. A ZAOGA pastor taught that Alick Macheso (a Zimbabwean popular musician) entertains people for money, but Christians do so to please God. The pastor encouraged the congregation to visit the sick and share with the poor and needy (5 May 2013). On a different occasion he also said:

> 2013 is a year of personal revelation as said by *baba* Guti, don't follow after crowd pullers, miracles, magic, Pentecostals are easy to mislead because many are after spectacular things yet your salvation is a miracle. Do not be greedy and come to church for a financial miracle. Guti refused money and buses that he was offered by a white man in America. We look poor outside but inside we are rich, worship God whole heartedly.
>
> (sermon 28 April 2013)

The significance of the above message is its sensitivity to dimensions of poverty which critics of the gospel of prosperity overlook. It is also important to note that Pentecostals have redefined poverty. Poverty is not lack, but it is a curse. When one is about to do something with his/her money something happens. Therefore, the poor have no poverty, and poverty is abundant among the rich people. Pentecostals diagnose poverty from a different angle. This is the perspective that is often missed by critics when pastors denounce poverty. It appears that they give the impression of denying the reality of material lack among Christians, especially in sermons that demonize poverty. Makandiwa became popular in rebuking the 'small house' (mistress) phenomenon that is widespread in Zimbabwe. In one of his sermons he declared: 'It is not God's intention for you to die poor. I know we are different and we have different destinies but what I refuse is to die in the wilderness (in poverty).'

This appears to be direct opposite to what a ZAOGA pastor taught his congregation in a Sunday service. He declared that there were many righteous people who will die poor. According to the pastor, poverty is not lack of finances because there were many rich people in Borrowdale, Glen Lorne and Shawasha (some of the leafy suburbs of Harare) who were very poor people. Material wealth is, therefore, not the yardstick to judge poverty or riches, but the relationship with God. Yet Makandiwa's message has to be examined in its context and matters surrounding the message. The researcher took time to analyse the whole message and context in which Makandiwa delivered his message. She noted that Makandiwa was encouraging members of UFIC not to give up in times of hardships and to be contended with their plight. Makandiwa acknowledged challenges in life but believers have to constantly 'fight' both spiritual and material poverty.

This is where we need to acknowledge that outside critics and insiders who advocate prosperity are coming from different ideological standpoints. The ZAOGA pastor was teaching on purity and its significance over and above material wealth. According to him, so many poor people die rich (spiritually). Makandiwa was teaching on fighting the vicissitudes of life and was encouraging his church not to surrender to the devil. Yet, taken and interpreted outside the context, the claims are that Makandiwa taught that Christians must not be poor. This is often the criticism levelled against Pentecostals such that many have labelled and viewed them as 'churches of the rich'. My argument is that Pentecostal churches have a mixed bag of clients from different confessional backgrounds because of the nature and character of Pentecostalism.

I argue that critics have often ignored the call to purity and shunning evil by the church leaders as they dwell more on the legitimacy of the prosperity gospel. The chapter does not overlook the challenges of the prosperity gospel. However, I argue that overemphasis on the financial dimensions of the gospel of prosperity has failed to do justice to other dimensions of the gospel of prosperity inherent in Pentecostalism. It is, therefore, imperative to document some of the injustices created by overemphasis on prosperity through examining how the Pentecostals have contributed to and impacted the socio-economic fabric of the nation of Zimbabwe.

Material prosperity versus social activism

As highlighted in the foregoing sections, Pentecostals view prosperity as both physical and spiritual. However, this section focuses on the material contributions by Pentecostals that critics of the gospel of prosperity either gloss over or ignore in their criticisms. One might question why people do not see the positive side enshrined in Pentecostal teachings on prosperity. Pentecostalism has the ability to amass wealth, through initiatives such as giving, working Talents (ZAOGA) and Altars (UFIC). These initiatives enable members to undertake entrepreneurial projects that benefit individuals and churches. Thus, there is need to pay attention to the contributions of these movements such that we present an accurate picture instead of scratching the surface of their gospel of prosperity. It appears many scholars have overemphasized that Pentecostals amass wealth but ignore their social activism that has strong political overtones and are making an economic contribution. For example, UFIC has donated to the orphans, the needy (especially street children) and to the hospitals. ZAOGA has established children's homes, schools (including preschool centres), a state-of-the-art hospital, colleges and a university. Other Pentecostals (though not under study) such as the AFM have established a children's home in Manhinga (Rusape, Zimbabwe), schools (Celebration Ministries International), alongside their theological colleges. These church properties require financial backing from the churches such that the messages and teachings on prosperity should be viewed and critiqued from this angle. Pentecostal churches, like other organizations, therefore, need to be engaged in generating income in order to sustain their activities.

In order to make this point clear, I interviewed some members of a mainline church who registered surprise at the very short time frame within which ZAOGA had established a university in Bindura. They pointed out that there was one mainline denomination which was failing to complete building a university because its members resisted contributing money. Yet the opposite is the case in Pentecostal churches. In many cases believers are not coerced to give but volunteer. For example, ZAOGA called upon every member to contribute US$100 towards building residential hostels for students at Zimbabwe Ezekiel Guti University (ZEGU) in Bindura, as well as for the salaries of staff. Within three months, the response had been overwhelming. It also appears that these movements are viewed as cash barons that do not run out of financial resources. Yet the above incident on ZAOGA shows that there was lack of funds to build the hostels and for salaries for the staff. Mismanagement of the funds is a possibility that critics cite that cannot be overlooked. While leaders have at times misused the funds and many in such positions have the potential also, I argue that a systematic and patient critique of the gospel of prosperity is crucial. Taking into account the contributions of Pentecostalism shows that the gospel of prosperity is multidimensional and that particular attention is required in order to avoid homogenizing in critiquing it.

Guti (1999) writes that

> [r]eal riches lie in the salvation of your soul, even if you have wealth here on earth, you need to be rich spiritually. We are training people who are balanced, we need people who work hard and get material wealth so that you impact the society. At the same time, maintain righteousness so that we please God.

The above quotation shows that Pentecostals encourage accumulation of wealth in order to serve and impact society. While the evils of such endeavours cannot be either underestimated or overlooked, it is a noble cause that needs to be acknowledged. Social activism should be commended. They are sensitive to the needs of the poor, the sick, the needy, the widows and extend proceeds from their churches to such individuals and groups.

Pentecostal discourses on prosperity have influenced social reforms. For example, the constitution-making process is one way that the EFZ demonstrated that they are concerned about the moral fabric of the nation. Sourcing from the Bible and culture, they denounce abortion, theft, greed and other sins that they thought had led to the disintegration of family life and the socio-economic fabric of the nation. While some of their ways of reading the Bible are problematic, they seek to influence ethical practice in society. EFZ teachings on prosperity and nation-building centre on establishing a God-fearing nation. Although the danger is the quest for a Christianized Zimbabwe, prosperity is defined broadly by Pentecostals. Many critics have missed this dimension. They focus on the financial, yet, as I pointed out earlier on, it is holistic. It is also important to note that testimonies from believers are varied. These testimonies touch on the areas of healing, giving and restoration of relationships that were broken. All these fall in the category of prosperity. It is from this that I argue that criticism of the gospel of prosperity has not been well balanced. For example, very few critics have acknowledged the socio-economic contributions of Pentecostalism in Zimbabwe and how they have empowered people (Togarasei 2011; Mapuranga 2018). Hence, in order to balance the argument, this chapter pays attention to some of the cases in Zimbabwe where it appears critics of the gospel of prosperity can be justified.

Spirit Embassy: Prosperity to the pastor and poverty for the people?

I pointed out earlier on that the Pentecostal message of prosperity is not homogenous in Zimbabwe. This is because of different Pentecostal churches that are in Zimbabwe and these churches have different and conflicting messages of prosperity. For example, many critics, including some Pentecostals, were infuriated by the founder of Spirit Embassy Uebert Angel's boastful messages and his castigation of poor people. For example, at the Midlands State University in October 2013, he declared that '[p]oor people are stupid'. He claimed that he had a lot of money from his business empire. Yet the majority of people are suffering because for more than a decade the economic crisis in Zimbabwe has paralysed the economy. One then wonders where the founder of Spirit Embassy (now Good News Church) gets such huge returns. Critics of Angel (including the researcher) have speculated that the money is from the believers who are desperate and poor. This gives weight to the economic explanations which advance the argument that people are not poor but that they are made poor by the global economic system. In this chapter, it is not the unfair economic system of the world that is creating poverty for believers. It is religious penny capitalism that has become an emerging giant in exploiting the masses, and it appears the push towards charging churches taxes in Zimbabwe becomes a noble idea. There is a proposal that churches should be taxed since they make a lot of money.

Angel also boasted that he was worth US$60 million (*NewsDay*). Related to such boastful messages are his claims that he is the most educated pastor. Such attitudes reveal the negative side of the gospel of prosperity in Zimbabwe. Closely related to such attitudes are contestable miracles of money (allegedly availed to members through mysterious ways) and babies that are conceived mystically. Though controversial, such miracles help to perpetuate the pastors like media personalities, creating a personality cult that cannot be questioned or declined (see Maxwell 2005; Biri 2013a). However, I argue that these controversial miracles should not lead to a blanket critique of Pentecostalism in Zimbabwe in relation to the gospel of prosperity. Contexts are significant in analysing the Pentecostal gospel of prosperity. I also argue that the 'gospel of prosperity' is a blanket term for varied Pentecostal views on the theology of dominion or success such that there is need to enumerate the specific area of dominion or success that is critiqued and also the denomination or ministry. Otherwise, the result will be making judgemental statements about Pentecostal gospel of prosperity outside contexts, misrepresenting other denominations.

The questions that one can pose at this juncture are: why has the gospel of prosperity received such widespread attention and criticism, and why there are often misconceptions and misrepresentations about Pentecostalism in the light of the above findings? I argue that scholars need to consider African world views in order to understand the gospel of prosperity.

Locating Pentecostal prosperity in the local context

Traditionally, evil forces have to be integrated into the community and kept under control. However, because of the disappearance of the mechanisms and structures that facilitated such processes, it explains the ministry of deliverance and prosperity (ter Haar 1998: 58). The missionaries proclaimed a gospel of soul's salvation and appeared to be silent on issues of man's politics, man's physical needs and his daily struggle for salvation; therefore, they did not spell out convincingly salvation for the entire man. This justifies Guti's teaching when he castigates the missionary gospel that emphasized joy in heaven and said what matters is what one does here on earth because when he/she receives Jesus she/he becomes heaven's candidate. Reading these messages outside contexts attracts criticisms of focusing on worldly matters only. For example, some critics say that the quest for earthly riches and temporary well-being is an illicit diversion, turning from God to self and wonders why Pentecostalism hankers after worldly concerns such as money and wealth.

Prosperity is interpreted in the widest sense and because money has become the medium of all the dimensions of prosperity, critiquing the gospel of prosperity requires different methodological approaches that do justice to the message of prosperity. For example, there is need for factoring in context, denomination, audience and even periodization. I argue that the emphasis on material prosperity should be read within the context of the decades of crisis in Zimbabwe. Preparing believers to soldier on in the face of the challenges, it was imperative to encourage hard work and accumulation of wealth in order to survive, as well as spiritual healing (because of the dysfunctional nature of the medical system). All these dimensions are crucial because when Pentecostals preach prosperity, they are influenced by these paradigms. Therefore, critiquing the message of prosperity outside the paradigms does not do justice to the gospel of prosperity.

Conclusion

'Serving God full time and overtime' encourages total allegiance and commitment to God, in spite of the situations that believers might be in. It is a statement that captures the Pentecostal attitude towards riches and poverty. This commitment is not only called for and grounded in material prosperity but even in times of lack, and also suggests spiritual prosperity. It appears Pentecostals in Zimbabwe have largely managed to balance the gospel of prosperity. Their social activism is testimony to how they discredit the myths and claims that they are after accumulation of material wealth and that they preach a 'cross less' Christianity. In fact, Pentecostals in Zimbabwe have empowered people; no wonder why their discourses resonate with the discourses of empowerment articulated by some politicians. It might be the reason why Pentecostal Christianity has managed to capture the imagination (see Maxwell and Lawrie (2002)) of many people because they address issues pertaining to both the spiritual and physical worlds. This is not to deny the presence of Pentecostal leaders who attract criticism through their controversial messages. It appears Pentecostals have also utilized these criticisms to reconfigure the gospel of prosperity by emphasizing the spiritual dimension of prosperity. While critics might have some basis for claiming that intense competition has led to distortions around the prosperity message, in this chapter I have highlighted how some of the leading denominations have continued to preach a moderate/balanced version of prosperity in Zimbabwean Pentecostalism.

12

Older and newer Zimbabwean Pentecostal churches' focus on the prosperity gospel: A comparative analysis

Phillip Musoni

Background

Since the start of the twenty-first century, Zimbabwe has witnessed a significant increase in the number of new millennium Pentecostal churches (NMPCs). These NMPCs seem to have attracted both the young and old, perhaps due to their gospel economy. This is a gospel economy that places emphasis on material 'blessings' that are acquired through the use of anointed objects purchased from the Church founders. This chapter theorizes a changing trend of the prosperity gospel within Zimbabwean Pentecostal churches. It reveals a shift from an entrepreneurial prosperity gospel, that is, a gospel that seeks to empower congregants economically with entrepreneurial skills, to a prosperity gospel that seems to be some form of entrepreneurship for church founders, hence the coining of the term 'gospreneurship'. The term 'gospreneurship' was first introduced in the Zimbabwean Pentecostal studies by Rejoice Ngwenya (2011), a Zimbabwean journalist, who criticized the newer Pentecostal church founders for commercializing the preaching of the gospel. Thus, to highlight this theological shift with regard to the prosperity gospel among the Zimbabwean Pentecostal Churches, this chapter compares the twentieth-century Zimbabwean Pentecostal founder Ezekiel Guti's focus on prosperity gospel deliberately, with two twenty-first-century Zimbabwean Pentecostal church founders', namely Emmanuel Makandiwa and Walter Magaya, focus on the prosperity gospel. The question raised throughout this chapter is, what are the negative socio-economic effects of this theological shift?

Introduction

This chapter interrogates the shift in the theology of the prosperity gospel within the Zimbabwean Pentecostal Christianity. Some scholars have noted that preaching the prosperity gospel is one of the major characteristics of African Pentecostal churches (Togarasei 2011). According to scholars who have published on the theme in Southern Africa, the Pentecostals' prosperity gospel has brought sustainable development for poverty reduction, particularly in Africa where poverty is deep-seated (Oosthuizen 1997; Togarasei 2011; Musoni 2013). However, this chapter argues that a transition has taken place within the Zimbabwean Pentecostal religious landscape where it seems the new millennium Pentecostal churches (NMPC) founders have taken the prosperity gospel as some form of entrepreneurship for their personal livelihood. Thus, instead of emphasizing the earlier entrepreneurial prosperity gospel that enriches church members by encouraging them to start up small businesses for survival, the NMPC founders have turned their churches into marketplaces for selling their anointed objects to miracle seekers.[1] Accordingly, this chapter argues that emphasizing prosperity that comes through the use of anointed objects purchased from church founders is a clear shift from the twentieth-century Pentecostal entrepreneurial prosperity gospel. This is a gospel which encourages entrepreneurship as a means and way of financial empowerment for ordinary church members by conveying entrepreneurial skills.

Thus, this chapter reviews the changing trends in the prosperity gospel within Zimbabwean Pentecostal Christianity critically by comparing Ezekiel Guti to Emanuel Makandiwa's and Walter Magaya's emphasis on the prosperity gospel. Ezekiel Guti is the founder of a twentieth-century Pentecostal church, the Zimbabwe Assemblies of God Africa (ZAOGA), while Emmanuel Makandiwa is the founder of the United Family International (UFI) Church and Walter Magaya is the founder of the Prophetic Healing and Deliverance (PHD) Ministries. These two are the twenty-first-century Zimbabwean Pentecostal churches. The above-mentioned churches were sampled to represent Zimbabwean Pentecostal churches as guided by a criterion set out for this chapter.

In the context of this chapter, the term 'Zimbabwean Pentecostal churches' is used narrowly to refer to churches founded by Zimbabweans in Zimbabwe and not by Western missionaries. The term is also used to refer to Zimbabwean churches whose emphasis is on speaking in other tongues/glossolalia as initial evidence of the Holy Spirit baptism for ALL members as these churches literally interpret (Acts 2:4): 'And they were ALL filled with the Holy Spirit and began to speak in other tongues as the Holy Spirit gave them utterance' (NKJV) (Musoni 2014). This gift of the Holy Spirit for the aforementioned Zimbabwean churches, unlike what is found in other Zimbabwean Spirit-type churches, is that ALL members, as guided by their literal interpretation of Joel 2:28, are capable of operating with spiritual gifts: 'And it shall come to pass afterward that I will pour out My Spirit on All flesh; and your sons and daughters shall prophesy, your old men shall dream dreams, Your young men shall see visions' (NKJV). The only difference between twentieth-century (older) Zimbabwean Pentecostal churches and the Zimbabwean NMPCs is that while everyone else exercises any spiritual gift within the twentieth-century (older) Zimbabwean Pentecostal churches, the NMPCs believe that only the gift of tongues is available to everyone while the gift of prophesy and healing is a unique gift of the church founders. Therefore, the commonality that is there, namely that the three church founders (Guti, Makandiwa and Magaya) are all Zimbabweans, sharing the same doctrine of glossolalia as initial evidence of the Holy Spirit and that every church member must speak in tongues, qualifies them to be referred to as the Zimbabwean Pentecostal churches in this chapter.

Accordingly, it is not coincidental that only ZAOGA was selected to represent the twentieth-century Zimbabwean Pentecostal churches. The reason why ZAOGA was the only church selected to represent the twentieth-century Zimbabwean Pentecostal churches is because it seems that it is the only Zimbabwean church founded in the twentieth century that fits the criterion developed specifically for this chapter to qualify as Zimbabwean Pentecostal churches. Guti, as the founder of ZAOGA, led a breakaway movement, first from the Apostolic Faith Mission (AFM) in 1950, and joined another Pentecostal church, the Assemblies of God, which he later broke away from again in 1957. This subsequently gave birth to the formation of the Assemblies of God Africa (AOGA) in 1960 (Maxwell 2006: 71). Guti is credited as being the 'founding father' of Zimbabwean Pentecostalism (Machingura et al. 2018). Though the AFM and Assemblies of God were the first Pentecostal churches in Zimbabwe, they do not fit into the category of the Zimbabwean Pentecostal churches particularly in this chapter because they were founded by white missionaries from outside the Zimbabwean borders. Thus, ZAOGA qualifies to be analysed as a 'typically Zimbabwean Pentecostal Church', as espoused above.

Methodology

A comparative historical narrative was used to discuss the changing trends in the prosperity gospel within Zimbabwean Pentecostal Christianity. Comparative historical analysis is a field of research characterized by the use of systematic comparison. It engages in the analysis of processes over time to explain large-scale outcomes such as religious evolutions, political regimes and welfare states (Mahoney 2004). Accordingly, a comparison was drawn between Guti's prosperity gospel and Emmanuel Makandiwa's and Walter Magaya's prosperity gospel. Although much has been written about Zimbabwean Pentecostal churches and the prosperity gospel, little has been done to identify the gaps between the older and the newer Zimbabwean Pentecostal churches' thrusts on the prosperity gospel. Thus, throughout this chapter, a comparison is drawn between Guti's focus on the prosperity gospel and Emmanuel Makandiwa's and Walter Magaya's focus on the prosperity gospel on the Zimbabwean religious landscape. The shift from a prosperity gospel designed to empower congregants with entrepreneurial skills to a prosperity gospel designed to create platforms for church founders to sell anointed objects to miracle seekers is discussed in this chapter. Makandiwa's and Magaya's emphasis on the prosperity gospel has been identified as *gospreneurship*, while Guti' concentration on the prosperity gospel has been identified as an *entrepreneurial* gospel.

The term 'gospreneurship' from the writings of Togarasei was used to refer to the amassing of wealth by the Zimbabwean Pentecostal church preachers for themselves by turning prosperity gospel platforms into some forms of entrepreneurship for themselves (Togarasei 2014: 121). This term, 'gospreneurship', is a combination of two words, namely 'gospel' and 'entrepreneurship'. Accordingly, in this chapter, the term 'gospreneurship' is used to capture the essence of creating the gospel platforms as survival means by church founders. This chapter argues that the emphasis on miracles associated with the use of anointed objects purchased only from church founders to miracle seekers is some form of business legalized to take place in church in order to benefit church founders. Several books, articles, journals and websites on Guti's, Makandiwa's and Magaya's approaches to the prosperity gospel were consulted.

The twentieth-century Zimbabwean Pentecostal prosperity gospel

Zimbabwean Pentecostal scholars, such as Togarasei (2011, 2018) demonstrate that Pentecostal churches in Zimbabwe are fast becoming sources of economic growth and poverty reduction, especially through encouraging entrepreneurship and positive thinking among their members. Similarly, the volume edited by Mapuranga (2018) has drawn attention to how women in Pentecostal churches in Harare deploy their religious identities for economic development. However, this prosperity gospel is not a new phenomenon among the Zimbabwean Pentecostal churches. This prosperity gospel started way back in North America (Yong 2012), although Zimbabwean/African Pentecostalism also has indigenous roots. For Yong, its most influential genealogical stream can be traced through the charismatic renewal and the Latter Rain revival movements of the mid-twentieth century, back to the teachings of popular writers such as Essek W. Kenyon, among others, in North America (Yong 2012: 15). The prosperity gospel was later adopted by the African Pentecostal churches as a tool to address contemporary socio-economic challenges as counter-reaction to most missionary teaching of 'good health and wealth in heaven' (Togarasei 2014: 112). However, for Wariboko, the future is no longer what African Pentecostal believers wait passively to happen to them in heaven (Wariboko 2012: 35). For him, the prosperity gospel helps church members to shape their future lives to be life-(abundance)-affirming rather than death-(poverty)-bringing (Warikobo 2012: 35). It is against this background that members of the older African Pentecostal churches are taught that they should pray and work hard that abundant life will happen in the here and now (Warikobo 2012). For Togarasei, the missionaries' gospel was like promising 'pie-in-the-sky' with what he referred to as 'wealth in heaven theology' (Togarasei 2014: 113).

Furthermore, Togarasei argues that the Western missionary theology of 'wealth in heaven' has made [Africans] think that possessing material wealth on earth is for sinners, whereas the righteous will only possess wealth in heaven (Togarasei 2014). Thus, the picture they painted in the hearts of Africans was: life will be better only in heaven and being poor in the flesh is God's design for Christians. Western missionaries were promising a good and pleasant life hereafter and not in the 'here and now' (Togarasei 2014). The author of this chapter grew up in a white missionary church in which he recalls the priest basing one of his sermons on Luke 16:19-31. The sermon was about poor Lazarus and the rich man who, when both died, had different destinies. Poor Lazarus went to heaven, while the rich man went to hell. The central teaching from that scripture was that it is better to be poor here on earth and be comforted when one dies and goes to heaven than to enjoy riches here on earth and go to hell. Using the vernacular, the priest would sum his sermon up by saying, '*Ngaitambure hayo panyika, ichafara kudhenga* [sic]'[2] ('Let it suffer here on earth for it shall rejoice one day in heaven') (wrongly pronounced). However, it is also imperative to note that the rise of Pentecostalism in Zimbabwe was not only in reaction to the missionary's 'wealth in heaven theology alone', but also due to the impact of modernity and its interaction with global Pentecostalism.

The twentieth-century Zimbabwean Pentecostal entrepreneurial prosperity gospel

For one to do justice to the discourse on the theological shift of the prosperity gospel from an entrepreneurial prosperity gospel to *gospreneurship*, one must first adopt a historical stance in order to understand what influenced the twentieth-century Zimbabwean Pentecostal churches to focus on the entrepreneurial gospel. David Maxwell (2006), who studied the ZAOGA church, argues that the entrepreneurial prosperity gospel was not first set up to empower congregants. He maintains that it was a means to sustain the running of the church. For Maxwell, church members, particularly women, were encouraged to engage in penny capitalism – small-scale production of foodstuffs and clothing to enhance church finances (Maxwell 2006: 94). The reason was that most African independent churches of that time were mainly composed of poor gardeners and maid servants whose incomes could not sustain the running of their families and the financial support of the church. However, although the money collected through small business/entrepreneurship would go into church coffers, for Maxwell, this practice created a culture of industry and entrepreneurship that sustained members as well (Maxwell 2006: 95).

The study on which this chapter is based observed that entrepreneurial prosperity gospel is not uniquely Guti's ideology, but a financial template for most black African indigenous churches. It was a model adopted during the colonial era. Zimbabwean African indigenous churches, in general, offer material advantages to their members, both in urban and rural settings (Sibanda and Maposa 2013). As illustrated by the Johane Masowe and Johane Marange Apostolic churches (pioneering African indigenous churches from the 1920s), there is strong community cooperation, to the extent that economic cooperatives have been formed within these churches. Most AICs are deeply involved in the vocational business. Members pool their resources in the basket- and tin-making cooperatives, wood-crafting cooperatives and cross-border trade. This signifies viable indigenous entrepreneurship, unlike foreign-funded mission churches (Sibanda and Maposa 2013: 128).

Ezekiel Guti and the entrepreneurial prosperity gospel

In order to facilitate the comparative thrust of the chapter, it is important to summarize rise of Guti's theology on prosperity gospel. The introduction of the entrepreneurial prosperity gospel in ZAOGA can be traced back to Guti's 1970 experiences in the United States at Christ for the Nation Institute in Dallas (Maxwell 1998). Upon the completion of his theological studies at Christ for the Nation Institute in Dallas, Guti met a certain wealthy white man who offered to give him money and buses for the propagation of the gospel in Africa (Guti 2014: 47). However, the offer had some conditions, namely that Guti had to accept working under this certain wealthy white man (Guti 2014: 25). Reading between the lines from the writings of Maxwell (2006) and Biri (2012), one could conclude that Guti was not going to accept the offer because Guti's colonial experiences would not allow any domination from the whites again.

Maxwell rightly points out that all the twentieth-century African black churches sought autonomy from whites (Maxwell 2006: 95). However, according to Guti, the reason why he did not accept the offer was that after many prayers the Holy Spirit told him that if he was going to work under this white man, God was going to take away his anointing (Guti 1999). Thus, it is against this background that Guti came back from the United States without the money and buses (Guti 2014: 45). Instead, he came back to Africa and started teaching his congregants to work using their hands in what he referred to as [the] 'School of Talents/*Matarenda*'. For Guti, the School of Talents/*Matarenda* is about teaching people how to start businesses, how to run businesses and how to save money (Guti 2015). This is how, to date, ZAOGA has built several preschools, primary schools, secondary schools and a university (the Zimbabwe Ezekiel Guti University in Bindura, Zimbabwe). For this reason, Togarasei passionately argues that the old criticism of Pentecostals lacking a social conscience cannot today be said of Pentecostal churches such as the ZAOGA (Togarasei 2014). ZAOGA is running not only a hospital, but also schools, a university and a television station as well (Togarasei 2014: 121). Guti has been critical of the younger churches and their version of the prosperity gospel. In a sermon entitled 'True Prosperity' uploaded on YouTube (YouTube 02 May 2018), Guti argues,

> Some people do not know that this gospel of miracle prosperity can cause people to be poor. Teaching people that someone can be rich without working hard is misleading. Teaching people that though you are not employed, and with no

project that brings income but believing that through a miracle one can become materially rich, is wrong and misleading teaching.

(YouTube 02 May 2018)

Guti clarified that he did not teach that kind of prosperity gospel. Instead, he indicated that he teaches people to use their hands and work hard so that they can prosper materially. For him, the prosperity gospel that says one can become rich miraculously can lead people to steal. In his sermon, Guti defined prosperity as having enough food and shelter, quoting from 1 Timothy 6:8. Guti attributed poverty in Africa to three sources:

- Laziness
- Lack of a culture of saving
- Lack of proper education or skills (YouTube 02 May 2018).

Guti defined laziness as idleness and being unwilling to use one's hands in order to earn a living. This is how men and women in ZAOGA are encouraged to start businesses using 'home-talents' (Biri 2014). In response to this, ZAOGA women composed a popular home talent song – *usagarira maoko* ('don't sit on your hands'). Furthermore, Guti taught his church members not to depend on a single income, but to make investments to create streams of income. For Guti, wealth that comes mysteriously also disappears mysteriously!

Apart from working by using one's hands, Guti taught his congregants a culture of saving; members of this church are encouraged to have bank accounts. To avoid a hand-to-mouth existence, he taught his church members that all money earned must be banked first before one decides to use it. He taught his members to grow financially, step by step. Guti argued that, in most cases, living hand to mouth is caused by being competitive, where one always wants to match one's peers, resulting in one spending more than one can afford. Furthermore, he discouraged his members from borrowing money. Therefore, members of this Pentecostal church (namely ZAOGA) are not allowed to borrow money but must learn to grow step by step, financially (Maxwell 1998: 353). Lack of saving is what is referred to by Togarasei as 'consumer mentality' (Togarasei 2014: 122). For Togarasei, a consumer mentality is defined as the spirit of always spending what one has, instead of thinking about investments (Togarasei 2014: 122).

In addition to working hard using one's hands and developing a culture of saving, Guti encourages all his congregants to pursue academic and professional courses. Thus, a lack of skills becomes a major source of Africa's poverty.

Acquiring a skill here is not just about acquiring a degree, but pursuing an accredited programme that empowers one with professional skills to make a living. In Zimbabwe, there was a time when bogus/unaccredited institutions were issuing degrees, including doctorates, without the commensurate academic training (Chitando and Biri 2016). Accordingly, Guti discouraged his pastors from registering at unaccredited institutions, but to register with reputable institutions to acquire skills (Ezekiel TV, Guti preaching during the 2015 Deeper-Life Leadership summit, Harare, Zimbabwe). For him, there is no miracle that brings wealth to a Christian without one having professional skills. It is such skills that position an individual strategically for job opportunities.

The study on which this chapter is based established that the twentieth-century Zimbabwean Pentecostal churches' entrepreneurial prosperity gospel emerged as a socio-economic protest. The entrepreneurial prosperity gospel model was chosen by ZAOGA and other AICs in a bid to be autonomous and free of white domination (Maxwell 2006: 95). Historically, for one to do justice when comparing the twentieth-century Zimbabwe Pentecostal churches to the twenty-first-century Zimbabwean Pentecostal churches, one has to appreciate the differences in the historical epochs. From 2000 onwards, Zimbabwe started to experience serious economic challenges. This is the very time that the Zimbabwean dollar depreciated dramatically to the extent that during prayer meetings, most Pentecostal churches would encourage their members to pray '*kuti dhora rive ne simba*' (that our Zimbabwean dollar will regain its value) (ZAOGA-2008 ten days prayer letter) (Interview 01 May 2019). It is against this background that the following section will discuss the historical development of what is referred to as gospreneurship among the NMPCs.

The twenty-first-century new millennium Pentecostal prosperity gospel

The rise of Makandiwa and Magaya has been adequately addressed in publications that have already appeared (see e.g. Chitando et al. 2013b; and Chitando and Biri 2016) and will not be described in detail in this chapter. However, it is imperative to note that these two churches can be used to represent many NMPCs. These NMPCs seem to have attracted both the young and old, perhaps due to their gospel economy. This is a gospel economy which emphasizes material 'blessings' that come from using anointed oil, water, branded wristbands and anointed handkerchiefs purchased from the church/

ministry founders. Accordingly, this section discusses the changing trend of the prosperity gospel within the Zimbabwean Pentecostal churches, revealing a shift from an entrepreneurial prosperity gospel to what is referred as African *gospreneurship* (making the gospel platforms business enterprises by church founders) (Togarasei 2014). This shift has been identified by Zimbabwean scholars and the media as a deviation from the old Zimbabwean Pentecostal entrepreneurial prosperity gospel, which was intended to empower congregants with entrepreneurial skills to a prosperity gospel that has become some form of entrepreneurship for church founders (Togarasei 2014: 121). 'Gospreneurship', as a term, was first used by Rejoice Ngwenya (2011) a Zimbabwean journalist who criticized the newer Pentecostal churches founders for commercialization of the gospel. The commercialization of the gospel, according to the critics of these newer Zimbabwean Pentecostalism, is based on the church founders' emphasis on prosperity which arises from

- Sowing of fat offerings/'tapping into the anointing' (giving money to the church founders)
- Selling of 'anointed' objects to miracle seekers
- Prosperity and deliverance through prophetic utterances by the founder.

The prosperity that comes through 'sowing a seed' or giving money to the church founders

It is imperative to note that almost all Zimbabwean churches, in one way or another, collect money offerings. Thus, even twentieth-century Pentecostal churches such as the ZAOGA collect money offerings. This chapter has already made the point that the ZAOGA founder (Guti) taught his members to work and to use their talents to support both themselves and the church since most AICs are self-supporting, self-administering and self-propagating churches (Oosthuizen 1997). The collection of money offerings in ZAOGA has made it possible for the church to have many houses of worship around the globe, buying church cars and church pastors' houses.

In contrast with the above, those who criticize the collection of money among most NMPCs contend that the bulk of the money collected at every service goes to the founder, hence, the reference to 'a God business' (Mahohoma 2017). This indicates that the church becomes a cash cow or business for the founders.

Nwadialor (2015) posits that these church founders (NMPCs) encourage a doctrine of prosperity in which the spiritual and material fortunes of a believer are dependent on how much one gives materially to God, often through the church founder who purports to be a representative of God on earth (Nwadialor 2015). This is what Nwadialor refers to as the commercialization of the gospel, 'giving to God in the name of sowing a seed' through giving to the church founder (Nwadialor 2015). The theology of giving more to obtain a blessing has created an environment for congregants to compete among themselves by giving to 'get a blessing' (Nwadialor 2015).

Giving willingly to God through 'the Man of God' has become the norm, especially in an environment where church founders have popularized a 'gap theory'. A gap theory entails ordinary church members only being able to approach God through the anointed 'Man of God'. This gap is created by projecting the believer as 'too unholy or too inferior' to connect with God personally without the aid of a church founder (Banda 2018b). Thus, NMPC founders project a huge gap between God and the ordinary believers and then position themselves as God's representatives on earth. An example is an audio recording that went viral on social media where Prophet Emmanuel Makandiwa urged his followers compellingly to bring him food and money, ostensibly because he is God's representative on earth (01 May 2019).

> *Unzai zvinhu kumba kwangu* (Bring things into my house.)
> *Unzai zvinhu kumba kwangu iyo, Bhuku ya Malachi 3 inodaro* (Bring things into my house, thus says Malachi Chapter 3.)
> *Unzai zvinhu kumba kwangu zvekudya/* (Bring things (food) into my house.)
> *Munoriverenga sei Bhaibheri, kune here one day yawakamboona Zino ra Mwari rakadhinda pa domasi?* (How do you read the Bible, is there any day you have seen God in His physical self, eating food/having His teeth imprinted on a tomato?)
> *Kunzi Mwari nhasi adya* (Or hearing people saying look!!! the plate which was full of food is now empty because God has eaten.)
> *Kwaari kuti unzai chikafu kune delegation yake* (Where God said to bring into the store house, it's where His prophets are.)
> *Mwari ane marepresentative anomudyira zvinhu panyika* (God has his earthly representatives who eat food on his behalf.)
> *Saka kana Mwari anzwa nokuda Pizza anoti, 'Makandiwa ndidyirewo pizza'* (If God has craved for pizza, He will say 'Makandiwa eat pizza for me.' Then you must bring pizza that I eat on God's behalf.)
> *Ndichitsenga pizza Mwari anengenge achinakirwa kuDenga* (As I will be chewing pizza, God in heaven will be enjoying the delicious pizza.)

At one point, Prophet Makandiwa taught and encouraged all his church members to set up altars in their houses so that if members encountered a significant problem, they would go to the altar and put money on it and offer prayers (Interview 01 May 2019). In his teaching, Makandiwa told his members that he, Makandiwa, would join the person at the altar in a spiritual form to answer his/her prayer because he is God's representative (Interview, an anonymous member of the UFIC 01 May 2019). Subsequently, the money put on the altar will be taken to the prophet of God as an offering (Interview 01 May 2019). This is a form of innovation, although it raises serious questions at the level of theology.

Another allegation raised against the approaches of NMPCs to the prosperity gospel is that while a twentieth-century Zimbabwe Pentecostal church such as ZAOGA is busy buying church property for worship, setting up permanent church offices and other valuable property using the money collected, NMPC founders were said to be buying guest houses and setting up personal businesses. At the time of the study, all the places of worship for the NMPCs were temporary structures and rented places. While money was being collected at every single service, it was alleged that the NMPCs had several guest houses – not as church property, but as personal property (Chibango 2016: 68). Importantly, these guest houses were a source of income for these church founders. They were located in the low-density areas, with title deeds in the founder's name, and not in the name of the church (Mahohoma 2017: 4). Members who would want to see the prophet one on one had to book rooms at these guest houses for a fee, which Mahohoma refers as 'double-dipping' (Mahohoma 2017: 6). For Mahohoma, 'double dipping' refers to church founders' collection of money from miracle seekers through accommodation fees they pay at church founders' lodges and a consultation fee paid to see the prophet one on one.

However, without disregarding the allegations raised above, one can also argue that it is superficial to argue that Makandiwa and Magaya do not have many houses of worship because they are collecting money for their personal benefit, especially when one considers the economic meltdown in Zimbabwe since they began their ministries. Perhaps one would argue that Guti, whose church was established many decades ago, has managed to accumulate resources over time. It is these resources that have enabled him to have many church properties. It is also imperative to note that ZAOGA and these two selected twenty-first-century Zimbabwean Pentecostal churches belong to different historical epochs; hence the fact that ZAOGA has property in contrast with the younger churches that do not have property is not enough evidence to accuse them of misappropriation of collected offerings in church.

Selling 'anointed' objects to miracle seekers

The use of anointed objects for healing and blessing has a long history that stretches from the Old Testament, through to the New Testament, the early church and various eras of church history (Banda 2018a). For example, Samuel used oil to consecrate David for kingship and James 5:14 says, *'Is there among you sick? Let him call for the elders of the Church and let them pray over him, anointing him with oil in the name of the Lord'* (ESV). The Apostle Paul used handkerchiefs and aprons to heal the sick, as recorded in Acts 19:12. However, critics of these movements are not against the use of anointed objects, but on the selling of such objects. Accordingly, what is clear from the Old Testament and New Testament narratives is that the priest or church elder would bring the anointing object with him to anoint someone to become a king or to heal the sick. In contrast, this is not the case with NMP church founders. Critics of these church movements argued that the selling of these anointing objects to miracle seekers becomes some form of entrepreneurship for these church founders. Thousands and thousands of bottles of 'anointed oil' are kept in storerooms to be sold to church members for 'spiritual blessings'. Congregants buy the oil because the church founders stress that 'anointing oil is a point of contact for spiritual warfare and symbol of the Holy Spirit' (Banda 2018a).

Furthermore, the churches stipulate that the anointing oil protects members from deadly diseases. One study participant, Ms Netsai Chawatama (not her real name), a former commercial sex worker and a member of one of the newer churches, testified that she had been HIV positive for two years but claimed to have been healed after using the prophet's anointed oil (Staff Editor, Daily News, 7 July 2014). She testified at church:

> I started using anointing oil, and my cervical cancer and pain went away. I kept on using the anointing oil, and I was healed of HIV. I am now HIV negative.
> (Staff Editor, Daily News, 7 July 2014).

Thus, the buying of oil is a continuous process because these NMPC founders teach that '[e]ven if you were anointed in 2016, it does not mean that you were still anointed in 2018, you need to buy fresh anointing for new challenges one would be facing at that time' (Banda 2018a). Accordingly, critics have argued that the NMPC founders turned the entrepreneurial prosperity gospel, which was intended to empower congregants with entrepreneurial skills, into a prosperity gospel, which has become some form of entrepreneurship for church founders.

The NMPC founders encourage their members to buy and wear wristbands branded with the name of the church founder. Not only do they sell wristbands, but they also sell anointed water, anointed pencils, anointed envelopes, anointed stickers, anointed pictures, anointed cups, anointed plates, anointed car keyholders, anointed bags, anointed wallets and anointed everything that money can buy (Mukondiwa 2017: 2).

What has been raised by critics of these movements is that some of the NMPC founders in smaller communities are enriching themselves at the cost of devout but naive followers. While one can argue that it cannot be feasible that oil is bought and handed out free of charge to thousands of followers, the only concern for the critics pertains to the profit motive by these church founders. Apart from the pure profit motives, many who use these anointed objects end up discontinuing their hospital medication, for most NMPCs assert that the use of scientific medication is a sign of a lack of faith in Jesus Christ (Chitando and Klagba 2013). Hence, this discontinuation of modern medicine, for example, antiretroviral therapy in the case of HIV and AIDS, will worsen the illness, resulting in unnecessary deaths.

Prosperity and deliverance through prophetic utterances by the founder

The young, charismatic Zimbabwean Pentecostal church founders, such as Makandiwa and Magaya, present a prosperity gospel that minimizes the need for people to engage in hard work (enterprise) as means of acquiring wealth. Instead, they promote a gospel that only encourages people to attend their miracle night services where they, the prophets, shout, '*Receive! Take it!*' Some incidents are recorded where these new Pentecostal church founders claim to have prayed for all congregants to get their wallets and pockets full of money (Mahohoma 2017). During the issuing of these 'Man of God' promises of wealthy living to their members during church services, members have to shout, in turn, '*I receive, Man of God. I believe, Man of God! Prophesy, Man of God! Go deeper.*' Whatever the prophet says is believed to be true. These NMPC founders teach that when a 'Man of God' pronounces a blessing, no one can reverse it.

Conclusion

The emergence of twenty-first-century NMPCs has transformed the twentieth-century Zimbabwean Pentecostal entrepreneurial prosperity gospel into becoming some form of entrepreneurship for church founders, hence the coining of the term 'gospreneurship'. In addition to turning gospel platforms into some form of entrepreneurship for these church founders, critics argue that the miracle gospel promotes idleness and laziness, since one will wait continuously for a miracle from heaven to place food on the table. This miracle gospel that seems to substitute hard work for a living continues to be a threat to economic development. This chapter has deliberately shown a bias towards the twentieth-century Zimbabwean Pentecostal churches' approaches to the prosperity gospel. Economically, these twentieth-century Zimbabwean Pentecostals and other Spirit-type churches are offering material advantages to their members in general. This is so because these churches are deeply involved in vocational businesses. Followers of these churches are encouraged to be entrepreneurs, thereby leading to employment creation. More importantly, members of these churches are encouraged to save money to avoid exhibiting a consumer mentality and are encouraged to develop themselves professionally by acquiring the necessary education for their development. This is not the case with NMPCs' prosperity gospel that emphasizes wealthy living through the use of anointed objects purchased from church founders.

13

At the mercy of 'the Man of God'? Sexual and gender-based violence in Zimbabwean Pentecostalism

Tapiwa Praise Mapuranga

Background

Many studies on Pentecostalism have noted how empowering it has been for women (see e.g. Soothill 2007; Bateye 2008; Mapuranga 2013a, 2018). It could be argued that Pentecostalism has brought with it space for women leadership and other roles as founders, prophets, evangelists among others. It is, therefore, reasonable to say that Pentecostalism has in so many ways empowered women in an area that was previously known as a male domain. Despite this empowerment, there has been an increase in the number of cases where women are at the mercy of some 'Men of God' in Pentecostalism. There has been a sharp increase in the rate at which cases of sexual abuse of women by church leaders are heard of in contemporary Zimbabwe. Despite its strengths, a careful rereading of some cases in Pentecostalism reveals an increase in the cases of sexual and gender-based violence both within the church and in the homes of some practitioners. Most studies hardly analysed this sad aspect that women encounter within Pentecostalism, fearing to project a negative image of a highly successful movement. The thrust of this chapter is to highlight some of these incidences of sexual and gender-based violence in Zimbabwean Pentecostalism. It examines the causes of the reported women's sexual abuse, particularly within the church, and suggests some recommendations to curb this problem within these institutions. Interviews were carried out with selected women (some of whom have been abused), religious leaders themselves and some members of society. The study upheld the relevant ethical protocols when researching into such a highly sensitive theme. The identities of study participants were protected.

However, a few of the high-profile cases that were already in the public domain were presented, as they were described in the media upon the conviction of perpetrators of sexual and gender-based violence by competent courts of law.

Introduction

The media in contemporary Zimbabwe is awash with news about prophets and Pentecostalism, with effects that are either positive or negative, in this particular case, with specific reference to women. This Pentecostal phenomenon had become prominent at the time of writing. Names of prominent prophets such as Emmanuel Makandiwa (United Family International Church), Walter Magaya (Prophetic Healing and Deliverance Ministries), Tavonga Vutabwashe (Heartfelt International Ministries) and Passion Java among many others are attracting larger congregants than previously.[1] There is an inexhaustible list of new Pentecostal churches in the country, and this chapter will not try to name them. The list is quite large, illustrating the vibrancy of Pentecostalism in Zimbabwe. All these divergent churches are evidence of the claim by Kalu (2008) that Pentecostalism represents the fastest-growing brand of Christianity in sub-Saharan Africa.

The rapid expansion of the sector has opened up the space for a number of fake prophets who simply want to abuse their congregants, especially women. Publications by earlier scholars confirm this worrying trend (see e.g. Chikafa-Chipiro 2016; Manyonganise 2016a; Parsitau 2019; Zimunya and Gwara 2019). All these scholars have confirmed the vulnerability of women to particularly some Pentecostal (and other) prophets/pastors. Pentecostal ministries seem to get more publicity as compared to mainline churches in relation to the sexual abuse of women. Critically, women have been left vulnerable to prophets in these Pentecostal churches, as they suffer sexual violence at the hands of some 'Men of God'. Believers are in search of prophecy about their anxieties, their future and various solutions to their problems. Many prophets have pounced mercilessly on desperate women. They have made their followers do wild things and have caused agony in different forms, and many have been stripped of cash and other goods. In particular, the sexual abuse of women has emerged as an area of concern. The thrust of this chapter is to analyse women's experiences at the hands of the 'Men of God' or the so-called prophets. It is, thus, necessary to start with a brief examination of the relationship between prophecy and Pentecostalism in Zimbabwe. This will facilitate an appreciation of the power that they have over their members and clients, including the women whom they end up abusing.

Prophecy and Pentecostalism in Zimbabwe: An overview

Prophecy is not a new phenomenon in Zimbabwe (Gunda 2012: 335). According to Chitando et al. (2013a: 157), 'the emergence of young prophets in Zimbabwe from 2010 is best understood using the metaphor of waves'. There have been different types of prophets emerging in Zimbabwe within different times and places. The era of Pentecostalism has seen the rising phenomenon of a unique wave of prophecy in Zimbabwe. In the earlier period of the 1920s, African instituted church (AIC) prophets emerged. They sought to combine Christianity with African culture, challenging the mainline/mission churches. In the 1950s and 1960s, some prophets emerged from mainline Pentecostal churches to establish independent Pentecostal movements/churches.

The rise in Pentecostalism in Zimbabwe has witnessed the rise of a somewhat different phenomenon of prophecy. For Chitando et al. (2013a: 159), Zimbabwe has witnessed the emergence of a plethora of prophetic ministries that are led by relatively young men. These have managed to attract large numbers of believers, particularly because of their healing ministries and their gospel of prosperity. It is justifiable to argue that one of the most probable reasons why Pentecostalism has managed to gain so much popularity in the country is because of its ability to address a diversity of human problems through prophecy. A survey in some newer Pentecostal churches in Harare revealed how much the members and clients are keen to be told of the 'unknown' through prophecy. This justifies the argument by Bourdillon (1993: 85) that 'the package of a religion affects people's choice of it'. According to Togarasei (2010: 26), 'Pentecostalism has been packaged to meet the needs and aspirations' of its followers.

Building upon the operations of prophets in African instituted churches (AICs), prophets in Pentecostalism sought to distinguish themselves and to create a category of 'white collar prophets' (Mangena and Mhizha 2013: 132). These 'white collar prophets' sought to project a more progressive and sophisticated outlook than that of the 'white garment' prophets who belonged to the older AICs. According to Mangena and Mhizha (2013), this phenomenon started with churches such as the Universal Church of the Kingdom of God (UCKG), followed by such churches as Celebration Ministries and Mathias and Mildred Ministries (Mangena and Mhizha 2013: 137). These largely paved the way for a unique type of prophecy that emerged as Pentecostalism grew in Zimbabwe. This new wave of Pentecostal prophecy is characterized by young, dynamic men who specialize in foretelling, healing and deliverance. They also preach a message of prosperity, promising their audiences radical transformation in their lives.

What is particularly striking about the latest wave of prophets in Zimbabwe is the power that individual prophets wield over their clients and overall standing in society. These prophets attract clients and members from diverse social classes, including senior politicians and business people. They are associated with sacred power and authority, and they claim to have privileged/special and even exclusive access to God. These prophets maintain that God speaks to them in unique ways that are not available to their members or clients. According to Kroesbergen:

> Ministries International are led by authoritarian big men – or women sometimes. It is the task of these big men or women to take care of the flock but, in return, the believers' strict obedience to their authority is required. The mutuality and reciprocity that exist in this relationship never take the form of equality or interchangeability.
>
> (Kroesbergen 2019: 239)

The next section examines some selected examples of alleged women abuse by some prophets especially in Pentecostalism.

Common headlines on women and sexual abuse in Pentecostal churches

The increase in the growth of Pentecostalism has seen an increase in abuse of women by pastors and prophets. There are common headlines, especially in the print media that portray this unfortunate development. Some of these include the following:

- 'Gumbura not the only one, ten more different Church Leaders accused of sexual abuse' (*iHarare* 2014)
- 'Adultery Scandal: Prophet Magaya Bought Married Girlfriend a US$ 10,000 Car' (*NewsDay* 2014)
- 'Are we in, or are we over the edge: as "prophets" prophesy ID numbers; Miracles, prosperity gospel takes over' (*The Sunday Mail* Mugauri 2011)
- 'Churches no longer Safe for Women' (*The Standard* 2014)

- 'RGM Church women belong to Gumbura' (*The Herald* 2013)
- 'Women pay price for belief in false prophets' (*NewsDay* 2011)
- 'Another Sex Scandal Hits Magaya' (*NewsdzeZimbabwe* 2014)
- 'EXCLUSIVE: Prophet Caught in Sex Scandal, Beaten Up' (*NewsdzeZimbabwe* 2014)

Admittedly, newspapers tend to sensationalize their headlines in order to attract attention to get people to buy them. However, it is clear that there is a silent epidemic of 'Men of God' within Pentecostal churches abusing women. These stories, among others, are the reason why certain practices of prophets within Pentecostalism should be approached with caution. Not all issues relating to women that emerge from Pentecostalism should be accepted as empowerment. Several women have been left vulnerable to sexual and gender-based violence within the church. This chapter unveils some of these cases as reported in the media in the upcoming section.

Selected cases of alleged sexual abuse: The 'Men of God' on the prowl

This section provides few examples of some 'men of God' who have been associated with sexual and gender-based violence in their respective ministries. These few examples serve to illustrate the urgent need for the church at large to act in more liberating ways and to be silent no more.

The most notable case that hogged the limelight is that of Martin Robert Gumbura of the RGM Independent End Time Message (see Chikafa-Chipiro 2016). According to Rupapa (2013), 'all women parishioners at RGM Independent End Time Message Church allegedly belong to the church leader Martin Gumbura and are given to their husbands on "loan", with Gumbura having the powers to recall them whenever he feels necessary'. Several women accused Gumbura of sexual assault in 2013. He went to court and was sentenced to forty years in jail at the beginning of 2014.

In an interview, Mrs Matando (not her real name) (August 2014), an elderly lady who goes to a Pentecostal church, reiterated that 'it is sad that women continue to be abused in the church, an institution that is supposed to proffer solutions to their problems or walk with them through their problems'.

In yet another incident, it is reported (*NewsdzeZimbabwe* 2014) that another 'Man of God' of the Tabernacles of Grace Church in Mutare (one of Zimbabwe's major cities) was involved in a sex scandal involving a congregant's wife. The pastor, who was caught in the act, was beaten by furious members present at the moment this happened. By the time of the report, the pastor was said to have fled to Zambia, perhaps as a sign of shame as he sought to flee from his alleged actions. As argued by Mlambo (Interview 2014), 'such cases are clear testimony to the fact that the church is not properly educating its leaders on issues regarding sexuality and the rights of congregants, especially women, who are supposed to seek comfort and consolation from this institution'. In another case, a pastor who raped a congregant on five different occasions and gave her anointing oil in a bid to buy her silence was sentenced to sixty years' imprisonment by a Harare magistrate (Chingarande 2017).

These cases of sexual and gender-based violence are not unique to Zimbabwe. The phenomenon is widespread. From South Africa, in an article entitled 'Women pay price for belief in false prophets' (Tsuma 2011: 7), the extent to which women have continuously fallen victim to controversial male 'healers' frequently accused of abusing women is discussed in greater depth. In this article, there is a story of a South African 'prophet' who allegedly dipped his fingers inside a young woman's sexual organ at a 'healing session'. In a different story in the same article, a prophet belonging to the Incredible Happening Church abused two female congregants as part of a ritual to exorcise them of demons. The authors of these articles note with concern how far 'prophecy' can lack authenticity and how far it can go in terms of affecting its female followers. These are some of the recorded cases in the media on how often women fall prey to these healers when they allegedly administer herbs inside women's sexual organs all in the name of healing, with the cunning ones going as far as using their male sexual organs to, as they often claim, 'push the medicine inside'. This illustrates how grave such prophecy can affect women in terms of the after-effects of these fake prophets: increase in vulnerability to HIV and AIDS being among one of the worst effects.

Similarly, in other cases which the study unearthed from attending court sessions, interviews and police briefings different pastors were imprisoned for raping their female congregants. A form-critical analysis of the cases shows a pattern. A desperate woman approaches a Pentecostal pastor, who is associated with the powers of healing and deliverance. The challenges that women face include infertility, 'spiritual husbands', problematic marriage, unemployment and others. The prophet/pastor promises 'healing/deliverance' by defeating the putative oppressive spiritual forces and invites the woman for private counselling and deliverance sessions. He takes advantage of the setting and rapes the woman. This pattern is replicated in the different incidents where the 'Men of God' violate women who come to them for spiritual support.

Pentecostalism as the breeding ground for sexual and gender-based violence? A critical analysis

The previous section examined some of the stories where clergy were alleged to have abused women. These few examples generally serve to illustrate how women have been vulnerable in the church in general, and in particular, in Pentecostalism. This section critically analyses why there has been a marked increase of women being sexually abused by the 'Men of God' in the country (and beyond). This study finds a relationship of this pattern with the general increase of Pentecostal activity in the country. The sheer growth of female believers turning to Pentecostalism as compared to the few male counterparts has a role to play on the unequal male to female proportion. Unfortunately, the few men in powerful positions tend to abuse women who go to them seeking help in various areas such as marital and fertility issues, poverty, health and other such problems. According to Maxwell (1995: 21) congregants in these Pentecostal churches look up to their prophets for protection from *ngozi* (avenging spirit), *chikwambo* (goblin) and for fertility, healing, success in public examinations, jobs and troubled marriages (as various forms of life challenges).

First and foremost, this study argues that there has been an increase in women abuse in Pentecostalism, most probably because the theology of submission is more intense in Pentecostalism. Mapuranga (2012) blames this on the wrong interpretation of such texts as 1 Corinthians 14:34-35 and 1 Timothy 2:11-14. The same is reiterated by Chitando (2012: 75) who argues that 'many men cite the scriptures of various religions to defend their authority to "discipline" women'. An abuse of sacred texts and traditions by men has allowed men to project having multiple sexual partners and using violence as 'divinely sanctioned'. This is in agreement with such scholars as Manyonganise (2010: 10) who argue that when relations between men and women are discussed in the churches, such scriptures that emphasize the subordination of women are stressed. According to Manyonganise (2013: 148):

> The church in Zimbabwe has perpetuated the notion that men are the heads of families. In other words, the church has maintained the patriarchal ideology as the springboard for socialization, thereby exposing women to the whims of

hegemonic masculinity. Married people are often bombarded with sermons that seek to maintain the status quo in terms of family hierarchies. The church itself is structured in such a way that women often find themselves in peripheral positions.

The Bible has and continues to be manipulated in many ways. Mapuranga (2013b: 217) gives more examples of such texts that have been twisted to suit those in power and authority over the weaker and vulnerable. In particular, self-styled Pentecostal prophets exploit their putative spiritual power.

Second, this study established that male leaders in these emerging independent/autonomous Pentecostal churches tend to enjoy too much independence and autonomy within their ministries. They decide what topics are open for discussion in the church and when. Most of these males who end up abusing women are founders of these ministries, and others have very high positions within their hierarchy. Consequently, by being leaders and founders, with patriarchal authority, they decide what to condone and what to rebuke. According to Chitando (2012: 75), most of these leaders maintain that as 'heads' they have the license to make decisions without consulting women. As such, issues on sexual and gender-based violence are hardly an issue in the church as they (in instances where the abuse occurs) tend to hurt the ego of these leaders and founders. It is not an issue for them that many women are vulnerable. Chitando and Chirongoma (2013: 10) wonder why male church leaders seem to have limitless energy when it comes to debates on homosexuality, but they appear frozen when it comes to confronting sexual and gender-based violence.

Third, there is a ripple effect of limited theological education from both the male leaders and the female congregants. Some 'Men of God', who have either been found guilty or have faced sexual and gender-based violence allegations, have got questionable theological training. Their academic qualifications are hardly mentioned in their biographies. A lack of a sound theological training leaves the prophets without the relevant ethical knowledge. This argument was supported in an interview by Moyo 2014 who feels that

> many of these young pastors and prophets especially in the Pentecostal ministries just wake up one day to start a church. They do not have any sort of theological training and as such do not know how to handle their congregants. At the end of the day, how would you expect such inexperienced men to interact ethically with women who come to seek counsel on various problems?

Generally, a church leader who has been exposed to some higher theological training and has been equipped to reflect on religion and gender would really appreciate the value of women as human beings and is not likely to be as abusive. Admittedly, there have been well-trained pastors who have abused their female members. However, they are fewer when compared to the Pentecostal prophets.

Fourth, apart from most male leaders of these charismatic ministries lacking adequate theological training, many female congregants themselves have not had any theological or academic training to instil in them their worth as women in church and society. This is also highlighted by Chimhanda (2003: 18) who argues that, for many centuries in the library of the church, women have been denied a place at the table of theological discourse. Thus, despite the influx of Pentecostalism, many women remain as followers of male prophets and pastors. They lack the capacity and charisma to start their own churches where they can lead their fellow women and thereby reduce the chances of instances of sexual and gender-based violence among ministry heads and their followers. Some few women pastors who have managed to rise to higher ranks have been reduced to be appendages of their husbands (Mapuranga 2013a). As such, these women too, according to Mate (2002), reinforce a Pentecostal discourse of femininity that tends to promote male dominance and female subordination, which, when misinterpreted, fuels sexual and gender-based violence.

Despite the fact that many women seek refuge in their Pentecostal churches, many have left these institutions in situations worse than where they started from, because of such reasons as highlighted. This does not discredit those instances where some genuine 'Men of God' have empowered their female congregants. In some instances, some women got empowered financially, where they have been taught the gospel of working hard and fending for their families (Proverbs 31). They joined Pentecostalism as poor and struggling women but have come to be 'virtuous women', 'women of valor' and 'precious stones', among other titles. This chapter appreciates such instances of women's empowerment. However, the concern comes with situations where women have been abused in the name of religion. Thus, where they joined their respective ministries as respectable, dignified and healthy women, some have returned as victims of sexual violence: tortured, raped and even infected with HIV and other sexually transmitted infections. According to Njoroge (2013: 23), 'sexual and gender-based violence has been identified as a major driver of HIV transmission and a barrier to HIV prevention, care support and treatment'. Some men have even divorced their wives after the discovery of their fate with the Men of God. Some have been accused of lying and have even lost their jobs. This is noted by Njoroge (2013: 22) who, with reference to the church at large, questions:

How many times have we heard stories of chaplains and theological educators, especially if they happen to be women, who report rape cases in our seminaries, and then are accused of lying, are silenced and sometimes even dismissed from their jobs?

All these are the ripple effects of sexual and gender-based violence on women in the church in general. For how long shall women continue to suffer in silence? With such abuse rife in the church, who shall pastor the pastors?

'Justice, not silence'[2]: The church in the struggle against sexual and gender-based violence

Theologians face a great challenge in curbing sexual and gender-based violence within the church. The church at large has widely been accused of silence which is 'in effect a death sentence and the church needs to be called to accountability' (Haddad 2003: 155). According to Chitando and Chirongoma (2013: 9), 'sexual and gender based violence … has emerged as one of the most demanding theological challenges of our time'. The church now needs to go beyond words and declarations. It is the time for the church to act. For Chitando and Chirongoma (2013: 10):

> Recognising the humanity of women goes beyond mere verbal articulation. It must be reflected in the churches' practices. It must be evident in the way that churches and theological institutions approach gender issues. It must be expressed in the churches' advocacy within the larger society.

Thus, the church should be silent no more but seek to be proactive in seeking justice for women within Pentecostalism. This is not to discredit some ministries in Zimbabwe that have been noted to be responding to the call against sexual and gender-based violence. Manyonganise (2013) and Biri (2013b) give examples of the United Family International Church and the Zimbabwe Assemblies of God, respectively. These Pentecostal churches have not remained silent in the face of sexual and gender-based violence. Instead, they have been actively involved in mobilizing church and society to address sexual and gender-based violence.

In terms of practical interventions, this chapter proposes that the absolute power and autonomy wielded by Pentecostal prophets be moderated in order to prevent the abuse of women. Thus, it is vital for the human dimension of the 'Men of God' to be emphasized. In other words, it is important to acknowledge that as flesh and blood human beings, they are susceptible to human vices, including the capacity to violate women. Therefore, the doctrine of the prophets being closer to God than other human beings must be challenged. This can be achieved through sustained campaigns by gender activists, including those from within the Pentecostal fold.

Second, there must be a process of training and awareness-raising on sexual and gender-based violence within the Pentecostal movement. As the church in Africa learnt from its engagement with HIV and AIDS, workshops that are well run are effective in changing attitudes. Therefore, there is need to invest in training Pentecostal prophets on sexual and gender-based violence, including on forms of expression, impact and prevention. All church members, including adolescents, must be targeted to ensure that there is a general appreciation of sexual and gender-based violence and how to prevent it.

Third, campaigns against sexual and gender-based violence that have been run by global ecumenical bodies such as the World Council of Churches need to reach Pentecostal churches as a matter of urgency. For example, the World Council of Churches' 'Thursdays in Black' campaign against sexual and gender-based violence is a powerful campaign that can change attitudes towards the violation of women in Pentecostal churches. Consequently, initiating and sustaining synergies between newer Pentecostal churches and older churches could be effective in minimizing sexual and gender-based violence.

Fourth, the empowerment of women (particularly through economic means and theological training) remains critical. I have already raised this point in the foregoing sections, but I will underscore it here yet again. When women are empowered economically, they become less vulnerable to the self-styled prophets. Furthermore, theological training equips women with the knowledge and skills to identify and largely prevent sexual and gender-based violence.

Conclusion

Pentecostalism is a double-edged sword in terms of women's empowerment and dignity with special reference to sexual and gender-based violence. While on the one hand some 'Men of God' have respected the dignity and worth of women, on the other hand there are those who have regarded women as sex objects. As I have demonstrated, such male religious leaders have sexually violated women in their churches. Though one could argue that there are a few bad apples, such instances have often caused some Pentecostal practices and practitioners to be treated with some suspicion. As the adage goes, 'one rotten apple spoils the barrel'. The fact that Pentecostal ethic renders women vulnerable must be critiqued as a matter of urgency. Furthermore, certain biblical interpretations should be reinterpreted to empower women against sexual and gender-based violence in their respective churches. Female followers in these Pentecostal ministries need to increase their levels of vigilance and note that the church is no longer a safe haven; they should no longer pray with both eyes closed. Furthermore, men in power must stop deploying theological ideas that enable them to capitalize on women's desperation. Male Pentecostal leaders in Zimbabwe must join men in other movements and across the world in taking a decisive stance against sexual and gender-based violence to enable women to enjoy life in abundance.

14

Lampooning prophetic Pentecostal Christianity in Zimbabwe: The case of Bustop TV

Ezra Chitando and Kelvin Chikonzo

Introduction

While prophetic Pentecostal Christianity (PPC) has been gaining momentum in Zimbabwe, especially in urban areas, its rise has not been without critique. The PPC movement has attracted considerable criticism over some perceived excesses. These include claims relating to faith healing, prophecies focusing on material prosperity (see the chapter by Musoni in this volume), the abuse of women (see the chapter by Mapuranga in this volume) and others. This chapter focuses on the use of drama to critique PPC in Zimbabwe. It focuses on one popular individual, 'Comic Pastor', and his group, Bustop TV, and analyses how they lampoon PPC. The first part of the chapter highlights the popularity of PPC in Harare, drawing attention to the contested dimensions. The second part of the chapter describes the critique of PPC by the Comic Pastor and Bustop TV. The third part analyses the strategies employed by the artists in their caricature of PPC. Four comic skits, namely *Vision* (2016), *New Miracle* (2017), *Kudenga kuna Mwari* (2016) and *Bus Stop Ministries* (2016), are analysed in this chapter. In conclusion, the chapter argues that the critique of PPC shows that its success has not been without contestation. Although the movement has captured the imagination of many, it has not escaped the critical eyes of actors.

Altering the religious map of Zimbabwe: The impact of prophetic Pentecostal Christianity and critical responses

Pentecostalism, a strand of Christianity that places emphasis on the visible manifestation of the Holy Spirit, having a personal experience of salvation and acknowledging the power of miracles in the contemporary period, has been part of the history of Zimbabwe. Older Pentecostal movements such as the Apostolic Faith Mission (Machingura 2011) and the Zimbabwe Assemblies of God Africa (ZAOGA) (Maxwell 2006) have been notable players on the country's spiritual market. If one adopts a broader definition of Pentecostalism to include African independent/indigenous/initiated or instituted churches (AICs) (Anderson 2013), then the impact of the phenomenon is even greater. However, with the emergence of the latest wave of PPC from the time of the Government of National Unity (GNU) or inclusive government (2009–2013) and the dollarization of the economy, Pentecostalism has assumed a higher profile.

Despite the popularity of Pentecostalism and its increasing profile, there have been a number of critical voices. These include the mainline Protestant churches and the Catholic Church. These churches claim to preserve 'proper' Christianity and regard PPC as an aberration. They are also feeling the impact of PPC by way of having fewer members, as PPC has attracted many of their members due to its dynamism and claims of deliverance. However, creative artists have also not been left behind in criticizing aspects of PPC. As we highlight below, they have drawn attention to some of the excesses of the movement, generating laughter in the process.

In a country going through severe economic challenges, comic offers a means of detonating loaded minds. The comic strips are, therefore, in demand, as an outlet of emotional anger (Anderson 1998: 2013). The emotional anger is on how the PPC leaders have presented themselves as holier than everyone else. They have assumed a prestigious position in Christian circles, yet they are portrayed as soiled by abominable crimes such as adultery, theft, murder. The comic strips become a way of revelation, giving light to congregants who think that they are following the Pentecostal light. The skits are a way of preaching intended to deliver the Pentecostal members, hypnotized by its discourse, out of that spiritual prison/bondage. The attack on Pentecostalism then becomes political, especially in a context where there are no attacks on other Christian denominations.

Background to Bustop TV and Comic Pastor

Established in 2014, Bustop TV is an online and youth-run television station that produces humorous videos and satirical skits that target mass audiences. The original name of this television station was PO BOX TV, whose original founders were Rolland Lunga (Boss Kedha), Admire Kuzhangaira (Bhutisi) and Lucky Aaaron. The trio split due to a misunderstanding. Lucky Aaron then engaged new faces, namely Prosper Ngomashi (Comic Pastor), Sharon Chideu (Maggie) and Samantha Kureya (Gonyeti.) They then changed the name to Bustop TV to avoid problems (Maguwu 2016). Bustop TV tackles topical current issues and probes lifestyles of prominent personalities in Zimbabwe in Shona and English and has a market threshold of 8000 viewers in Zimbabwe. Their mission is to afford Zimbabweans a platform to talk, discuss and laugh about issues of common interests in the country.

In an interview, Lucky Aaron told Maguwu (2016) that the name 'Bus Stop' came out of the realization that '[i]t is at the bus stop where people meet and you get to hear gossip as well. It is at the bus stop where people talk'. The emergence of this station, just like its contemporaries such as Zambezi News, Madam Boss and Bhanditi TV, has a direct connection with the idea of widening democratic spaces in a country characterized by rigid control of media platforms by the state. The 'bus stop' is therefore a public sphere and a liberated terrain where citizens use comedy to probe society about social and political ills that need attention. Bustop TV is, therefore, a grassroots rebellious platform that allows constructive engagement by means of humour. Because they seek to lambast and lampoon figures of authority, they cannot rely on mainstream media. The Zimbabwe Broadcasting Corporation (ZBC) does not tolerate dissenting voices. Furthermore, it does not have the money to pay for content. Bustop TV is, therefore, both an entrepreneurial and business enterprise that markets goods and services by means of humour. The social media platform enables Bustop TV to reach a different market with traceable patterns of consumption and viewership. Thus, corporates can quantify the advertising output of Bustop TV. They offer advertising services at cheaper rates than mainstream media owing to the relatively affordable technology of internet television production which Bustop TV uses. Furthermore, they offer customers direct, real-time and interactive exchanges with viewers.

The use of humour is a strategy of avoiding censorship, as this humorous branding allows the station to attack and mock authorities, however, without being seen as threats to the status quo. Humour allows Bustop TV to be sidelined as youthful jokes and as an activity of unemployed youth who are just whiling up their time in anticipation of serious jobs. This humorous branding makes them look unthreatening so much that some of the institutions that they mock actually give them business and are proud to be associated with Bustop TV. This development has made Bustop TV popular so much that the anchors of the station such as Gonyeti and Comic Pastor have become reputable Directors of Ceremonies and have presided over significant and important national and corporate functions in Zimbabwe.

The morphology of lampooning

A greater chunk of Bustop TV satirical skits mock and attack Pentecostalism. These attacks range from PPCs' methods of prayer, its inclination towards the gospel of prosperity, its sycophantic deification of pastors/prophets, and its claims to stupendous miracles and powers of healing. Although Pentecostalism is not new to Zimbabwe, in recent times there emerged Pentecostal churches that differed in approach from traditional Pentecostal churches such as the Apostolic Faith Mission, the Zimbabwe Assemblies of God Africa and the Family of God. These new Pentecostal denominations centred their practice on prosperity issues. The most notable of these include Emmanuel Makandiwa's United Family International Church, Walter Magaya's PHD Ministries and Uebert Angel's Spirit Embassy. Commenting on why he mocks Pentecostal churches, Prosper Ngomashi or Comic Pastor from Bustop TV remarks:

> *Dambudziko riripo nderekuti most pastors brag, nhau yekuti akangoita kamiracle one akutomhanya kumapaper, aphotoshoppa maphotos ake achiita kunge ari kudenga otoenda kumapaper.* I don't like it.
> (The reason is that most pastors brag about their miracle powers, they run to the media after performing any miracle, even when they photoshop photos of themselves in Heaven. I detest such actions.)

The relevance of the comic skits rests on their ability to relate to current issues in a particular society. Jokes must be fresh and popular. Pentecostal movements provide these incentives. Pentecostal churches clamour for attention. Their leaders perform miracles in public and comment on issues of national importance. They have an insatiable desire for popularity which is also Comic Pastor as he rides on the popularity of these movements. The advent of prophets who have been commanding their flock to perform unimaginable acts in honour of the prophets has made them quite popular and topical in Zimbabwean society. By dealing with a subject that is current and popular, Bustop TV and Comic Pastor ride on the wave of popularity which catapults them into popular sites that deal with contemporary popular culture in Zimbabwe. The Pentecostal subject markets the station and it, therefore, becomes a viable marketing strategy on the part of Bustop TV and Comic Pastor.

The million-dollar question is why and in what ways does Bustop TV use humour to attack Pentecostal churches in Zimbabwe? According to Obadare (2009), laughter/humour serves a variety of functions for the oppressed African subject – as 'vengeance', 'coping mechanism', a 'means of escape', 'subversion', not to mention as a means of 'resistance'. Veenhoven et al. (1997: 20) add that humour

> appears to be one of the most important means by which the majority define, 'get even with', and 'resist' the power elite and the dominant power relations. Humor is also vital to the way in which ordinary people endure social asperities, as well as negotiate, shape, and contest the public domain of critical deliberation.

Humour is ambivalent. On one level, the comic skits seem to be celebrating the trickster skills of the Pentecostal leaders in the same manner in which Hare's trickster motive is to celebrate in traditional folk tales. This is evident in a skit called 'Vision' where Tinashe approaches his pastor to inform him about the vision of 'Biti Money' which the Holy Spirit showed him during a fasting session in the mountains. The Comic Pastor listens and then interjects Tinashe by asking him rules about vision in his ministry. The Comic Pastor tells Tinashe that *'Vision dzese dzinotanga naMfundisi, saka vision yako iyoyo ndeyangu'* ('The pastor sees all spiritual visions before anyone, hence I own your vision'). The pastor then turns the tables against Tinashe and informs him that Tinashe was actually obscuring his prophetic and visionary powers by claiming to be a visionary. The Comic Pastor advises Tinashe to find a girlfriend who should entertain him rather than concentrating on making visions. However, the skit ends on a comical note with the Comic Pastor asking Tinashe to give him rights over the vision.

'Vision' ridicules the basis of prophetic powers by Pentecostal pastors. It reveals how prophesying is actually a collective effort which is, however, presented to congregants as the effort of an individual pastor with super powers. The spectator wonders why Tinashe submits to the Comic Pastor when he has more spiritual powers than the pastor. The skit reveals ironies of power inherent in Pentecostal pastoralism and questions unwarranted submission and vassalage of congregants to con artists masquerading as 'Men of God'. For this reason, the viewer laughs at the weaknesses of the victims of these churches. The skits reveal the victim as the one who is quite stupid and very ungodly as they fail to read the world beyond the church dogma. 'Vision' points out that the followers willingly allow leaders of Pentecostal churches to abuse them. 'Vision' reveals that it is the followers who have elevated ordinary church leaders into deities.

Consequently, when these human-made deities exploit their congregants, they are operating within the confines and purview of the power bestowed upon them by the congregants. The trickster approach is used in comic skits to point out the laughable elements of congregants' behaviour, which fuels abuse of power by Pentecostal leaders.

Yet in lampooning the congregants as victims of bad pastors, the comic skits reveal that the misfortunes of the congregants are laughable because they are human-made. By constructing the church as a human-made entity, the comic skits are demystifying and unmasking the myth and mask of Godliness and the Holy Spirit which the Pentecostal churches use to undermine resistance and reasoning among their followers. For example, in 'Bus Stop Ministries', the Comic Pastor creates his own Pentecostal ministry. He then claims that he has healing and deliverance powers. In this skit, the Comic Pastor invites John (Cde Fatso), a white man, to give a testimony about how he received a miracle that transformed him from being black to white. In his 'testimony', John says he comes from Muzarabani (rural Zimbabwe) where he was born Fatso. John says he was born with a very dark complexion like people from Uganda such that his peers nicknamed him Matsito (charcoal). But after 'deliverance and healing' from the Comic Pastor, he is now so white that he cannot even speak any Shona. He 'confesses' that he saved a lot of money from going for plastic surgery or using dangerous chemicals to bleach his skin and fulfil his desire to be a white person. The idea of a black person undergoing a miracle in order to become white is preposterous. Thus, in 'Bus Stop Ministries', Bustop TV uses irony to satirize and question the healing powers of Pentecostal pastors. They reveal miracles as stage-managed so much that one who believes in them ought to be very naive. The skit interrogates why congregants believe in testimonies rather than seeing the actual miracle in action. Thus, the skit suggests abuse of faith in Pentecostal churches.

Pentecostal leaders claim to be operating under the guidance of the Holy Spirit when they lead their followers. They claim that they are the only ones who speak with God and, owing to that, they cannot be questioned. In '*Kudenga Kuna Mwari*' (There Is God in Heaven) a junior pastor (played by Doc Vikela) visits the Comic Pastor's wife where he tells her about his recent visit to heaven. The junior pastor is wearing very short cargo pants which reveal his thighs suggesting that apart from desiring to tell the pastor's wife about his mission to heaven, he also has other earthly desires with the pastor's wife. The junior pastor narrates what he saw in heaven and then he concludes his narrative expressing his shock at seeing Judas Iscariot in heaven when all along he thought, like everyone, that Judas is in hell since he betrayed Jesus. The junior pastor is in this instance quite blasphemous as he also claims that he saw God who happens to be an old man who does not want to leave the throne as is the norm with old people in Zimbabwe who do not want to vacate leadership posts. The Comic Pastor's wife realizes that the testimony borders on insanity, so she tells the junior pastor that '*Maragado uite mashoma*' (Reduce your dosage of drugs). In laughing at the activities of the church, the comic skit attacks the core of Pentecostal authority as they reveal these leaders to be ordinary people who command their flock to execute tasks that are ungodly. The comic skits use humour to hit back at 'the anointed', whom they perceive as an enemy/misfit who is tearing apart the respectability of the church as a moral institution. Because the anointed are untouchable in real life, comic skits make them touchable in the world of humour where the comedians gain the power to invent these esteemed figures in their own imaginations. Lawrence Levine advances that 'the need to laugh at our enemies, our situation, ourselves, is a common one, but it often exists the most urgently in those who exert the least power over their immediate environment; in those who have the most objective reasons for feelings of hopelessness' (cited by Gilbert 1997: 325). Obadare (2009: 243) cites Mbembe and Roitman reinforcing the same idea that comics

> aim to travesty, avenge, scare the evil spirits and appease them or to exercise reprisals on 'the signs of the thing' that cannot be overcome otherwise. As rites of expiation, laughter and derision give way to an imaginary well-being; they allow for distance between the subject who laughs and the object of mockery. The division thus realized is precisely what permits the laughing subject to regain possession of self and to wear the mask, that is, to become a stranger to this 'thing' that exercises domination – and then to deride torture, murder, and all other forms of wretchedness.

In this process of hitting back against Pentecostal leaders, their followers are then reminded that this situation and predicament can be reversed; it is a mere construction and, therefore, can be undone. By removing the veil of supernaturalness by which the pastors invent themselves, the church skits sensitise followers to the dangers of organized religion and the dangers of uncritical and blinkered worship. They present the ills inherent in Pentecostal movements with the idea of initiating discussion and engagement with these ills. They reveal a problem and leave the viewer with a suggestion: do something about this. The comic skits eliminate and interrogate the notions of fate and blind faith because the plight of the followers is revealed as not God given and hence it is changeable. In revealing the trickery and cunningness of the pastors, the comic skits attack the very establishment of Pentecostal image, where leaders of faith are ordained by God.

It is critical to note that the comic skits possess the ability to say sensitive and emotional issues in a manner which does not deepen the gravity of the issues. This is illustrated by the skit, *New Miracle*. In this skit, the Comic Pastor goes on a holiday with friends, spending the congregants' money. He comes back broke and asks his wife about the state of church funds. The wife responds that '*Vanhu vari kubvisa chegumi kunge vakaita kubhejerwa zvekuti ndatofa necash*' (The congregants are paying their tithes as if they are possessed/have bets placed on them. I am loaded with cash). The pastor is delighted to know that church coffers have been replenished through congregants' tithes. He then asks whether the salaries of church employees have been paid. He is not amused to learn that the praise and worship guys, band members, plus the people responsible for writing sermons have not yet been paid. The skit discusses a sensitive issue regarding the fate of church funds. It opens reflections on the contentious issue of these church entities as purely business adventures rather than spaces for spiritual replenishment. In fact, the Comic Pastor urges his wife to use a money transfer system which is a better way of taking money from congregants than anointed oil. These are very sensitive issues that are, however, openly discussed owing to the power of humour.

New Miracle deploys post-dramatic performance techniques which dismantle empathy and identification with characters and actors, as well as the situation which they are presenting. This is done to dilute the depth of realism in the skit so much that it appears just as a humorous and rushed piece of work rather than a serious video that demands emotional and psychological attachment. The character of the Comic Pastor, apart from being volcanic and tricksterish, is not defined or integral so much that it prevents identification with the character being played or the issues being raised by the skits. Prosper Ngomashi plays his character of Comic Pastor with great mischief, complemented by laughter-provoking gestures, body images, costumes and vocalizations that fragment psychological acting and its consequential oppressive spectatorship and identification. Pieter J. Fourie (1988: 79) observes that

> [i]n simplistic terms, identification is the human ability to pick up another person's vibes, to empathise with others. Such feeling is based on shared values, a common background, education, culture and the like, in fact, anything that makes intersubjective fellowship possible.

Identification operates through empathy, which Boal (1985: 102) defines as

[t]he emotional relationship between the character and the spectator and which provokes, fundamentally, a delegation of power on the part of the spectator, who becomes an object in relation to the character: whatever happens to the latter happens vicariously to the spectator.

The spectator, according to Boal, becomes a victim of character so much that he/she attaches him-/herself emotionally to the character. The spectator identifies with a character so much that he/she abides by its decisions and experiences. The Comic Pastor, by virtue of playing a comical character, has a way of disintegrating the dramatic character so much that the viewer is reminded that what they are watching is a piece of drama, not reality. Sometimes, the Comic Pastor deliberately looks into the camera, thereby disrupting the fourth wall through which television realism acquires its depth of reality.

Another dynamic character, Gonyeti's acting, just like all the characters, violates the dictates of method acting or psychological realism where the actor totally becomes the character and conveys the emotions of the character in an emotional way. Gonyeti does not get into character; she remains a half actor who does not forget herself. She does not convey emotions and the skits, by virtue of being short, do not provide an emotional journey to their audiences. Her voice is highly stylized; her dialogue is pedestrian and ordinary. It is nowhere near proper dramatic and realist dialogue. She does not act to convey emotions; rather she simply acts to present a situation and she clearly reminds the spectator that she is acting. Even when she attempts to be serious, she retains humorous features on her face and she will be on the brink of laughing. She laughs at what she is acting; she laughs at the predicaments of her character and indeed other characters in the skits. This style of acting disintegrates depth of realism so much that even if the issues that she raises are sensitive, her acting dismantles any sense of attachment to these roles on the part of the spectator.

The narrative structure of the skits is organized in such a way that they fragment the normative construction of a story from the perspective of an oedipal/dramatic text. Normally, a story follows stages of linear progression characterized by exposition, inciting incident, rising action, climax and falling action/denouement. The skits violate this narrative structure as they begin and end abruptly. The skits are of short duration so much that the actors concentrate on presenting the joke in a small scene rather than develop a scene or scenes with well-constructed levels of conflict, plot mechanisms and super objectives for the characters. This disruption is augmented by the fact that, apart from being short, the skits are episodic so much that each skit is a stand-alone entity. There are no sequels or a well-defined thread in terms of linear progression that makes the skits become scenes of one entity, as in soapies. Although the skits usually have the same actors, the situations they present are so diverse and loosely connected that what really binds them together is the fact they are just Bustop TV programmes. Such production aesthetics heighten the humorous effect of the skits as they disintegrate identification of any sort with either the characters or the themes of the skits.

When new actors are introduced in some skits, there is a careful audition system that selects actors on the basis of their well-known prowess in acting for comedy-related genres. For example, actors such as Doc Vikela, Amai Titie, Cde Fatso, Dereck Nziyakwi and Madam Boss have a well-known track record as comical performers. When they appear in any skit, the spectator is mesmerized by Bustop TV's ability to assemble such stars together in a comical skit. The comical value attached owing to their interaction with them as Director of Ceremonies at various events reinforces in the spectator the idea that 'these are just a bunch of comedians, don't take them seriously'. It is, however, worth noting that although these comical elements do not make people angry, they also have a tendency to make people not to seriously value issues that these skits raise. There is a great danger that people laugh and move on, rather than engage. There is also a danger that since the issues are being delivered by laughable elements in society, they are not real. They can dangerously be viewed as mere constructions by attention-seeking drama queens and kings. It is, however, at this point that comedy/humour becomes so ambivalent that its consumers and even the ridiculed institutions do not know exactly how to respond to the work of Bustop TV. Wilson (2008: 41) points out the complexity of this ambivalence:

> When there is a gap between *verifiable facts* and *statements of fact* made by the narrator, we have a true unreliable narrator. When there is a gap between the *interpretation of facts* by the narrator via her/his story and the interpretation attributed to the implied author, we call this a discordant narrator .... Comics can be both and these distinctions (between stated and known facts and between stated and held interpretations) cause problems for rhetorical evaluation. Yet, because any narrator is always prone to unreliability, always capable of interjecting discord, we never have to believe what they say. It is this very condition that creates a space for the comic author to say whatever s/he chooses.

This ambivalence gives Bustop TV the licence to do as they please. Their strategies make them impervious to counter actions of any type.

The elimination of emotional orgies is important because it keeps the spectator in the critical frame of mind. The spectator focuses on the situation because the situations are presented in a manner that is devoid of attachment. When the situation seems as if it is about to get emotional, the skit ends to ensure that the build-up of emotions is curtailed. When the viewer becomes engaged by the skit, the skit ends. The skits always end humorously, thereby dismantling negative energies they may have generated. The comic skit, therefore, encourages critical reason because it eliminates emotions during its presentation, which enables the viewer to be critical of the Pentecostal churches. Martin Esslin (1959: 127) advances that

> [b]y keeping the (viewer) in a critical frame of mind it prevents him from seeing the conflict entirely from the view of the characters involved in it and from accepting their passions and motives as being conditioned by 'eternal human nature.' Such a theatre will make the audience see the contradictions in the existing state of society; it might even make them ask themselves how it might be changed.

The comic skits then pose a question to the viewer: 'are you aware that this is happening in Zimbabwe? Now that you know, what are you going to do about it?' They simply present a problem and laugh about it without taking sides or prescribing a course of action. Post-dramatic acting, according to Wright (2007: 83), entails a process of de-representation which 'maintains a specific level of presentation, yet deliberately eschews a clear reading in order to create a fluctuating multiplicity of interpretations'.

The skits are open-ended: they do not take a position about the issues they generate so much that the viewer is left neither happy nor angry, but he/she laughs at the absurdity of the human conditions espoused by the skits. This tactic is critical as a strategy of evading backlash from the concerned authorities. When journalists write stories about these leaders they are accused of taking sides, of being paid in order to tarnish the images of the 'Men of God' because newspapers are factual; they talk about the names of leaders and the day where a particular event transpired. In comparison, Bustop TV's skits do not use names of churches or of individuals. They simply portray a situation or occurrence (see also Freud 1976).

Their lack of clarity became their way of out-manoeuvring the censorship of followers of these leaders. They cannot be held accountable for defamation, yet what they present is not imaginary; it is based on real events. Gilbert (1997: 319) notes that in comic skits, there is humorous discourse that reminds the audience not to take it (or themselves) seriously with every punchline. Indeed, humor is a rhetoric unique in its ability to undermine its own power with the 'only joking' disclaimer.

In this vein, the comic skits present themselves as mere jokes, artistic constructions by some loafers who own a company which specializes in producing comedy. They are not to be taken seriously since they are just some stupid humour just to make people laugh. The comic strategy is, therefore, critical in undermining legal backlash by Pentecostal leaders or their followers. The comic strips present themselves just as mere jokes that people can watch just to get by and forget the hardships prevailing in Zimbabwe. Bustop TV and the Comic Pastor reveal their work as some stupid jokes. Yet in being 'stupid and not so serious', the Comic Pastor and Bustop TV get the poetic licence to make serious comments on the churches, while pretending to be non-subversive. This is clearly a strategy of avoiding trouble with the politically connected Pentecostal movement in Zimbabwe. Moreover, the sketches do not point out any specific church; neither do they point out any specific scenario or event that has happened. Bustop TV and the Comic Pastor do not claim to base their work on real-life stories or events. Rather, the sketches remain fictitious so much that it is difficult for any leader or movement to press charges on the Comic Pastor. There are no laws that incriminate joking, especially on issues where no specific names of individuals, places or organizations are used. Humour then becomes a way of talking about things that many people would not openly talk about. It is also a way of evading any legal action from those that are criticized.

The mode of presentation on social media is also quite important because, apart from relying on humour to evade censorship and legal backlash, they rely on social media which cannot be censored locally. They do not need to negotiate with any broadcaster to be aired; they do not need any large sums of capital to be on air. Their skits are accessible to millions of viewers, yet they are not capital-intensive in terms of production costs. Social media gives these emerging media houses the means to speak to power as and when they wish. This level of independence and media freedom enables Bustop TV and the Comic Pastor to proffer an alternative understanding of Pentecostalism. They are a subaltern critique of Pentecostal practice. They represent the voice of the youth who wish to critique social ills of society. It is this branding which generates interest in their initiatives in a country where rights to broadcast are tightly controlled by the state.

Conclusion

This chapter has analysed how Bustop TV, which is an online television station, uses humour as a strategy of lampooning what they believe is wayward behaviour by some prophets, pastors and congregants of emerging Pentecostal churches in Zimbabwe. The chapter has revealed how ridicule, satire and irony serve as techniques of humour which serve different functions. Borrowing from Afrocentric approaches to humour and psychological theorizations on humour, the chapter has unpacked the contextual and efficacy issues that inform the turn towards humour as a strategy of ridicule. The chapter has argued that humour enables Bustop TV to evade censorship and backlash through the manner in which Bustop TV humorously brands itself. Whereas competition has forced newer Pentecostal churches to resort to extreme forms of creativity and innovation, artists such as those who are behind caricatures of the prophets challenge them through the strategy of ridicule.

Notes

Chapter 2

1. A practice usually done at the Apostolic Faith Mission in Zimbabwe (AFM) where newly born babies are symbolically given to the church in order to be guided and protected from harm throughout their lives.
2. The extended family is considered the core of the African family system.
3. In the form of prayers, anointed oils, anointed cloths and a variety of other anointed material, including bricks, are generally sold at high prices.
4. The authors are yet to come across anyone with a sticker on their car declaring them to be proudly ATR.

Chapter 3

1. Within Christianity, Pentecostals have the highest growth rates per year. According to Barrett et al. (2001: 19–21), annual growth rates among Christians are as follows: Pentecostals (8.1 per cent), Evangelicals (5.4 per cent), All Protestants (3.3 per cent) and Roman Catholics and Others (1.3 per cent).
2. Millenarianism is the belief that Christ's return to earth is imminent, and that when he does return there will exist a thousand years during which holiness will prevail and Christ will reign on earth (Chalfant et al. 1981: 231).

Chapter 11

1. It is reiterated in ZAOGA that Guti refused money and buses that the white men offered him when he was in America (see History of ZAOGA). This has been interpreted to mean that Guti is not after material things but to serve people.
2. The study agrees with the views of Obvious Vengeyi. Vengeyi is a biblical studies scholar at the University of Zimbabwe who has always argued that in spite of the 'noise' that people make in dismissing Pentecostal teachings on miracles, prosperity and healing, one cannot even cite a verse from the Bible to disprove them because there is nothing new and outside the Bible that the Pentecostal miracle workers do.

Chapter 12

1 Passing a verdict on this dimension of the NMPCs does not suggest evaluating their overall impact.
2 The proper term should have been '*kudenga*', but the missionary mispronounced it as '*kudhenga*'. Referring to indigenous believers as '*ngaitambure*' (let it suffer) was also condescending.

Chapter 13

1 The listing of these prominent prophets in this chapter is not in any way linking them to the theme of this chapter, namely the abuse of women. It is only to draw attention to their popularity.
2 This title is taken from *Justice Not Silence: Churches Facing Sexual and Gender Based Violence,* edited by Ezra Chitando and Sophia Chirongoma (eds.), Stellenbosch: EFSA, Sun Press, 2013.

References

Achunike, H. 2004. *The Influence of Pentecostalism on Catholic Priests and Seminarians in Nigeria*. Onitsha: Africanan First Publishers.

Adogame, A. 2004. 'Engaging the Rhetoric of Spiritual Warfare: The Public Face of Aladura in Diaspora', *Journal of Religion in Africa* 34, 494–522.

Adogame, A. 2012. 'Dealing with Local Technology: Deliverance Rhetoric in the Mountain of Fire and Miracles Ministries', *Journal of World Christianity* 5(1), 75–101.

Adogame, A. 2013. *The African Christian Diaspora: New Currents and Emerging Trends in World Christianity*. London: Bloomsbury.

Afolayan, A., O. Yacob-Haliso and T. Falola. (eds.). 2018. *Pentecostalism and Politics in Africa*. Cham, Switzerland: Palgrave Macmillan.

Amanze, J. 2014. 'Conflict and Cooperation: The Interplay between Christianity and African Traditional Religions in the Nineteenth and Twentieth Centuries', in C. N. Omenyo and E. B. Anum (eds.), *Trajectories of Religion in Africa: Essays in Honour of John S. Pobee*. New York: Rodopi, 281–313.

Anderson, A. 2002. 'The Newer Pentecostal and Charismatic Churches: The Shape of Future of Christianity in Africa?', *Pneuma: The Journal of the Society for Pentecostal Studies* 24(2), 167–84.

Anderson, A. 2004. *An Introduction to Pentecostalism*. Cambridge: University of Cambridge Press.

Anderson, A. H. 2013. *To the Ends of the Earth: Pentecostalism and the Transformation of World Christianity*. New York: Oxford University Press.

Asamoah-Gyadu, J. K. 2010. 'Pentecostalism in Africa', in D. B. Stinton (ed.), *African Theology on the Way: Current Conversations*. London: SPCK, 56–67.

Asamoah-Gyadu, J. K. 2015. *Sighs and Signs of the Spirit: Ghanaian Perspectives on Pentecostalism and Renewal in Africa*. Oxford: Regnum Books International.

Asamoah-Gyadu, A. J. K. 2007. '"Born of Water and the Spirit": Pentecostal/Charismatic Christianity in Africa', in O. U. Kalu (ed.), *African Christianity: An African Story*. New Jersey: Africa World Press, 339–58.

Atkinson, D. J. and D. H. Field. (ed.). 1995. *The New Dictionary of Ethics and Pastoral Care*. Leicester: Inter-Varsity Press.

Attanasi, K. 2012. 'Introduction: The Plurality of Prosperity Theologies and Pentecostalism', in K. Attanasi and A. Yong (eds.), *Pentecostalism and Prosperity: The Socio-Economies of the Global Charismatic Movement*. New York: Palgrave Macmillan, 1–12.

Attanasi, K. and A. Yong. (eds.). 2012. *Pentecostalism and Prosperity: The Socio-Economics of the Global Charismatic Movement*. New York: New York: Palgrave Macmillan.

Baffour, A. K. 2018. 'Healing and Deliverance in Pentecostal and Charismatic Christianity in Ghana', *Journal of Applied Thought* 6(1), 268–81.

Bakare, S. 2007. *Drumbeat of Life*. Geneva: World Council of Churches.

Banda, C. 2018a. 'Not Anointing, but Justice? A Critical Reflection on the Anointing of Pentecostal Prophets in a Context of Economic Injustice', *Verbum et Ecclesia* 39(1), a1870. https://doi.org/10.4102/ve.v39i1.1870

Banda, C. 2018b. 'Complementing Christ? A Soteriological Evaluation of the Anointed Objects of the African Pentecostal Prophets', *The Journal of the South African Theological Seminary* 12(1), 55–69.

Bankston, C. 2002. 'Rationality, Choice and Religious Economy: The Problem of Belief', *Review of Religious Research* 43(4), 311–25.

Barrett, D. B., G. T. Kurian and T. M. Johnson. 2001. *World Christian Encyclopedia: A Comparative Survey of Churches and Religions in the Modern World, Vol 1*. New York: Oxford.

Bateye, B. O. 2008. 'Paradigmatic Shift: Reconstruction of Female Leadership Roles in the New Generation Churches in South-Western Nigeria', in A. Adogame, R. Gerloff and K. Hock (eds.), *Christianity in Africa and the Diaspora: The Appropriation of a Scattered Heritage*. London: Continuum, 113–25.

Bepete, L. and M. Gagare. 2015. 'Magaya Disappoints Hundreds of Followers', *The Chronicle*. 1 April.

Berger, P. 1990. 'Social Sources of Secularization', in J. C. Alexander and S. Seidman (eds.), *Culture and Society: Contemporary Debates*. Cambridge: Cambridge University Press, 229–48.

Biri, K. 2012. 'The Silent Echoing Voice: Aspects of Zimbabwean Pentecostalism and the Quest for Power, Healing and Miracles', *Studia Historiae Ecclesiasticae* 38 (Supplement), 37–55.

Biri, K. 2013a. 'African Pentecostalism and Cultural Resilience: Zimbabwe Assemblies of God Africa', Unpublished DPhil, Department of Religious Studies, Classics and Philosophy, University of Zimbabwe.

Biri, K. 2013b. 'The Response of the Zimbabwe Assemblies of God Africa (ZAOGA) to Gender-Based Violence: An Analysis', in E. Chitando and S. Chirongoma (eds.), *Justice Not Silence: Churches Facing Sexual and Gender Based Violence*. Stellenbosch: EFSA, 157–68.

Biri, K. 2013c. 'Religion and Politics in Post-Colonial Zimbabwe: A Comparative Analysis of Robert Mugabe and Ezekiel Guti Leadership Styles', in E. Chitando (ed.), *Prayers and Players: Religion and Politics*. Harare: SAPES, 111–24.

Biri, K. 2014. 'Migration, Transnationalism and the Shaping of Zimbabwean Pentecostal Spirituality', *African Diaspora* 7, 139–64.

Biri, K. and L. Togarasei. 2013. '"… but the One Who Prophesies, Builds the Church": Nation Building and Transformation Discourse as True Prophecy: The Case of Zimbabwean Pentecostal Women', in E. Chitando, M. R. Gunda and J. Kügler (eds.), *Prophets, Profits and the Bible in Zimbabwe: Festschrift for Aynos Masocha Moyo*. BiAS. Bamberg: University of Bamberg Press, 79–94.

Boal, A. 1979. *Theatre of the Oppressed*. London: Pluto Press.
Boal, A. 1985. *Theatre of the Oppressed*. New York: Theatre Communications Group.
Bond, P. and M. Manyanya. 2002. *Zimbabwe's Plunge: Exhausted Nationalism, Neoliberalism and the Search for Social Justice*. Harare: Weaver Press.
Bourdillon, M. F. C. 1986. *The Shona Peoples: An Ethnography of the Contemporary Shona, with Special Reference to Their Religion*. Gweru: Mambo Press.
Bourdillon, M. F. C. 1993. *Where Are the Ancestors: Changing Culture in Zimbabwe*. Harare: University of Zimbabwe Publications.
Brooks, S. 2013. *Where Are the Mantles?* Maitland, FL: Xulon Press.
Bruce, S. 2002. *God Is Dead: Secularization in the West (Religion and Spirituality in the Modern World)*. Oxford: Blackwell.
Chalfant, H., R. Beckley and C. Palmer. 1981. *Religion in Contemporary Society*. California: Alfred.
Chaves, M. and D. E. Cann. 1992. 'Regulation, Pluralism, and Religious Market Structure: Explaining Religion's Vitality', *Rationality and Society* 4(3), 272–90.
Chavunduka, G. 1978. *Traditional Healers and the Shona Patient*. Gweru: Mambo Press.
Chaya, V. 2015. 'Macheso Performs at Magaya's PHD', *Daily News*. 4 May.
Chese, S. 2014. 'Magaya Donates 18K to Xaba', *The Herald*, 7 October.
Chesnut, A. 2007. 'Specialised Spirits: Conversion and the Products of Pneumacentric Religion in Latin America's Free Market of Faith', in T. J. Steigenga and E. E. Cleary (eds.), *Conversion of a Continent: Contemporary Religious Change in Latin America*. New Brunswick: Rutgers University Press, 72–92.
Chesnut, R. A. 2003. *Competitive Spirits: Latin America's New Religious Economy*. Cary, USA: Oxford University Press.
Chibango, C. 2016. 'Prosperity Gospel, a Pathway out of a Socio-Economic Crisis? The Case of the PHD Ministries of Walter Magaya, Zimbabwe', *Modern Research Studies* 3(1), 55–82.
Chikafa-Chipiro, R. 2016. 'Discoursing Women, Christianity and Security: The Framing of Women in the Gumbura Case in Zimbabwean Media', *Agenda* 30(3), 60–9.
Chimhanda, F. H. 2003. 'The Word Became Flesh: A Shona Women's Christology', *Mukai-Vukani* 24, 16–20.
Chingono, N. 2014. 'Walter Magaya Calls for Calm', *Daily News*, 23 November.
Chiroro, P., A. Mashu and W. Muhwava. 2002. *The Zimbabwean Male Psyche with Special Reference to Reproductive Health, HIV, AIDS and Gender Issues*. Harare: University of Zimbabwe Publications.
Chitando, E. 2007. 'A New Man for a New Era: Zimbabwean Pentecostalism, Masculinities and HIV', *Missionalia* 35(3) 2007, 112–27.
Chitando, E. 2012. 'Religion and Masculinities in Africa: Their Impact on HIV and Gender Based Violence', in J. J. Hendriks et al. (ed.), *Men in the Pulpit, Women in the Pew? Addressing Gender Inequality in Africa*. Stellenbosch: EFSA, Sun Press, 71–84.
Chitando, E. 2013. 'Prophets, Profits and Protests: Prosperity Theology and Zimbabwean Gospel Music', in E. Chitando, M. R. Gunda and J. Kugler (eds.), *Prophets, Profits and the Bible in Zimbabwe*. Bamberg: University of Bamberg Press, 95–112.

Chitando, E. 2018. 'The Religions of Zimbabwe in Their Plurality', in L. Togarasei (ed.), *Aspects of Pentecostal Christianity in Zimbabwe*. Cham, Switzerland: Springer, 15–32.

Chitando, E. and K. Biri. 2016. 'Walter Magaya's Prophetic Healing and Deliverance (PHD) Ministries and Pentecostalism in Zimbabwe: A Preliminary Study with Particular Reference to Ecumenism', *Studia Historiae Ecclesiasticae* 42(2), 72–85.

Chitando, E. and S. Chirongoma. 2013. 'Introduction', in E. Chitando and S. Chirongoma (eds.), *Justice Not Silence: Churches Facing Sexual and Gender Based Violence*. Stellenbosch: EFSA, 9–14.

Chitando, E. and S. M. Kilonzo. 2018. 'Towards a "Proverbs 31 Man?" Pentecostalism and the Reconstruction of Masculinities in Kenya', *Journal of Gender and Religion in Africa* 24(1), 60–78.

Chitando, E. and C. Klagba. (eds.). 2013. *In the Name of Jesus: Healing in the Age of HIV*. Geneva: World Council of Churches.

Chitando, E., M. Manyonganise and B. Mlambo. 2013a. 'Young, Male and Polished: Masculinities, Generational Shifts and Pentecostal Prophets in Zimbabwe', in E. Chitando, M. R. Gunda and J. Kügler (eds.), *Prophets, Profits and the Bible in Zimbabwe*. Bamberg: University of Bamberg Press, 153–70.

Chitando, E., M. R. Gunda and J. Kugler. 2013b. 'Introduction: Back to the Future! A Reader on the Bible, Prophets and Profits in Zimbabwe', in E. Chitando, M. R. Gunda and J. Kugler (eds.), *Prophets, Profits and the Bible in Zimbabwe*. Bamberg: University of Bamberg Press, 9–13.

Chitando, E., M. R. Gunda and J. Kügler. (eds.). 2013c. *Prophets, Profits and the Bible in Zimbabwe: Festschrift for Aynos Masocha Moyo*. BiAS. Bamberg: University of Bamberg Press.

Chitemba, B. 2016. 'Makandiwa's Mysterious Tale'. *The Sunday Mail, Religion*, 28 August, 2.

Chiwara, A. and N. T. Taringa. 2010. 'Phenomenology of Religion'. Harare: Zimbabwe Open University.

The Chronicle. 2015. 'Magaya Followers Flood Botswana', 1 July.

Comstock, W. R. 1984. 'Toward Open Definitions of Religion', *Journal of the American Academy of Religion* 52(3), 499–518.

Connell, R. 1995. *Masculinities*. California: University of California Press.

Connell, R. W. 1995. *Masculinities*. Cambridge: Polity Press (2nd edition, 2005).

Corner, M. 2005. *Signs of God: Miracles and Their Interpretation*. Hampshire: Ashgate.

Counted, V. 2012. 'Youth in Pentecostal and Charismatic Churches and Factors Accounting for Their Attraction to Pentecostalism', Nigerian Pentecostal Charismatic Research Conference.

Cox, H. 1996. *Fire from Heaven: The Rise of Pentecostal Spirituality and Reshaping of Religion in the Twenty-First Century*. Reading, Mass: Addison.

Cox, J. L. 1993. *Changing Beliefs and an Enduring Faith: A Reformulation of Christian Beliefs in Response to Five Major Obstacles for Faith*. Gweru: Mambo Press.

Cox, J. L. 1996. *Expressing the Sacred: An Introduction to the Phenomenology of Religion*. Harare: University of Zimbabwe Publications.

Daily News. 6 November 2014. Harare.
Daneel, M. L. 1970. *Zionism and Faith – Healing in Rhodesia: Aspects of African Independent Churches.* Mouton: The Hague.
Dayton, D. W. 1987. *Theological Roots of Pentecostalism.* Michigan: Zondervan.
Deena, F. (ed.). 2012. *Pentecostalism and Development: Churches, NGOs and Social Change in Africa.* Basingstoke: Palgrave Macmillan.
Deuschle, T. 2003. *How a Church Can Change the Nation: Building People, Building Dreams.* Wheaton: Tyndale Publishers.
Diara, B. C. D. and G. Onah. 2014. 'The Phenomenal Growth of Pentecostalism in the Contemporary Nigerian Society: A Challenge to Mainline Churches', *Mediterranean Journal of Social Sciences* 5(6), 395–402.
Droogers, A. 2005. 'Pentecostalism', in J. de Santa Ana (ed.), *Religions Today: Their Challenge to the Ecumenical Movement.* Geneva: World Council of Churches, 258–70.
Dube, E. E. N. 2019. 'Desperation in an Attempt to Curb Modern-Day Prophets: Pentecostalisation and the Church in South Africa and Zimbabwe', *Conspectus: The Journal of the South African Theological Seminary* 27, 25–34.
Dube, Z. 2015. 'Jesus and Afro-Pentecostal Prophets: Dynamics within the Liminal Space in Galilee and in Zimbabwe', *HTS Teologiese Studies/Theological Studies* 71(1), Art. #2748, 6 pages. http://dx.doi.org/10.4102/hts.v71i1.2748
Dunn, J. D. G. 1990. *Unity in Diversity in the New Testament.* London: SCM Press.
Einstein, M. 2008. *Brands of Faith: Marketing Religion in a Commercial Age.* London: Routledge.
Elphick, R. 1997. 'The Benevolent Empire and the Social Gospel: Missionaries and South African Christians in the Age of Segregation', in R. Elphick and R. Davenport (eds.), *Christianity in South Africa: A Political, Social and Cultural history.* Cape Town: David Phillip, 347–69.
Esslin, M. 1959. *Brecht: A Choice of Evils, a Critical Study of the Man, His Work and Opinions.* London: Heinemann.
eTV. 2010. 'Faith Healing Advertorial Fatal: *South African Medical Journal SAMJ-S* Afrmed.j.vol.100n.10', Cape Town.
Fourie, P. J. 1988. *Aspects of Film and Television Communication.* Kenwyn: Juta and Co. Ltd.
Fenga, V. F. 2018. 'Prophetic Preaching in Neo-Pentecostal Christianity during the Socioeconomic and Socio-political Crisis of Zimbabwe (2000–2012): A Practical Theological Exploration'. Unpublished PhD thesis, Practical Theology, University of Pretoria, South Africa.
Freeman, D. (ed.). 2012. *Pentecostalism and Development: Churches, NGOs and Social Change in Africa.* Basingstoke: Palgrave Macmillan.
Freud, S. 1976. *Jokes and Their Relation to the Unconscious.* London: Routledge.
Gabaitse, R. M. 2015. 'Pentecostal Hermeneutics and the Marginalisation of Women', *Scriptura* 114(1), 1–12.
Gadzikwa, W. 2020. '"Wolves in Sheep's Clothing"? Mugabe and the Media Agenda on the Prosperity Gospel', in E. Chitando (ed.), *Politics and Religion: The Deification of Robert Mugabe.* London: Routledge, 126–38.

Gaidzanwa, R. B. 2015. 'Grappling with Mugabe's Masculinist Politics in Zimbabwe: A Gender Perspective', in S. J. Ndlovu-Gatsheni (ed.), *Mugabeism? History, Politics and Power in Zimbabwe*. New York: Palgrave Macmillan, 157–79.

Gauthier, F. and T. Martikainen. (eds.). 2013. *Religion in Consumer Society: Brands, Consumers and Markets*. Burlington, VT: Ashgate.

Gelfand, M. et al. 1985. *The Traditional Medical Practitioner*. Gweru: Mambo Press.

Gewald, J.-B., A. Leliveld and I. Peša. 2012. 'Introduction: Transforming Innovations in Africa; Explorative Studies on Appropriation in African Societies', in J.-B. Gewald, A. Leliveld and I. Peša (eds.), *Transforming Innovations in Africa: Explorative Studies on Appropriation in African Societies*. Leiden: Brill, 1–15.

Gibson, T. 2003. 'Prophet vs. Politician: Evaluating the Role of Charismatic Leadership in the Promotion of Political Stability', Unpublished paper, Kentucky Political Science Association's Annual Meeting.

Gifford, P. 1990. 'Prosperity: A New and Foreign Element in African Christianity', *Religion* 20(4), 373–88.

Gifford, P. 2004. *Ghana's New Christianity: Pentecostalism in a Globalising African Economy*. Bloomington: Indiana University Press.

Gilbert, J. 1997. 'Performing Marginality: Comedy, Identity and Cultural Critique', *Text and Performance Quarterly* 17, 317–30.

Godheswar, B. M. 2008. 'Building Brand Identity in Competitive Markets: A Conceptual Model', *Journal of Product and Brand Management* 17(1), 4–12.

Golden, A. V. 2006. 'Material Culture', in D. A. Stout (ed.), *Encyclopedia of Religion, Communication and Media*. New York: Routledge, 234–6.

Goredema, B. 2015. 'An Afternoon with a Prophet Magaya Follower'. Online. http://thesovereignstate.org/an-afternoon-with-a-prophet-magaya-follower.

Gifford, P. 2009. *Christianity, Politics and Public Life in Kenya*. London: Hurst and Company.

Grillo, L. S., A. van Klinken and H. J. Ndzovu. 2019. *Religions in Contemporary Africa: An Introduction*. London and New York: Routledge.

Gukurume, S. 2017. 'Singing Positivity: Prosperity Gospel in the Musical Discourse of Popular Youth Hip-Hop Gospel in Zimbabwe', *Muziki* 14(2), 36–54.

Gunda, M. R. 2012. 'Prediction and Power: Prophets and Prophecy in the Old Testament and Zimbabwean Christianity', *Exchange* 41, 335–51.

Guti, E. 1999. *A History of ZAOGA FIF: The Book of Remembrance. How It Began, Where It Is Going*. Harare: EGEA.

Guti, E. 2007. *Tithes, Prosperity That Comes through Obedience in Tithing*. Harare: EGEA.

Guti, E. 2018 "True Prosperity – Apostle Dr Ezekiel H Guti – YouTube: Deeper Life Conference for Deacons in Harare Zimbabwe." Tuesday, April 25th, 2012. Uploaded by FIFMI ZAOGA. Accessed 18 April 2019.

Guti, E. n.d. *Prosperity That Comes through Obedience: To Be a Millionaire Starts with Spending Less Than You Earn, Giving Is Proof That You Have Conquered Greed*. Harare: EGEA (ND).

Guti, E. H. 2014. *History of ZAOGA Forward in Faith: The Book of Remembrance How It Began and Where It Is Going Fifth*. Harare: EGEA Publications.

Guti, E. H. 2015. *Talents/Matarenda: Go and Teach Them to Use Their Hands*. Harare: EGEA Publication.

Haddad, B. 2003. 'Choosing to Remain Silent: The Links between Gender Violence, HIV/AIDS and the South African Church', in I. Phiri et al. (ed.), *African Women, HIV/AIDS and Faith Communities*. Pietermaritzburg: Cluster Publications, 149–67.

Haralambos, M. and M. Holborn. 2004. *Sociology: Themes and Perspectives*. London: HarperCollins.

The Herald. 2015. 'Magaya Speaks on Makandiwa'. 9 November.

Holland, R. F. 1965. 'The Miraculous', *American Philosophical Quarterly* 2(1), 43–51.

Hunt, S. 2002. *Religion in Western Society*. New York: Palgrave.

Hunt, S. 2003. *Alternative Religions: A Sociological Introduction*. Hampshire: Ashgate.

Hunt, S. (ed.). 2020. *Handbook of Mega Churches*. Leiden: Brill.

Hunt, S., M. Hamilton and T. Walter. 1997. 'Introduction: Tongues, Toronto and the Millennium', in S. Hunt, M. Hamilton and T. Walter (eds.), *Charismatic Christianity: Sociological Perspectives*. London: Macmillan, 1–6.

Iannaccone, L. R. 1990. 'Religious Practice: A Human Capital Approach', *Journal of the Scientific Study of Religion* 29(3), 297–314.

Iannaccone, L. R. 1994. 'Why Strict Churches Are Strong', *American Journal of Sociology* 99, 1180–211.

Iannaccone, L. R. 1998. 'Introduction to the Economics of Religion', *Journal of Economic Literature* 36(3), 1465–95.

Iannaccone, L. R. and E. Berman. 2006. 'Religious Extremism: The Good, the Bad, and the Deadly', *Public Choice* 128(1), 109–29.

Iheanacho, N. N. and C. A. Ughaerumba. 2016. 'The Rising Paradigm of Pentecostapreneurship in Nigeria: Impacts on National Development', *Open Journal of Philosophy* 6, 165–82.

International Defence and Aid Fund for Southern Africa. 1977. *Zimbabwe: The Facts about Rhodesia*. London: International Defence and Aid Fund.

Jeater, D. 2016. 'Masculinity, Marriage and the Bible: New Pentecostal Masculinities in Zimbabwe', in A. Cornwall et al. (ed.), *Masculinities under Neoliberalism*. London: Zed Books, 165–82.

Jelen, T. G. (ed.). 2002. *Sacred Markets, Sacred Canopies: Essays on Religious Markets and Religious Pluralism*. Lanham: Rowman and Littlefield.

Kalu, O. 1998. 'The Third Response: Pentecostalism and the Reconstruction: Christian Experience in Africa from 1970–1995', *Studia Historiae Ecclesiasticae* 24(2), 1–34.

Kalu, O. U. 2003. '"Globecalisation" and Religion: The Pentecostal Model in Contemporary Africa', in J. L. Cox and G. T. Haar (eds.), *Uniquely African? African Christian Identity from Cultural and Historical Perspectives*. Trenton: Africa World Press, 215–40.

Kalu, O. U. 2008. *African Pentecostalism: An Introduction*. Oxford: Oxford University Press.

Kamhungira, T. and V. Chaya. 2014. 'Magaya Draws 350 000 at the Church', *Daily News*. 10 November.

Kamhungira, T. and V. Chaya. 2016. 'Magaya Opens Up', *Daily News*. 6 November.

Kangwa, J. 2016. 'The Role of the Theology of Retribution in the Growth of Pentecostal-Charismatic Churches in Africa', *Verbum et Ecclesia* 37(1), a1542. http://dx.doiorg/10.4102/ve.v37i1.1542

Kaunda, C. J. 2016. 'Neo-Prophetism, Gender and "Anointed Condoms": Towards a *Missio Spiritus* of Just-Sex in the African Context of HIV and AIDS', *Alternation* 23(2), 64–88.

Kaunda, C. J. 2018. *The Nation That Fears God Prospers: A Critique of Zambian Theopolitical Imaginations*. Minneapolis: Fortress Press.

Kay, W. K. 2009. 'Pentecostalism and Religious Broadcasting', *Journal of Beliefs and Values* 30(3), 245–54.

Keddy, P. A. 2001. *Competition*. Dordrecht: Kluwer Academic.

Kelso, A. 2006. 'Advertising', in D. A. Stout (ed.), *Encyclopedia of Religion, Communication and Media*. New York: Routledge, 1–4.

Klaits, F. 2017. '"Catch the Word": Violated Contracts and Prophetic Confirmation in African American Pentecostalism', *HAU: Journal of Ethnographic Theory* 7(3), 237–60.

Klassen, P. E. 2011. *Spirits of Protestantism: Medicine, Healing, and Liberal Christianity*. London: University of California Press Ltd.

Kroesbergen, H. (ed.). 2017. *Neo-Pentecostalism in Southern Africa – Some Critical Reflections*. Wellington, South Africa: Christian Literature Fund.

Kroesbergen, H. 2019. *The Language of Faith in Southern Africa: Spirit World, Power, Community, Holism*. Cape Town: AOSIS.

Kuzma, A. T. et al. 2009. 'How Religion Has Embraced Marketing and the Implications for Business', *Journal of Management and Marketing Research* 2, 1–9.

Laguda, D. O. 2013. 'Religious Pluralism and Secularization in the Nigerian Religious Sphere', in A. Adogame, E. Chitando and B. Bateye (eds.), *African Traditional Religion in the Study of Religion, Diaspora and Gendered Societies*. London: Ashgate, 25–33.

Lindhardt, M. 2015. 'Men of God: Neo-Pentecostalism and Masculinities in Urban Tanzania', *Religion* 45(2), 252–72.

Lovemore, T. (ed.). 2018. *Aspects of Pentecostal Christianity in Zimbabwe*. Cham, Switzerland: Springer.

Lyer, G. and D. Soberman. 2000. 'Markets for Product Modification Information', *Marketing Science* 19(3), 203–25.

Ma, W. 2017. 'The Holy Spirit in Pentecostal Mission: The Shaping of Mission Awareness and Practice', *International Bulletin of Mission Research* 41(3), 227–8.

Machingura, F. 2011. 'The Significance of Glossolalia in the Apostolic Faith Mission, Zimbabwe', *Studies in World Christianity* 17(1), 12–29.

Machingura, F. 2012. *The Messianic The Messianic Feeding of the Masses: An Analysis of John 6 in the Context of Messianic Leadership in Post-Colonial Zimbabwe*. Bamberg: University of Bamberg Press.

Machingura, F., L. Togarasei and E. Chitando (eds.). 2018. *Pentecostalism and Human Rights in Contemporary Zimbabwe*. Newcastle upon Tyne: Cambridge Scholars Press.

Mackie, J. L. 1982. *The Miracle of Theism*. Oxford: Clarendon

Magesa, L. 1997. *African Religion: The Moral Traditions of Abundant Life*. Maryknoll, New York: Orbis Books.

Magezi, V. and C. Banda. 2017. 'Competing with Christ? A Critical Christological Analysis of the Reliance on Pentecostal Prophets in Zimbabwe', *In die Skriflig* 51(2), a2273.

Maguwu, S. 2016. 'PO BOX Rebrands to BUS STOP TV', https://www.dailynews.co.zw/articles/2016/04/04/po-box-rebrands-to-bus-stop-tv, Accessed 12 April 2018.

Mahohoma, T. C. 2017. 'A Theological Evaluation of God Business: A Case Study of the Prophetic Healing and Deliverance Ministries of Zimbabwe', *HTS Teologiese Studies/Theological Studies* 73(2), a4529. https://doiorg/10.4102/hts.v73i2.4529

Mahoney, J. 2004. 'Comparative-Historical Methodology', *Annual Review of Sociology* 30(1), 81–101. https://doi.org/10.1146/annurev.soc.30.012703.110507

Maimela, S. S. 1985. 'Salvation in African Traditional Religions', *Missionalia* 13(2), 63–77.

Makandiwa, E. 2013. Sermon, Harare, 4 May.

Mangena, F. and S. Mhizha. 2013. 'The Rise of White Collar Prophecy in Zimbabwe', in E. Chitando, M. R. Gunda and J. Kügler (eds.), *Prophets, Profits and the Bible in Zimbabwe*. Bamberg: University of Bamberg Press, 133–54.

Manica Post 5 September 2014. Mutare, Zimbabwe.

Manyonganise, M. 2010. 'From Safety Zones to Public Spaces: Women's Participation in Sport in Zimbabwe', in J. Shehu (ed.), *Gender, Sport and Development in Africa: Cross-Cultural Perspectives on Patterns of Representation and Marginalisation*. Dakar: CODESRIA, 13–26.

Manyonganise, M. 2013. 'Pentecostals Responding to Gender-Based Violence: The Case of the United Family International Church in Harare', in E. Chitando and S. Chirongoma (eds.), *Justice Not Silence: Churches Facing Sexual and Gender-Based Violence*. Stellenbosch: EFSA, 145–56.

Manyonganise, M. 2016a. 'Zimbabweans and the Prophetic Frenzy: Fertile Ground for Women's Sexual Abuse?', in J. Hunter and J. Kügler (eds.), *The Bible and Violence in Africa*. Bamberg: University of Bamberg Press, 269–83.

Manyonganise, M. 2016b. 'The Church, National Healing and Reconciliation in Zimbabwe: A Womanist Perspective on Churches in Manicaland (CiM)'. A PhD thesis submitted to the University of Pretoria.

Mapuranga, T. P. 2012. 'The Politics of Pentecostalism and Women's Ministries in Zimbabwe: An Interpretation of 1 Corinthians 14:34-35 and 1 Timothy 2:11-14', in M. R. Gunda and J. Kugler (eds.), *The Bible and Politics in Africa*. Bamberg: University of Bamberg Press, 379–94.

Mapuranga, T. P. 2013a. 'Bargaining with Patriarchy: Women Pentecostal Leaders in Zimbabwe', *Fieldwork in Religion* 8(1), 74–91.

Mapuranga, T. P. 2013b. 'Shona Christians and Gender-Based Violence: Appropriating Resources from African Traditional Religion and Christianity', in E. Chitando and S. Chirongoma (eds.), *Justice Not Silence: Churches Facing Sexual and Gender-Based Violence*. Stellenbosch: EFSA, Sun Press, 215–27.

Mapuranga, T. P. 2013c. 'AICs as a Gendered Space in Harare, Zimbabwe: Revisiting the Role and Place of Women', *Studia Historiae Ecclesiasticae* 39(2), 303–17.

Mapuranga, T. P. (ed.). 2018. *Powered by Faith: Pentecostal Businesswomen in Harare*. Eugene, OR: Resource Publications.

Mapuranga, T. P., E. Chitando and M. R. Gunda. 2013. 'Studying the United Family International Church in Zimbabwe: The Case for Applying Multiple Approaches to the Study of Religion and Religious Phenomena', in E. Chitando, M. R. Gunda and J. Kugler (eds.), *Prophets, Profits and the Bible in Zimbabwe*. Bamberg: University of Bamberg Press, 299–321.

Marongwe, N. and R. S. Maposa. 2015. 'PHDs, Gospreneurship, Globalisation and the Pentecostal "New Wave" in Zimbabwe', *Afro-Asian Journal of Social Sciences* 6(1), 1–22.

Martin, D. 1990. *Tongues of Fire: An Explosion of Protestantism in Latin America*. Cambridge: Basil Blackwell.

Martin, D. 1996. *Forbidden Revolutions: Pentecostalism in Latin America and Catholicism in Eastern Europe*. London: SPCK.

Maseno, L. 2017. '"The Glory Is Here!" Faith Brands and Social Rituals for Self-Affirmation for Social Responsibility in Kenya', *Alternation Special Edition* 19, 252–67.

Mashau, T. D. 2016. 'Moving to Different Streams of Healing Praxis: A Reformed Missionary Approach of Healing in the African Context', *Verbum et Ecclesia* 37(1), a1508. http://dx.doi.org/10.4102/ve.v37i1.1508.

Maskens, M. 2015. 'The Pentecostal Reworking of Male Identities in Brussels: Producing Moral Masculinities', *Etnográfica* 19(2), 323–45.

Masvotore, P. 2016. *Prosperity Gospel: To Save or to Enslave*. Saarbrüeken: LAP Lambert Academic Publishing.

Mataire, L. 2015. 'Magaya Defends Gospreneurship'. *The Herald*, 3 June.

Matandare, S. and M. Mugomba. 2015. 'Charismatic Leadership and the Socio-Economic Transformation of the Church', *International Journal of Humanities and Social Science* 5(6), 169–74.

Mate, R. 2002. 'Wombs as God's Laboratories: Pentecostal Discourses of Femininity in Zimbabwe', *Africa* 72(4), 549–68.

Matsilele, T. 'I Am a Trillionaire: Claims Zimbabwean Prophet', *CNBCAFRICA.com*, Accessed 25 February 2016.

Matsilele, T. 2015. 'I am a Trillionaire: Prophet Magaya', https://www.pazimbabwe.com/main-news-7970-i-am-a-trillionaire-prophet-magaya.html, Accessed 22 November 2017.

Maxwell, D. 1995. '"Witches, Prophets and Avenging Spirits:" The Second Christian Movement in North East Zimbabwe', *Journal of Religion in Africa* 25(3), 309–39.

Maxwell, D. 1998. '"Delivered from the Spirit of Poverty": Pentecostalism, Prosperity and Modernity in Zimbabwe', *Journal of Religion in Africa* 28(3), 309–37.

Maxwell, D. 2005. 'The Durawall of Faith: Pentecostal Spirituality in Neo-Liberal Zimbabwe', *Journal of Religion in Africa* 35(1), 4–32.

Maxwell, D. 2006. *African Gifts of the Spirit: Pentecostalism and the Rise of a Zimbabwean Transnational Religious Movement*. Harare: Weaver.

Maxwell, D. 2008. 'Post-Colonial Christianity in Africa', in H. McLeod (ed.), *The Cambridge History of Christianity: World Christianities c1914–c2000*. Cambridge: University of Cambridge Press, 401–21.

Maxwell, D. and I. Lawrie. (eds.). 2002. *Christianity and the African Imagination: Essays in Honour of Adrian Hastings*. Leiden: Brill.

Mayrargue, C. 2008. *The Paradoxes of Pentecostalism in Sub-Saharan Africa*. Paris: Istitut Francais Relations Internationales Sub-Saharan Africa Programme, 1–19.

Mbiti, J. S. 1969. *African Religions and Philosophy*. Oxford: Heinemann.

McCauley, J. F. 2012. 'Africa's New Big Man Rule? Pentecostalism and Patronage in Ghana', *African Affairs* 112(446), 1–21.

Meyer, B. 1998. 'Make a Complete Break with the Past: Memory and Post-Colonial Modernity in Ghanaian Pentecostalist Discourse', *Journal of Religion in Africa* 28(3), 316–49.

Mike. 2014a. *'I Had Sex with Zimbabwean's Leading Prophet and He Was Ready to Marry Me', Says Beverly Sibanda*, Accessed 3 September 2015.

Mike. 2014b. *'Bev Sibanda Exposes Magaya in Mutare, "the Whole Thing Is Well Ostracized Money Spinning Venture"*, 5 September 2015.

Miller, D. E. 2003. *Emergent Patterns of Congregational Life and Leadership in the Developing World: Personal Reflections from a Research Odyssey*. Durham, NC: Duke Divinity School

Miller, K. D. 2002. 'Competitive Strategies of Religious Organizations', *Strategic Management Journal* 23(5), 435–56.

Ministries, B. S. 2016. Bus Stop TV Skit, YouTube. https://www.youtube.com/watch?v=1gaODAtCDhw, Accessed 10 March 2017.

Miracle, N. 2017. Bus Stop TV, YouTube. https://www.youtube.com/watch?v=i7HvmHUkTNU&t=139s, Accessed 18 July 2017.

Moyo, A. M. 1987. 'Religion and Politics in Zimbabwe', in K. H. Petersen (ed.), *Religion, Development and African Identity*. Uppsala: Scandinavian Institute of African Studies, 59–72.

Moyo, S. 2013. 'Indigenous Knowledge Systems and Attitudes towards Male Infertility in Mhondoro-Ngezi', *Zimbabwe*. https://doi.org/10.1080/13691058.2013.779029. Accessed 20 June 2018.

Moyo, S. and I. Muhwati. 2013. 'Socio-Cultural Perspectives on Causes and Intervention Strategies of Male Infertility: A Case Study of Mhondoro-Ngezi, Zimbabwe', *African Journal of Reproductive Health* 17(2), 89–101.

Moyo, S. and Y. Mine. 2016. *What Colonialism Ignored: 'African Potentials' for Resolving Conflicts in Southern Africa*. Bamenda: Langaa RPCIG.

Mtethwa, N. 2016. 'Religion in a New Era: The Encounter between Ndau Traditional Religion and Pentecostalism in the Prophetic Healing and Deliverance Ministry in Zimbabwe', Unpublished BA Hons Dissertation, Harare: University of Zimbabwe.

Muchemwa, K. and R. Muponde. (eds.). 2007. *Manning the Nation: Father Figures in Zimbabwean Literature and Society*. Harare: Weaver.

Mugabe, T. 2015. 'Magaya Buys Grace Mugabe Book for 50K', *The Herald*. 27 July.

Mukondiwa, R. 2017. 'How Does Prophet Bushiri Make Money? Here Are the Top 10 Ways, Number 3 Will Surprise You'. Online. https://doi.org/10.1186/1471-2458-12-114.

Mundondo, N. 2015. 'Gospel of Prosperity and Women in the Prophetic and Healing and Deliverance Ministries in Zimbabwe', Unpublished BA Hons Dissertation, Harare: University of Zimbabwe.

Mushava, E. 2015. '*Magaya Gets His Power from Snakes: Vapostori*', *NewsDay*. 29 February.

Musoni, P. 2013. 'African Pentecostalism and Sustainable Development: A Study on the Zimbabwe Assemblies of God Africa, Forward in Faith Church', *International Journal of Humanities and Social Science Invention* 2(10), 75–82.

Musoni, P. 2014. 'Glossolalia: A Theological Position in Pentecostal Christianity: A Case Study of Zimbabwe Assemblies of God Africa Forward in Faith (Z.A.O.G.A F.I.F) Spirituality', *International Journal of Innovative Research and Development (IJIRD)* 3(6), 134–40.

Mutsagondo, S. and J. Makanga. 2014. 'Dollarization, Exit Illegal Informal Dealers: How the Adoption of the Multi-Currency System Hit the Illegal Informal Sector in Zimbabwe', *International Journal of Innovation and Scientific Research* 9(2), 440–7.

Mutsagondo, S., E. Karimanzira and J. Makanga. 2016. 'Ndau Women, Informal Cross-Border Trade and the Changing Socio-Economic Dispensation in Zimbabwe', *Paradigms: A Research Journal of Commerce, Economics, and Social Sciences* 10(2), 1–13.

Mwari, K. K. 2016. Bus Stop TV Skit, YouTube. https://www.youtube.com/watch?v=uPXBKi2N7Wg, 18/7/17

Nagel, J. 1998. 'Masculinity and Nationalism: Gender and Sexuality in the Making of Nations', *Ethnic and Racial Studies* 21(2), 242–69.

Ncube, X. 2015. 'Magaya, Makandiwa War a Sign of the Times: AFM Pastor'. *The Standard*, 22 November.

'Nehanda Radio', Accessed 15 February 2015.

Netland, H. A. 1991. *Dissonant Voices*. Grand Rapids, Michigan: B. Eerdmans Publishing Company.

NewsDay. 2011. 'Women Pay Price for Belief in False Prophets', https://www.newsday.co.zw/2011/05/08/2011-05-08-women-pay-price-for-belief-in-false-prophets/, Accessed 26 November 2014.

NewsDay 9 February 2015. Harare.

NewsDay 6 November 2015. Harare.

News Reporter. 2015. 'My Dream Is to Meet President Mugabe: Says Popular Prophet Magaya', 3 July.

Ngbea, G. 2015. 'Influences of Pentecostalism on the Mainline Churches in Nigeria', *Archives of Business Research* 3(3), 67–76.

Njoroge, N. 2013. 'Preach the Gospel and Tell HER Story!', in E. Chitando and S. Chirongoma (eds.), *Justice not Silence: Churches Facing Sexual and Gender Based Violence*. Stellenbosch: EFSA, 17–33.

Norris, P. and R. Inglehart. 2004. *Sacred and Secular. Religion and Politics Worldwide*. Cambridge: Cambridge University Press.

Norris, P. and R. Inglehart. 2011. *Sacred and Secular: Religion and Politics Worldwide*. New York: Cambridge University Press.

Nwadialor, K. 2015. 'Pentecostal Hermeneutics and the Commercialization of the Gospel Message in Nigeria', *International Journal of Research* 2(2), 1270–87.

Nyambi, O. 2016. 'Of Weevils and Gamatox: Titles, Names and Nicknames in ZANU PF Succession Politics', *African Identities* 14(1), 59–73.

Nyamnjoh, F. B. and J. A. Carpenter. 2018. 'Introduction: Religious Innovation and Competition in Contemporary African Christianity', *Journal of Contemporary African Studies*. 10.1080/02589001.2018.1492096

Obadare, E. 2009. 'The Uses Of Ridicule: Humour, "Infrapolitics" and Civil Society in Nigeria', *African Affairs* 108(431), 241–61.

Obayi, P. M. and I. O. Edogor. 2016. 'Nigerian Audiences' Perception of Pentecostal Churches' Ownership of Satellite Television Channels', *Global Journal of Arts, Humanities and Social Sciences* 4(3), 12–29.

Online Correspondents. 2013. 'Night of Turnaround Explained: Is Magaya Really a True Prophet of God?' Accessed 20 April 2016.

Oosthuizen, G. C. 1997. *African Independent Churches and Small Business Spiritual Support for Secular Empowerment*. Pretoria: HSRC Printers.

Orobator, A. E. 2018. *Religion and Faith in Africa: Confessions of an Animist*. Maryknoll, NY: Orbis Books.

Paley, W. 1743–1805. *Natural Theology, or, Evidences of the Existence and Attributes of the Deity*. Boston: Gould and Lincoln.

Parrinder, E. G. 1961. *West African Religion*. London: SPCK.

Parsitau, D. 2019. 'Violent Theologies, Women's Bodies, and Church "Business" in Kenya', *Elephant*. https://www.theelephant.info/features/2019/10/31/violent-theologies-womens-bodies-and-church-business-in-kenya/

Pasura, D. and A. Christou. 2018. 'Theorizing Black (African) Transnational Masculinities', *Men and Masculinities* 21(4), 521–46.

Patton, M. Q. 1990. *Qualitative Evaluation and Research Methods*. Newbury Park, CA: Sage.

PHD Ministry member. 2016. *Interview*. Harare. 30 March. www.phdministries.org/about_phd.html, Accessed 1 April 2015.

Phillips, J. 1987. *Bible Explorer's Guide: How to Understand and Interpret the Bible*. Grand Rapids: Kregel Publications.

Platvoet, J. G. 1988. *Essays on Akan Traditional Religion: A Reader*. Harare: Unpublished, University of Zimbabwe.

Platvoet, J. G. 1999. 'To Define or Not to Define: The Problem of the Definition of Religion', in J. G. Platvoet and A. L. Molendijk (eds.), *The Pragmatics of Defining Religion: Contexts, Concepts & Contests*. Leiden: Brill, 245–66.

Pongweni, A. 1983. *What's in a Name? A Study of Shona Nomenclature*. Gweru: Mambo Press.

Price, F. K. C. 2005. *Name It and Claim It! The Power of Positive Confession*. Benin City: Marvellous Christina Publication.

Religion Writer. 2016. 'Magaya Ready for Night of Turnaround' *The Sunday Mail, Religion*. 30 October, 2.

Robbins, J. 2003. 'On Paradoxes of Global Pentecostalism and the Perils of Continuity Thinking', *Religion* 33(3), 221–31.

Rosenau, P. V. 2003. *The Competition Paradigm: America's Romance with Conflict, Context and Commerce*. Lanham, MD: Rowman and Littlefield.

Sachikonye, L. 2011. *When a State Turns on Its Citizens: 60 Years of Institutionalised Violence in Zimbabwe*. Auckland Park, SA: Jacana.

Santa Anna, J. (ed.). 2005. *Religions Today: Their Challenge to the Ecumenical Movement*. Geneva: World Council of Churches.

Schleiermacher, F. 1999. *The Christian Faith*. Translated by H. R. MacIntosh and J. S. Stewart. Edinburgh: T&T Clark.

Shoko, T. 2007. *Karanga Indigenous Religion in Zimbabwe: Health and Well-Being*. Aldershot: Ashgate.

Shoko, T. 2009. 'Healing in Hear the Word Ministries Pentecostal Church in Zimbabwe', in D. Westerlund (ed.), *Global Pentecostalism*. London: I.B. Tauris, 43–55.

Shoko, T. 2010. 'Traditional Healing in Harare: Continuity and Change', in L. Togarasei and E. Chitando (eds.), *Faith in The City: The Role and Place of Religion in Harare*. Uppsala: Swedish Science Press, 85–106.

Shoko, T. 2015. 'The Pastoral Identity of Emmanuel Makandiwa: A Discussion of the United Family International Pentecostal Church's Gospel of Prosperity and the Shona Traditional Practitioner in the Context of Poverty in Zimbabwe', in H.

Moyo (ed.), *Pastoral Care in a Globalised World: African and European Perspectives*. Pietermaritzburg: Cluster Publications.

Shoko, T. and A. Chiwara. 2013. 'The Prophetic Figure in Zimbabwean Religions: A Comparative Analysis of Prophet Makandiwa of United Family International Church (UFIC) and the *N'anga* in African Traditional Religion', in E. Chitando, M. R. Gunda and J. Kügler (eds.), *Prophets, Profits and the Bible in Zimbabwe*. Bible in Africa Studies (BiAS) Bamberg: Bamberg University Press, 1–17.

Sibanda, F. 2016. 'Avenging Spirits and the Vitality of African Traditional Law, Customs and Religion in Contemporary Zimbabwe', in P. Coertzen, M. C. Green and L. Hansen (eds.), *Religious Freedom and Religious Pluralism in Africa: Prospects and Limitations*. Stellenbosch: AFRICAN SUN MeDIA, 345–59.

Sibanda, F. and N. Madzokere. 2013. 'Where Are the Ancestors? Theological Reflections on the Impact of Inter-Denominational Sunday Services at Great Zimbabwe University', *AARJMD* Vol. 1(7) March, 176–89.

Sibanda, F. and R. S. Maposa. 2013. 'Behind the Smokescreen: African Instituted Churches and Political Processes in Zimbabwe', in E. Chitando (ed.), *Prayers & Players: Religion and Politics in Zimbabwe*. Harare: SAPES, 125–42.

Soothill, J. E. 2007. *Gender, Social Change and Spiritual Power: Charismatic Christianity in Ghana*. Leiden: Brill.

Spickard, J. V. 2015. 'Religion in Consumer Society: Brands, Consumers and Markets', *Journal of Contemporary Religion* 30(1), 155–7. www.divineyardchurch.org/about/john-chibwe, Accessed 1 June 2016.

Staff Editor, *Daily News*. 2014. 'You Can't Fight God – Magaya'. 7 July. https://dailynews.co.zw/articles-2014-07-07-you-can-t-fight-god-magaya/

Staff Reporter. 2015. 'PHD Is Not a Church: Magaya', *NewsDay*. 4 July.

Stark, R. and L. R. Iannaccone. 1994. 'A Supply-Side Interpretation of the "Secularization" of Europe', *Journal for the Scientific Study of Religion* 33, 230–52.

Stark, R. and R. Finke. 2000. *Acts of Faith: Explaining the Human Side of Religion*. Berkeley: University of California Press.

Stark, R. and R. Finke. 2002. 'Beyond Church and Sect: Dynamics and Stability in Religious Economics', in T. D. Jelen (ed.), *Sacred Markets, Sacred Canopies: Essays on Religious Markets and Religious Pluralism*. Lanham: Rowman and Littlefield Publishers, 31–62.

Stewart, E. 2016. 'We'll Make a Man Out of You Yet: The Masculinity of Peter in the Book of Acts', *HTS Teologiese Studies/Theological Studies* 72(4), a3433. http://dx.doiorg/10.4102/hts.v72i4.3433

Stolz, J. 2010. 'A Silent Battle: Theorizing the Effects of Competition between Churches and Secular institutions', *Review of Religious Research* 51(3), 253–76.

Sunday Mail 6 March 2016. Harare.

Swinburne, R. 1968. 'Miracles', *Philosophical Quarterly* 18, 320–8.

Taru, J. and F. Settler. 2015. 'Patterns of Consumption and Materialism among Zimbabwean Christians: A Tale of Two Indigenous Churches', *Journal for the Study of Religion* 28(2), 113–37.

Tarusarira, J. 2016. 'An Emergent Consciousness on the Role of Christianity on Zimbabwe's Political Field: A Case of Non-Doctrinal Religio-Political Actors', *Journal for the Study of Religion* 29(2), 56–77.

Taylor, M. C. (ed.). 1998. *Critical Terms for Religious Studies*. Chicago: University of Chicago Press.

Ter Haar, G. 1998. *Half Way to Paradise: African Christians in Europe*. Cardiff: Cardiff Academic Press.

Togarasei, L. 2005. 'Modern Pentecostalism as an Urban Phenomenon: The Case of Family of God Church in Zimbabwe', *Exchange* 34(4), 349–75.

Togarasei, L. 2010. '"Churches of the Rich?": Pentecostalism and Elitism', in L. Togarasei and E. Chitando (eds.), *Faith in the City: The Role and Place of Religion in Harare*. Uppsala: Swedish Science Press, 19–40.

Togarasei, L. 2011. 'The Pentecostal Gospel of Prosperity in African Contexts of Poverty: An Appraisal', *Exchange* 40, 336–50.

Togarasei, L. 2013. 'The Bible and Healing: Reflections in the Light of HIV and AIDS in an African Context', in E. Chitando and C. Klagba (eds.), *In the Name of Jesus! Healing in the Age of HIV*. Geneva: WCC Publications, 39–56.

Togarasei, L. 2014. 'African Gosprenuership: Assessing the Possible Contribution of the Gospel of Prosperity to Entrepreneurship in Light of Jesus's Teaching on Earthly Possessions', in H. Kroesbergen (ed.), *In Search of Health and Wealth: The Prosperity Gospel in African, Reformed Perspective*. Eugene: Wipf & Stock Publishers, 110–25.

Togarasei, L. (ed.). 2018. *Aspects of Pentecostal Christianity in Zimbabwe*. Cham, Switzerland: Springer.

Ukah, A. 2003a. 'The Redeemed Christian Church of God (RCCG), Nigeria. Local Identities and Global Processes in African Pentecostalism'. Doctoral thesis submitted to the University of Bayreuth, Bayreuth, Germany.

Ukah, A. 2007. 'African Christianities, Features, Promises and Problems', *Arbeittspapiere/ Working Papers 79*, 1–20. Johannes Guttenberg Universitat Mainz.

Ukah, A. 2015. 'Managing Miracles: Law, Authority, and the Regulation of Religious Broadcasting in Nigeria', in I. J. H. Rosalind and B. F. Soares (eds.), *New Media and Religious Transformations in Africa*. Bloomington: Indiana University Press, 175–201.

Ukah, A. F. 2003b. 'Advertising God: Nigerian Christian Video Films and the Power of Consumer Culture', *Journal of Religion in Africa* 33(2), 203–31.

Ukwuegbu, B. et al. (eds.). 2014. *Material Wealth and Divine Blessings in the Bible*. ACTS OF THE CATHOLIC BIBLICAL ASSOCIATION OF NIGERIA (CABAN), Vol. 5. Port Harcourt: CABAN.

Van Dijk, R. 2000. 'Christian Fundamentalism in Sub-Saharan Africa: The Case of Pentecostalism' Occasional Paper, Centre of African Studies, University of Copenhagen.

Van Dijk, R. 2001. 'Time and Trans-Cultural Technologies of Self in the Ghanaian Pentecostal Diaspora', in R. M. Fratani and A. Corten (eds.), *Between Babel and Pentecost: Transnational Pentecostalism in Africa and Latin America*. Bloomington: Indiana University Press, 216–34.

Van Djik, R. A. 1997. 'From Camp to Encompassmen: Discourses of Transsubjectivity in the Ghanaian Pentecostal Diaspora', *Journal of Religion in Africa* 27(2), 135–59.

Van Klinken, A. 2014. *Transforming Masculinities in African Christianity: Gender Controversies in Times of AIDS*. Farnham: Ashgate.

Van Klinken, A. S. 2016. 'Pentecostalism, Political Masculinity and Citizenship: The Born-Again Male Subject as Key to Zambia's National Redemption', *Journal of Religion in Africa* 42(3), 129–57.

Veenhoven, R., M. J. DeJong and A. C. Zijderveld. 1997. *The Gift of Society*. Nijkerk: Enzo Press.

Vengeyi, O. 2013. 'Zimbabwean Pentecostal Prophets: Rekindling the "True and False Prophecy" Debate', in E. Chitando, M. R. Gunda and J. Kugler (eds.), *Prophets, Profits and the Bible in Zimbabwe*. Bamberg: University of Bamberg Press, 29–54.

Walker, A. 1997. 'Thoroughly Modern: Sociological Reflections on the Charismatic Movements from the End of the Twentieth Century', in S. Hunt, M. Hamilton and T. Walter (eds.), *Charismatic Christianity: Sociological Perspectives*. London: Macmillan, 17–42.

Wariboko, N. 2012. 'Pentecostal Paradigms of National Economic Prosperity in Africa', in K. Attanasi and A. Yong (eds.), *Pentecostalism and Prosperity: The Socio-Economics of the Global Charismatic Movement*. New York: Palgrave Macmillan, 35–59.

Wariboko, N. 2014. *The Charismatic City and the Public Resurgence of Religion: A Pentecostal Social Ethics of Cosmopolitan Urban Life*. New York: Palgrave Macmillan.

Wilkinson, J. 1998. *The Bible and Healing: A Medical and Theological Commentary*. Grand Rapids: Eerdmans.

Wilson, M. 1966. *The Church Is Healing*. London: SCM Press.

Wilson, N. 2008. 'Was That Supposed to Be Funny? A Rhetorical Analysis of Politics, Problems and Contradictions in Contemporary Stand-Up Comedy', Unpublished DPhil Thesis, University of Iowa.

Wright, S. M. 2007. 'Unstable Acts: A Practitioner's Case Study of the Poetics of Post-Dramatic Theatre'. Doctor of Philosophy, Creative Industries, Queensland University of Technology.

Yidana, A. and M. Issahaku. 2014. 'Pentecostal Creative Ideas, Inspiring Vision, and Innovation in Ghana: A Bane of Pentecostal Continued Plausibility', *American Journal of Sociological Research* 4(1), 1–10.

Yong, A. 2005. *The Spirit Poured Out on All Flesh: Pentecostalism and the Possibility of Global Theology*. Grand Rapids: Baker Academic.

Yong, A. 2012. 'Typology of Prosperity Theology: A Religious Economy of Global Renewal or a Renewal Economics?', in K. Attanasi and A. Yong (eds.), *Pentecostalism and Prosperity: The Socio-Economics of the Global Charismatic Movement*. New York: Palgrave Macmillan, 15–33.

Yong Yin, I. 2007. 'Multiples Roles of Branding in International Marketing', *International Marketing Review* 24(4), 384–408.

Zaleski, P. A. and C. E. Zech. 1995. 'The Effect of Religious Market Competition on Church Giving', *Review of Social Economy* Vol. LIII(3), 350–67.

Zimdisapora: The Voice of the Voiceless. 2013. 'Zimbabweans Rush to Prophet Magaya PHD Ministries for Miracle Healing', 29 July.

Zimdisapora: The Voice of the Voiceless. 2014. 'Pretty Xaba Dies', 7 December.

Zimunya, C. T. and J. Gwara. 2013. 'Pentecostalism, Prophets and the Distressing Zimbabwean Milieu', in E. Chitando et al. (ed.), *Prophets, Profits and the Bible in Zimbabwe*. Bamberg: University of Bamberg Press, 187–201.

Zimunya, C. T. and J. Gwara. 2019. '"Do Not Touch My Anointed!" (Ps 105) – An Analysis of Sexual Violations in Zimbabwean Religious Movements', in J. Kügler, R. Gabaitse and J. Stiebert (eds.), *The Bible and Gender Troubles in Africa*. Bamberg: University of Bamberg Press, 115–28.

Zuze, L. 2016. 'Magaya Strategy of Righteousness by Condemnation', *The Zimbabwean*. 11 February.

Sources

Oral sources

Client X, testimony Yadah TV, 13 September 2014.
Magaya, W. sermon 8 November 2014.
Mashoko, P. interview 20 December 2015.
Moyo, C. interview 12 May 2016.
Shumba, B. interview 2 April 2015.
Tine, S. interview 12 February 2016.

Websites

Dale, C. 2014. 'The demons of African Pentecostalism', www.firstthings.com/blogs/firstthoughts/2014/01/pentecostals-and-the-demonic.

http://www.herald.co.zw/magaya-crusade-creates-international/, Accessed 2 October 2015.

http://newsvyb.com/7-life-lessons-we-can-all-learn-from-prophet-walter-magaya/#. V2qO6xJV6M8, Accessed 22 June 2016.

http://www.whydidtheydisappear.com/soap/pentecostal.html, Accessed 23 June 2016.

Karibu. 'Modern Ghana', http://www.karibu-stenger.net/en/articles/atr.shtml, Accessed 28 January 2013.

Lloyd Harrison. http://www.bible.ca/t-why-I-left-pentecostalism.htm, Accessed 30 June 2016.

Video clips

DCOHP, 'Deliverance from the Spirit of Snake, Generational Curses, Rejection and Prostitution', www.divineyardchurch.org, Accessed 20 April 2016.

DCOHP, 'Deliverance from Familiar Spirits and Satanic Forces', www.divineyardchurch.org, Accessed 10 May 2016.

DCOHP, 'Deliverance from the Spirit of False Prophets and Ancestral Spirits', www.divineyardchurch.org, Accessed 20 May 2016.

DCOHP, 'Healing of a Fractured Wrist', www.divineyardchurch.org, Accessed 20 May 2016.

DCOHP, 'A Must Watch!!! A Fall from Grace: Are Anointed Items of God Meant to Be Sold?', www.divineyardchurch.org, Accessed 20 May 2016.

DCOHP, 'Satanist Prostitute Spills It All: The Deep Secrets of Satanism Part 1 – 8 February 2015', www.divineyardchurch.org, Accessed 10 May 2016.

DCOHP, 'Witchcraft!!! Anointed Ash Saved a Man from a Vicious Attack by a Demon Possessed Cat', www.divineyardchurch.org, Accessed 20 May 2016.

DCOHP, 'Zimbabweans, You Are Foolish!!! You Run after GMO Miracles', www.divineyardchurch.org, Accessed 2 May 2016.

Interviews

Matando, T. E. August 2014. Elderly member in one of the Pentecostal Churches in Harare.

Mlambo, O. B. 2014. Pastor in one Pentecostal Church (consented to the use of his real name)

Moyo, M. 2014. Lecturer in the Department of Religious Studies, Classics and Philosophy, University of Zimbabwe, 13 August 2014 (consented to the use of his real name).

Private interview 1 July 2019, member of UFIC, Chitungwiza, Harare.

Private interview 1 May 2019, Senior Elder of PHD ministry, Waterfalls Zindoga, Harare.

Private interview 1 May 2019, ZAOGA church Elder, Seke 1, Chitungwiza, Harare.

Private interview, 1 May 2019, Senior member of UFIC, Chitungwiza, Harare.

Newspaper articles

Chingarande, D. 2017. 'Pastor Gets 60 Years for Raping Congregant', *NewsDay*, 3 November. Accessed 1 December 2019.

iHarare. 2014. 'Gumbura Not the Only One, Ten More Different Church Leaders Accused of Sexual Abuse', *iHarare*. http://www.iharare.com/gumbura-not-the-only-one-ten-more-different-church-leaders-accused-of-sexual-abuse/, Accessed 8 July 2014.

Laiton, C. 2014. 'Adultery Scandal: Prophet Magaya Bought Married Girlfriend a US$ 10,000 Car', *NewsDay*. http://www.zimeye.com/adultery-scandal-prophet-magaya-bought-married-girlfriend-a-us10000-car/, Accessed 15 September 2014.

Mugauri, G. 2011. 'Are We in, or Are We Over the Edge: As "Prophets" Prophesy ID Numbers; Miracles, Prosperity Gospel Takes Over', *The Sunday Mail*. http://www.bulawayo24.com/index-id-opinion-sc-blogs-byo-4524-article-Are+we+in,+or+we+are+over+the+edge!.html, Accessed 24 November 2014.

Mugugunyeki, M. 2014. 'Churches No Longer Safe for Women', *The Standard*, 19 January. http://www.thestandard.co.zw/2014/01/19/churches-longer-safe-women/, Accessed 26 February 2014.

Rupapa, T. 2013. 'RGM Church Women Belong to Gumbura', *The Herald*. http://www.herald.co.zw/rgm-church-women-belong-to-gumbura/, Accessed 20 December 2013.

Zimbabwe mail, 2014. 'Another Sex Scandal Hits Magaya', *NewsdzeZimbabwe*. http://www.newsdzezimbabwe.co.uk/2014/10/another-sex-scandal-hits-magaya.html, Accessed 10 November 2014.

Zimbabwe News, 2014. 'EXCLUSIVE: Prophet Caught in Sex Scandal, Beaten Up'. *NewsdzeZimbabwe*. http://zimbabwenewsday.co.uk/exclusive-prophet-caught-sex-scandal-beaten/, Accessed 10 October 2014.

Index

Achunike, H. 164
Adogame, A. 1, 11, 31
Afolayan, A. 1, 164
African Independent Churches (AICs)
    26–8, 77, 91, 152, 156, 180, 183–4,
    193, 204
African indigenous religions 9
African Initiated Churches or *mapositori* 91
African Pentecostalism
    anthropological beliefs 125–33
    branding 14
    distinctive features 23
    emergence 1–2
    health and wellbeing quest 25
    spirit-driven'. histories of 6–7
    ultra-competitive nature 3, 9
African religious market 2
    new adherents and clients 3, 14, 16
African traditional healers 15, 25, 78, 119,
    131, 156. *See also n'angas*
African traditional religion (ATRs)
    anthropological beliefs 118, 125–33
    divining and healing practices 25–6
    health and well-being practices 22–3
    indigenous practice 156
    miracles, beliefs in 38–9
    Pentecostalism and 21–2
    prophets vs 15, 17, 33
Amanze, J. 117
Anderson, A. 135, 152, 164, 166, 204
Anderson, A. H. 6, 204
Angel, Uebert 75, 91, 106, 149, 172, 206
anointing
    artefacts 26–7
    clothes and regalia 27–8
    holy oil 26
Antony, Tinashe Romeo (Shinsoman) 114,
    159
Apostolic Faith Mission (AFM) 11, 14,
    40, 46, 65, 68, 90–1, 140–1, 164–5,
    170, 177
Asamoah-Gyadu 1, 79, 90, 152–3

Attanasi, K. 65, 164
Azusa Street revival in 1906–09 90, 135

bad luck (*munyama*) 31
Baffour, A. K. 8
Bakare, S. 27
Banda, C. 72, 185, 187–8
Banda, 'Dr' Kamwelo 15
Bankston, C. 107
Barrett, D. B. 46, 49
Bateye, B. O. 191
Bepete, L. 154
Berger, P. 107, 118
Biri, K. 4, 17, 19, 21–2, 27, 29–30, 84, 141,
    150–1, 156–7, 163, 165, 172, 181–3,
    200
Boal, A. 210–11
Boateng, Victor Kusi 92
Bond, P. 10, 69
Bourdillon, M. F. C. 83, 142, 193
Brooks, S. 110
Bruce, S. 46
Bushiri, Shepherd 75
Bustop TV
    background 204–6
    marketing strategy 206–14

Carpenter, J.A. 2
Chalfant, H. 50
charismatic renewal movement 90
Chaves, M. 2
Chavunduka, G. 25
Chaya, V. 113, 150, 160
Chese, S. 158
Chesnut, A. 97, 118–19
Chibango, C. 90–1, 94–5, 186
Chibwe, Mr John 123–5, 133. *See also*
    DiVineyard Church of His Presence
    against 'gospelneurship' 130
Chikafa, Chipiro 192, 195
Chikonzo, K. 19, 72, 203
Chikwinya, N. 76

Chimhanda, F. H. 199
Chirongoma, F. 18, 103, 198, 200, 217
Chiroro, P., A. 61
Chitando, E. 1, 4, 8–9, 13, 18–19, 21–3, 61, 72, 91–2, 94–5, 117, 124, 126, 130, 141, 149–51, 183, 188, 193, 197–8, 200, 203–4
Chitemba, B. 145–6
Chiwara, A. 78, 81, 83–4, 121
Christianity
    factionalism 103
    rebranding 91–6, 92–6
classical Pentecostal churches 90
competition
    categories 9
    creativity and innovation 108
    definition 104
    inter and intra religion 105–6
    key dimensions 14–16
    problematic practices 3
    religious groups 103–4
Comstock, W. R. 6
Connell, R. 13, 63, 70
contentious theory 46
Corner, M. 35, 141–2
Counted, V. 159
Cox, H. 46, 49–50, 59
Cox, J.L. 121

Daneel, M. L. 76
Dayton, D. W. 46
Deuschle, T. 168
Diara, B. C. D. 7, 150
DiVineyard Church of His Presence (DCOHP)
    anthropological beliefs 125–33
    historical background 123–5
    ShekhinahGlory TV 125
    Shekhinah Home of Hope 125
    on social media 125
    traditional beliefs 118
divorce 13, 34, 133, 199
Droogers, A. 46–50, 58
Dube, E. E. N. 16
Dube, Z. 12, 69, 160
Dunn, J. D. G. 148

Edogor, I. O. 96
Elphick, R. 138
Emmanuel television station 76

empowerment 11, 19, 55, 59, 115, 174, 176, 191, 195, 199, 201
Enlightened Christian Gathering 75
Esslin, M. 213
Evangelical Fellowship of Zimbabwe (EFZ) 163, 171
Exodus 86
Ezekiel 11

fast-track land reform programme (FTLRP) 10
Father's Day celebration 93
Fenga, V. F. 6
Finke, R. 107, 118, 136–7
Finke, Roger 118
Fourie, P. J. 210
Freeman, D. 113, 164
Freud, S. 213

Gabaitse, R. M. 13, 92
Gadzikwa, W. 73
Gagare, M. 154
Gaidzanwa, R. B. 61
Gauthier, F. 2
Gelfand, M. 81
Gewald, J. B. 2
Gibson, T. 62
Gifford, P. 22, 29, 135, 164
Gilbert, J. 209, 213
Global South. 64
God's actions
    of miracles 37–8
    supernatural intrusion 36–7
Golden, A. V. 95
Good News Church 75, 149, 172
Government of National Unity (GNU) 62, 64–6
Grillo, L. S. 9
Gukurume, S. 11
Gunda, M. R. 193
Guti, E. 21, 28, 30, 59, 163, 165–8, 170–1, 173, 175–8, 180–4, 186. *See also* Zimbabwe Assemblies of God Africa (ZAOGA)
Gwara, J. 40, 192

Haddad, B. 200
Haralambos, M. 46
Heartfelt Ministries of Apostle Tavonga Vutawashe 106

Holborn, M. 46
Holland, R. F. 36
Holy Spirit 6–7, 47–9, 68, 78, 82, 85, 90, 110–11, 155, 176–7, 181, 187, 203, 207–8
Hunt, S. 1, 46–9

Iannaccone, L. R. 2, 63, 111, 137
Iheanacho, N. N. 15
Inglehart, R. 108, 136–7
innovation. *See also* Magaya, Walter; Makandiwa, Emmanuel
  and competition 1–19, 66–71
  creativity and 108
  key dimensions 14–16
  social 114
Islamophobia 40

Java, Passion 90
Jeater, D. 61
Jelen, T. G. 2
Joshua, T. B. (Prophet) 26, 76–8, 92, 124–5, 133, 141, 151, 155

Kalu, O. 6, 9, 26, 29–30, 126–8, 130, 132, 152–3, 192
Kamhungira, T. 150–1, 157
Kaunda, C. J. 1, 3, 12
Kay, W. K. 14, 96
Keddy, P. A. 104
Kelso, A. 96
Klaits, F. 8
Klassen, P.E. 158
Kroesbergen, H. 1, 8, 194
Kuzma, A. T. 4, 10

Laguda, D.O 105
Lindhart, M. 61
Lovemore, T. 17, 45
Lyer, G. 112

Macheso, Aleck 76, 113, 159–60, 168
Machingura, F. 1, 64–5, 177, 204
Mackie, J. L. 36
Magaya,Tendai 27
Magaya, Walter. *See also* Prophetic Healing and Deliverance (PHD) Ministry
  Aguma product 15
  anointing oil, use of 85, 94
  artefacts, use of 27, 94
  background information 5, 22, 45
  business seminars 116
  creativity and innovation 4
  criticism on 72–3
  demonization of 28
  exorcism and philanthropism 68–9
  father (papa) status 63, 66–7
  gender ideologies 13
  health and wealth teaching 158–60
  holy oil distribution 26
  holy place, idea of 86
  life story 150–2
  Marine Spirits: Mweya Yemumvura (Water spirits) 156
  masculine brands 69–71
  miracles, focus on 35
  naming of ministry 25
  prophecy, healing and deliverance 21, 24, 67, 78–9
  prosperity messages 11, 28–30, 65
  religious vitality 31
  spiritual father 78
  traditional healing methods 15
  zunde ramambo, distribution of 30
Magesa, L. 122–3
Magezi, V. 72
Maguwu, S. 205
Mahohoma, T. C. 63, 184, 186, 188
Mahoney, J. 178
Maimela, S. S. 7, 122
Makandiwa, Emmanuel. *See also* United Family International (UFI) Church
  approach to divorce 13
  artefacts, using 26–7, 94
  background information 5, 22, 45
  business seminars 115
  creativity and innovative ideas 4, 11–12
  criticism of 72–3
  demonization of 28
  family and extended family concept 23–4
  father (papa) status 23, 63, 66–7
  health and wealth teaching 65, 68
  holy oil distribution 26, 94
  masculine brands 69–71
  miracles, focusing 35
  prophesying, healing and deliverance 24, 31, 67
  prosperity messages 28–30, 65

social activism 30
traditional healing 15
zunde ramambo, distribution of 30
Makandiwa, Ruth 21–2
Mangena, F. 193
'Man of God' 1, 6, 8. *See also* prophets
Manyanya, M. 10
Manyonganise, M. 18, 21, 72, 89, 91, 93–4, 192, 197, 200
Mapfumo, Thomas 63
Maposa, R. S. 91, 138, 142, 180
Mapuranga, T. P. 1, 11, 13, 19, 21, 72, 120, 139, 144, 146, 152, 164, 171, 179, 191, 197–9, 203
Marongwe, N. 91, 138, 142
Martikainen, T. 2
Martin, D. 18, 49, 51, 58, 149, 195, 213
masculinity
  gender studies 61
  nationalism and 63–4
  religion and 61
  social context 62
  spiritual marketing and 69–70
Maseno, L. 67
Mashau, T. D. 131
mashavi 123
Maskens, M. 61, 70–1
Masvotore, P. 16, 153–4
Mataire, L. 93
Matandare, S. 68
Mate, R. 199
Matsilele, T. 151
Matthew 35, 136, 147
Ma, W. 7
Maxwell, D. 1, 6, 48, 50–1, 58–60, 65, 77, 90, 135, 155, 164, 172, 174, 177, 180–3, 197, 204
Mayrargue, C. 90–1
Maziwisa, Psychology 76
Mbare Chimurenga Choir 62
McCauley, J. F. 72
mega prophets 2, 5, 15, 45, 59, 62
Meyer, B. 79
mhondoro 22, 39, 76, 150, 156
Miller, D. E. 90
Miller, K. D. 97, 99, 108
miracles and magic
  background 33
  coincidences and 35–6
  definition 34–5, 91

God's action and intervention 36–8
traditional specialists 39–40
transformation, reasons and possibilities 40–4
Mlambo, O. B. 17, 33, 196
modern Pentecostal churches (MPCs) 90
Moyo, A. M. 119
Moyo, S. 156
Mtethwa, N. 83–4, 86
Mtukudzi, Oliver 114
Muchemwa, K. 61
Mudzimumukuru 122
Mugabe, Robert 10–12, 18, 27
  fatherhood 63–5
  against homosexuality 64
Mugabe, T. 157
Mugomba, M. 68
Mujinga, Rev M. 18, 149
Mukondiwa, R. 188
Mundondo, N. 80–1
Mushava, E. 156
Musikavanhu 122
Musoni, P. 14, 19, 72, 175–7, 203
Mutsagondo, S., E. 138–40
Muyambo, T. 18, 135
Muzembi, Walter 76
Mwari, K. K. 121–2, 185, 203, 208

Nagel, J. 63
*n'anga*s 24–7, 30–1, 38
nationalism
  definition 63
  inclusive government or government of national unity (GNU) 64–5
  masculinity and 63–4
Ncube, X. 98, 115
Ndlovu, L. 17, 45, 110
neo-charismatic 'catch all' category 90
neo-Pentecostal churches 152, 159
Netland, H. A. 121
New Age spirituality 136
New International Dictionary of Pentecostal and Charismatic Movements 90
new Pentecostal churches (NPCs) 90
ngozi 123
Nigerian Pentecostalism 1–2, 7, 15, 26
Njoroge, N. 199
Nkomo, Joshua ('Father Zimbabwe') 63
Norris, P. 108, 136–7

Nwadialor, K. 185
Nyadenga 122
Nyambi, O. 11
Nyikadzimu 122

Obadare, E. 207, 209
Obayi, P. M. 14, 96
Onah, G. 7, 150
Oosthuizen, G. C. 176, 184
ordinary believers 54–8
Orobator, A. E. 9
Oyakhilome, Pastor Chris 125

Paley, W. 37
Pambuka, Oscar 76
Parrinder, E. G. 83
Parsitau, D. 3, 192
Pasura, D. 61
patriarchy 12–13, 18, 64, 70, 72, 92, 197–8
Patton, M. Q. 138
Pentecostal churches
    classification 90
Pentecostalism
    fatherhood doctrine 91
    miracle deliverances 33–4, 91
    seven tenets 153–8
    universal definition 5
Pentecostal movements 23, 33–4, 43–4, 46, 80, 90, 97, 101, 116, 124, 136–8, 140–1, 193, 204, 206, 209
    various forms 90
Pentecostal prophetic movements (PPMs) 92, 98
Phillips, J. 110
Platvoet, J. G. 6, 80
Pongweni, A. 23
Prayzah, Jah 113
Price, F. K. C. 153
prophetic healing 140–1
Prophetic Healing and Deliverance (PHD) Ministries 4, 14, 17–19, 21–5, 27–9, 31–2, 45
    ATRs and 21
    background 76, 106–7, 140–1
    'back to sender' slogan 31
    branding 109–10
    deliverance and healing 81–2, 141–5, 158
    elements, use of 84–5
    exorcism 83–4
    gender ideology 32

giving concepts 79
holy ground 86
housing projects 115
mantles, use of 110
masculinity concepts 62
media, use of 95, 98
mentorship 77–8
miracles 83
music 112–13, 159–60
naming system 25
n'anga practice 80
night prayers 113–14, 145–7, 159
payment for service 80–1
precipitation and growth 77
prosperity messages 79–80, 94
rebranding of Christian faith 89
religious icons, use of 29–32
rivalry and collaboration with UFIC 99–101, 147–8
seeding money 94
singing and dancing 85–6
social engagement 86–7, 114
socio-economic and political contexts 45
spirits, belief in 79–80
wristbands, concepts 112
Yadah TV (television channel) 68–9, 95, 98
prophetic Pentecostal Christianity (PPC) 203–4
Prophetic Pentecostalism 6, 8, 90–1
prophets 1–2
    African traditional religion (ATRs) vs 15, 17, 33
    artefacts, keeping 27–8
    branding 14
    challenging claims 3
    creativity 9
    emergence of ministries 11
    financial resources 29–30
    gender ideology 12–13, 18
    internal competition 4–5
    political environment 11–12
    power and authority 3, 6, 8
    prosperity themes 7
    spiritual market 14–16
    titles, significance 26
    women abuse 19
prostitution 123, 126, 128, 133
Psalms 85, 110

Redeemed Christian Church of God
    (RCCG) 98
religious economy in society. *See
    also* African Pentecostalism;
    DiVineyard Church of His Presence
    (DCOHP)
  beliefs, classification 120–3
  research methodology 119–20
  theoretical framework 118–19
religious/spiritual market
  comparison of services 96
  competition and branding 66–71
  consumer culture 118
  radical pluralism 9
research, religion's role in unsettled times
    47. *See also* Zimbabwe Assemblies
    of God Africa (ZAOGA)
  analysis 54–8
  background 45
  data collection 52–3
  empirical study 51–60
  key concepts 47–9
  literature review 49–51
  methodology 49–51
  ordinary believers 55–8
  pastors 54–8
  Pentecostalism 47–8
  prosperity ministries 48
  questionnaire 51–2
  respondents 52
  results 58–9
  type of problems 53
  Zimbabwe's geographical area 48–9
Robbins, J. 130–1
Rosenau, P. V. 104

Sachikonye, L. 77
Satan/Lucifer 126, 128
secularization theory 46–7, 136
Sermon, Harare 29
shavi renjuzu 39
Shoko, T. 1, 18, 25, 75, 78, 81–5, 122–3,
    128–9, 153, 155–6
Shona
  epistemological insights 19
  healers 25
  Musikavanhu 38
  naming system 23
  n'anga, visiting 25, 31
  traditional beliefs and practices 21

Sibanda, F. 18, 117, 123, 180
Soberman, D. 112
social activism 28, 30, 169–71, 174
Soothill, J. E. 13, 191
Spickard, J. V. 119
Spirit Embassy 91, 106, 149, 206. *See also*
    Angel, Uebert
  prosperity gospel, negative side
    171–2
spiritual father 26, 43, 76, 78, 92, 124, 151,
    155, 165
Stark, R. 107, 118, 136–7
Stark, Rodney 118
Stewart, E. 68
Stolz, J. 135, 137
Swinburne, R. 36
Synagogue, Church of All Nations
    (SCOAN) 76, 124

Taringa, N.T. 121
Taru, J. 153, 159
Tarusarira, J. 11
Taylor, M. C. 5
Tendai, Magaya 27, 76–7, 150, 157
Togarasei, L. 1, 6–7, 65, 90, 135, 143,
    152–3, 157, 159, 164, 171, 176,
    178–9, 181–2, 184, 193
traditional specialists 39, 41–3
transformation
  business analogies 42–4
  reasons for 40–2

Ukah, A. 1, 14, 93, 96, 98–9, 152–3,
    155–8
Ukwuegbu, B. 1
United Family International (UFI) Church
    4, 11, 14, 17–19, 21–4, 27–9, 29,
    31–2, 45. *See also* Makandiwa,
    Emmanuel
  anointing oil, use of 110–11
  ATR's and 21
  background 106–7, 139–40
  'back to sender' slogan 31
  branding 109–10
  Christ TV (television channel) 68, 95,
    98
  gender ideology 32
  healing and deliverance 22–3, 141–5
  housing projects 114
  mantles, use of 110

masculinity concepts 62
media, use of 95, 98
music 112–13
naming system 23–4
'*ndiri mwana womuProfita*' 66
night prayers 113–14, 145–7
prophecy 22–3, 142–3
prosperity gospel 28–9, 94, 163–6, 170, 186
rebranding of Christian faith 89
religious icons, use of 29–32
rivalry and collaboration with PHD 99–101, 147–8
social innovations 114
socio-economic and political contexts 45
wristbands, concepts 112
United States
　megachurch phenomenon 10
　religious market 3
University of South Africa (UNISA) 4

vadzimu 122–3
Van Dijk, R. 23–4
Van Klinken, A. 13, 61
Veenhoven, R., M. 207
Vengeyi, O. 135, 149–50, 152, 157

Walker, A. 46, 50
Wariboko, N. 11, 164, 179
Weber, views on Protestantism 7
Wilkinson, J. 143
Wilson, M. 143
Wilson, N. 212
witchcraft 22, 31, 33–4, 48, 82, 123, 125–6, 128–9, 145, 156
Wright, S. M. 213

Yidana, A. 4, 9, 97, 105–6
Yong, A. 90, 109, 164, 179
youthful male prophets 65–7
　as alternative sources of power 65

Zacharia, Nicholas 76, 113
Zaleski, P. A. 119
ZANUPF party 62
Zech, C. E. 119
Zhakata, Leonard 113–14
Zimbabwe. *See also* Zimbabwean Pentecostalism
　economic, political and social crises 10–11, 45–7, 90–1, 138–9
　masculinity and fatherhood 63–5
Zimbabwean Pentecostalism
　branding 66–70
　brotherhood and sisterhood 96
　characteristics of new churches 152–8
　definitional predicament 5–8
　diversity and complexity 165
　gender ideology 12–13
　innovation and competition 1–19, 66–71
　key characteristics 6, 8
　masculinity 66–70
　new Pentecostal movements 90–3
　new wave 138
　socio-economic and political context 10–12
　survival of the fittest 103–16 (*see also* Prophetic Healing and Deliverance (PHD) Ministry; United Family International (UFI) Church
　upsurge 138–9
　working definition 6
Zimbabwe Assemblies of God Africa (ZAOGA)
　competitors 59
　gender ideologies 61, 65
　prosperity gospel 163–8, 170, 176–7, 180–4, 186
　secular dynamics 40, 46
　spiritual guidance and shared economic principles 11, 14, 19, 48
　struggle with the devil 60
Zimunya, C. T. 17, 33, 40, 192
Zuze, L. 156

www.ingramcontent.com/pod-product-compliance
Lightning Source LLC
Chambersburg PA
CBHW072142290426
44111CB00012B/1947